LET'S KEEP TALKING

Dearest Lili

Thank you so very much for having me to the Freud Museum. It was such a treat and lovely to meet you and see your moving art.

to be continued...

Paul

LET'S KEEP TALKING
Lacanian Tales of Love, Sex, and Other Catastrophes

Yael Baldwin

KARNAC

First published in 2016 by
Karnac Books Ltd
118 Finchley Road
London NW3 5HT

British Library Cataloguing in Publication Data

A C.I.P. for this book is available from the British Library

ISBN-13: 978-1-78220-307-0

Typeset by V Publishing Solutions Pvt Ltd., Chennai, India

Printed in Great Britain by TJ International Ltd, Padstow, Cornwall

www.karnacbooks.com

This book is for those who speak and those who listen.

It is with untellable love and appreciation that I dedicate this book to my dearest family and incredible friends (you know who you are).

CONTENTS

ACKNOWLEDGEMENTS

For encouraging me to write case studies, and for his superb mentorship and friendship, I am most grateful to Bruce Fink. Over the years, I have greatly benefited from the fellowship and feedback of Lacanians in the Affiliated Psychoanalytic Workgroups (APW)—in particular Dan Collins, Kareen Malone, Stijn Vanheule, Patricia Gherovici, and Dany Nobus. And immense appreciation goes to the tireless Russell Grigg for his encouragement and contributions. For their particular approaches to psychoanalysis and their willingness to impart them to me, I thank Joel Kovel, Jonathan Lear, and Anna McClellan.

A number of people have read parts of this work and offered helpful comments: Thank you Paul Richer, Russell Walsh, and Elaine Bleakney. Two more read every word: Paul Fugelsang is the finest and tallest cheerleader an author could have. And Sarah Patten is the best writing partner and friend a gal could ask for (though I never needed to ask)— thank you for each smile offered upon seeing my furrowed brow from across our writing table and every walk to clear our heads.

Thank you to Mars Hill University—to the students who inspire me to search for ever more meaning in this thing we call psychology, to my outstanding colleagues, and to the administration for all their support. And a most hearty thank you to the Appalachian College

Association for granting me the fellowship that made my sabbatical year possible—that was a true gift.

I am much obliged to the most detailed reader I know, Hillary Modlin; without you this book would have so many mistakes in it, it's not even funny. And to the gracious people at Karnac: Oliver Rathbone for answering that you would be delighted to publish my book, my editor Rod Tweedy, Cecily Blench, Martin Pettitt, Constance Govindin, and Rachel Rathbone.

A heartfelt thank you to my beloved family: The late Mark Goldman, Toby Goldman, James and Lucy Baldwin, Elizabeth, John, Naomi and Hugo Chun, Grace Frenzel and Leonard Kahn, for supporting me in the educational journey that culminated in this book. I also extend my profound appreciation to the friends who make my life brighter and better by being in it and offer respite from things like writing about Lacan.

A deep bow of loving gratitude to Matthew Baldwin for steadfastly standing by my side through every single stage of this book, the writing of which took well over a decade. And to Lena and James Z, it is with bountiful love that I thank you for being in my life; you both blow me away every day.

Most of all, I am indebted to my clients, without whom this book simply would not be. These case studies present only my interpretations of our work together; they do not and cannot offer the final word on their subjects. To be sure, the richness of all our lives surpasses all words and theories.

ABOUT THE AUTHOR

Dr. Yael Baldwin is a psychologist, associate professor of psychology, and chair of social sciences at Mars Hill University. She is a member of the Affiliated Psychoanalytic Workgroups, a co-editor of *Lacan and Addictions: An Anthology*, and the author of various anthology chapters and articles on Lacan.

Talking as the best medicine

Let us face facts: current trends in clinical practices and psychological research regarding the treatment of mental suffering reveal that two people talking therapeutically, narrating and investigating a person's tribulations and triumphs, is becoming a rarity in favour of psycho-pharmacology and other biological models. Moreover, even when talk therapy is employed, increasingly manuals offering step-by-step instructions guide these conversations, very specifically, leaving little room for human improvisation.

Such trends away from people actually speaking with one another mirror our broader technological cultural milieu.[1] In this climate, people seeking psychological or physiological assistance have even been referred to as "iPatients"[2], reduced to the information found in computer files, images, and lab reports; the bulk of their communications with clinicians are done through technology rather than face to face.[3] I have witnessed people, in dire distress, speak with mental health professionals who rarely look up from their screens while entering information about a person's afflictions into the computer before them, for the entire session. These clinicians are often working under the gun of the demands of expediently charting and attending to as many people as possible, but in so doing risk not actually seeing the person before them. Indeed, too often the individual who comes for help feels neither seen nor heard. These truly are missed encounters.[4]

Recently, following a lecture on psychopathology, a student came up to me after class and apologised if she seemed "out of it". She explained her primary care physician had prescribed her an anti-anxiety medication and it was making her feel "woozy and weird". I invited her to my office to speak. She narrated how she told her doctor that she was feeling anxious and he sent her home with a prescription. I asked what she had been feeling anxious about and she relayed that she was having difficulties getting along with her university soccer coach. I knew this young woman to be bright, ambitious, hardworking, social, and friendly. In my estimation, the conflict with her soccer coach would have been better approached as a life lesson, one in which the young student would be encouraged to further articulate her distress and desires, to work through the particular situation and relationship, and arrive at a different, more manageable place. In so doing she would come to know herself better and open possibilities for how she relates to others and the world. She would do this, in my book, through speech, not through taking a pill. This happening saddened but did not surprise me. Believe me when I say there are definitely times and places for physiological treatments such as psychotropic medications, but these days psychopharmacology is too often the *first* line of defence in mental health treatment, when we could be talking something through.[5] What are we teaching young people, if when they try to speak to us about cares and concerns, we bypass speech and jump immediately to a pill?[6]

Over a century ago, Sigmund Freud realised that speaking with the people he worked with helped them eradicate or lessen their troublesome symptoms, move fixations, and positively changed their lives. Freud recognised that people improved by being encouraged to say whatever was on their mind, free from censorship, to another person. Via free association, people could work through what had been repressed but returned to haunt them in menacing ways (in their thoughts and behaviours). Psychoanalysis, the "talking cure",[7] was created as a method for accessing repressed psychic material that wreaks havoc on our lives and moves us, repeatedly, in ways in which we are unaware. It was a radical idea, and, I would argue, it still is. Where else in our society are we encouraged to say whatever comes to mind—the good, the bad, and the ugly—to another person who is trained not to judge us, allot punishment, or demand penitence, but to listen to us in a meaningful way, such that we may also hear ourselves differently in order to improve our own lives? Now, more than ever, we need this radical endeavour of analytic talk therapy.

Thankfully the ritual and art of talk therapy is not dead. Speaking, questioning, listening, and being-with, in the mitigation of suffering in order to expand one's life experience, is at the heart of talk therapy. Part of my overarching ambition for this book is to emphasise the usefulness of open-ended (*vs.* manual-based), person-centred (*vs.* problem-centred) talk therapy in fostering positive psychological change. Many open-ended talk therapies are available to clinicians and clients. In my journey, I have found the Lacanian orientation to be an approach that provides a rigorous avenue into the workings of the unconscious by highlighting the importance of the role of speech and language to our very beings. Ultimately for Lacan, a truly psychoanalytic approach is one that stays true to the importance of the signifier (signifiers being a linguistic term, following Ferdinand de Saussure, for the *sounds* we produce and hear during speech) in the formations of the unconscious.[8] Thus, when speaking about the art of talk therapy, and what it can (still) offer and do for us, the work of Jacques Lacan is a worthy contribution.

Lacan's focus on speech and language

When people inquire about my clinical "orientation" or what I write about, and I reply that my specialty is Lacanian psychoanalysis, more often than not, further explanation is needed. Many people, particularly in the United States, including those who study and practice psychology, have never heard of the Parisian psychoanalyst, Jacques Lacan (1901–1981). Even those who have ventured to read Lacan's work and find it theoretically and philosophically interesting, often ask me how a clinical practice is founded upon such writings. "How does Lacan's theory actually translate into therapy? What does it look like in practice? How does adopting a Lacanian perspective affect one's listening and understanding?" Many people cannot imagine how Lacan's complicated musings on philosophers, anthropologists, and linguists, about people like Merleau-Ponty, Lévi-Strauss, and de Saussure, to name but a few of the thinkers Lacan addresses, function in the clinic and help to allay psychic suffering. Even in mental health circles, when therapeutic approaches are discussed in the United States, Lacan is often left out of the conversation (his work is much more prominent in other parts of the world, such as Europe and South America). And the published literature on Lacan is often highly theoretical and thus not particularly accessible to those not already steeped in his work.[9] This is unfortunate because Lacan's is a very useful clinical approach that emphasises, arguably more than others, how we can utilise language and speech to promote therapeutic change and well-being. Clinicians and anyone interested in talk therapy may question how learning about Lacan will affect and benefit their understanding, practices, and case conceptualisations. This book is my response to such questions.

Lacan's oeuvre is indeed clinically relevant. Jacques Lacan was first and foremost a psychoanalyst, one interested in training other analysts. He explicitly stated, "The aim of my teaching has been and still is the training of analysts" (1978, p. 230). To fully make use of Lacan's teachings, we must resituate and return them to the clinical arena. We need to distinguish what makes his theory and technique unique, and we must not rely upon characterisations of Lacan as an obscure French thinker whose work is only of interest to political and cultural theorists and feminist film critics (although cheers to the aforementioned for using Lacan!). As Malone states, "There has been so little contact between American clinicians and Lacanian approaches that any American characterisation of Lacanian clinical work is […] premature" (2000, p. 5). In order to bring Lacan to the table of the broader clinical discourse, clinicians who utilise this theory in their practices need to articulate their actual experiences. Ultimately, this is part of a larger task, which involves demystifying therapeutic practices in general.

This book helps define the difference that utilising a Lacanian model of talk therapy, which focuses on the transformative role of speech, can make. Of course, Lacanians believe in biology; however, as Lacan emphasised, *because we are speaking beings, biology always intersects with language.* And how we speak influences our biology. This is an important idea for health professionals who may become lost in the mire of medicalisation. Indeed, Lacan warned of psychology's tendency to biologise without recognising the profoundly altering (and alienating) role of image and signifier upon our physiology. Lacan believes that to think of the body as a biological entity divorced from image and signification, is a "delusion," and that analytic work withers if it "forgets that its first responsibility is to language" (2006, p. 721/606).[10]

Lacan foregrounds language and desire, and the intricate intersection of both, upon our personhood. As speaking beings, we are always already alienated in the Other's language and desire (it is how we are born). And while all neurotics are alienated, Lacan highlighted (based on Freud's categories) how hysterics and obsessionals tend to be alienated in different ways. Those readers not already familiar with Lacan and Freud might be wondering about these two categories, hysteria and obsessional neurosis, so let me address them and their status in current day nosology.

Hysteria and obsessional neurosis today

Freud famously observed and theorised two psychological structures, hysteria and obsessional neurosis, and how these structures are lived phenomenologically. He was describing what he saw when he worked with people and how these structures profoundly and systematically affected their adopted stances towards themselves, others, and the world. For example, Freud noticed and recorded how people's symptoms "joined in the conversation"[11] somewhat differently according to whether one fell under either category (the hysteric tends towards somatic conversion in symptom formation—i.e., a somatisation—and the obsessional tends towards rumination and ritual, for example). Many of Freud's texts laid out how he saw these categories operate in people's lives, particularly their struggles and victories.

Lacan also emphasised these diagnostic categories, although he provided a more structural understanding of them. The Lacanian diagnostic scheme, as the following cases demonstrate in close detail, thus differs from the current psychiatric diagnostic bible, *The Diagnostic Statistical Manual-5* (*DSM-5*). Lacan, following Freud, used three main categories—neurosis, psychosis, and perversion—for describing adopted stances towards the world. In this book, I take up neurosis, particularly the hysteria and obsessional neurosis divide, but I will not take up phobia, the less prevalent subcategory of neurosis.[12]

Some people think these diagnostic categories, hysteria and obsessional neurosis as Freud encountered them, have disappeared from our current milieu. The "hysteric" category is no longer in the *DSM*. And the *DSM*'s compulsive disorder, while a distant relative to the original diagnostic category of obsessional neurosis, is really not the same thing at all.[13] And yet, as I believe the case studies in this book will reveal, we continue to see these two structures everywhere, very much alive (and sometimes well) in life and in the clinic, and, furthermore, these existential structures are remarkably useful clinically. The two structures remain, today, distinctive subject positions and variant ways of relating to others, the world, and ourselves.

The cases comprising this book present pictures of modern-day hysteria and obsessional neurosis, and readers will hopefully come away with a renewed appreciation for the hysteric and obsessional divide, and how the observations set forth by Freud and Lacan are still seen today, albeit in a different historical-cultural context, and above all, how knowledge of these structures is still a useful guide for clinicians.

Existential dilemmas—now and then

The following case studies illustrate how we find very similar, powerful existential forces operating upon clients today, in the twenty-first century, that Freud's patients encountered in the nineteenth century. The cases address the existential issues of how people confront the task of living a life. I try to capture how therapy is a place where people do not just get better (by eradicating symptoms and inhibitions), but confront the big existential dilemmas of their lives, like intimacy and mortality. Indeed, some locate Lacanian psychoanalysis in the existential field of the discipline, because it presupposes and entails an ethics of autonomy, meaning, and responsibility.

The ethics of Lacanian treatment revolves around enlarging a person's realm of autonomy and possibilities rather than curing a particular symptom. Analysis works towards subjective responsibility, and it is through speech that subjects achieve these goals. Lacanian clinicians do not have preconceived goals for the work, but rather hold open the position of what Lacan calls the analyst's desire, that appetition for analysands or clients to speak more fully, procure full speech, and explore the subject-specific unconscious meanings of their symptoms. These cases will serve to show what that looks like in practice.

Obstacles, detours, and treatment variations

Available Lacanian case studies are few and far between for a reason. Myriad obstacles present themselves to authors of any psychotherapy case study, including issues of confidentiality, complexity, author subjectivity,[14] and the generally intimidating experience of opening oneself up to criticism by presenting one's clinical work. Let me address these concerns from the outset.

To be sure, I have given utmost consideration to disguising my clients' identities; absolutely no identifying information is given. Rather, the material concerns desires, fears, fantasies, symptoms, dreams, and parapraxes, such as slips of the tongue. I write about what is sometimes referred to as depth-psychological material as opposed to identifiable life facts. Freud describes

> the paradoxical truth that it is far easier to divulge the patient's most intimate secrets than the most innocent and trivial facts about him; for, whereas the former would not throw any light on his identity, the latter, by which he is generally recognised, would make it obvious to every one. (1909d, p. 156)

It is an interesting and perhaps rather sad commentary upon our society that this remains very much the case—perhaps even more so now that our "connections" are mediated via electronic devices and social media. We rarely know people by their intimate desires and fears. We know their names, their jobs, and where they live. We know what they present to us, their public face. In the absence of demographic facts, we are hard-pressed to recognise our dearest friends and family members by their deepest concerns, wants, wishes, and struggles.

Regarding the particularity of my experience, a few words about the cases are needed. First, the treatment I present in these cases is a variation on any "standard" Lacanian treatment, keeping in mind that Lacan would likely label the very notion of a "variation of standard Lacanian treatment" a pleonasm, if not an oxymoron.[15] My clinical practice is guided by Lacanian theory. However, I consider this work analytic-psychotherapy, not psychoanalysis.[16] I call what I do analytic-therapy because psychoanalytic theory, particularly Lacanian theory, grounds my practice.[17] Also, the work presented in these cases was part of my doctoral training and took place in a university setting, under certain conditions that affected the work discussed as well as the language employed in these cases. For example, there were particular restrictions on time and money. From an analytic viewpoint ideally, a clinician sees her or his clients as often as needed for as long as necessary, at the set and appropriate price, to be determined between the therapist and client. My fee was determined by clinic policy, and while time management was more or less afforded to me in differing degrees, there were some restrictions. Some clients I saw once a week, others I saw up to three times a week, some clients for less than one year, others for three. In a number of cases, when my work at the clinic was completed, it brought a premature end to the therapeutic work, as described within the cases.

While ideally Lacanian therapy is open-ended, it is appropriate to discuss how it can be used in a time-limited mode, as the growing trend is towards briefer therapy. Many mental health settings now offer brief and very brief therapy. Brief therapy is loosely defined and can connote any length from six sessions to once a week for a year. Very brief is often defined as one to five sessions in total. Freud discusses time-limited therapy, and says it is meant to meet the "haste of American life" (1937c, p. 216).[18] In order to adapt to the requests of clients and to accelerate the often-slower progress of analysis, time-limited therapy is nowadays commonplace.

Although the latter is not ideal, Lacanian tenets can indeed be applied to time-limited therapy when necessary. Given the prevalence of briefer work, which is due in part to the pressures from the health insurance industry and, in some areas, to a growing demand for treatment and a lack of available resources, articulating how Lacanian theory can be used in briefer therapy seems a worthy task. In general, demonstrating how Lacanian guidelines can be used in different therapeutic settings and within various limitations seems advantageous.

Another example of how my use of Lacanian theory is a variation on a theme is the way I employ scansion. Lacan is famous for his use of scansion—ending a session earlier or later than expected, or what is known as the variable-length session. Lacan argues "we must free the [session's] ending from its routine framework and employ it for all the useful aims of analytic technique" (2006, p. 209/44). He claims ending a session earlier or later than expected serves to punctuate the client's discourse and leave the client questioning the meaning of her or his speech. Lacan states,

> It is, therefore, a propitious punctuation that gives meaning to the subject's discourse. This is why the ending of the session—which current technique makes into an interruption that is determined purely by the clock, and, as such, takes no account of the thread of the subject's discourse—plays the part of a scansion which has

the full value of an intervention by the analyst that is designed to
precipitate concluding moments. (2006, p. 252/44)

Clients cannot strategically waste time to fill up a session if they do not
know how long they will be expected or allowed to speak. To be sure, we
act differently when we know the time we are to finish and leave than
when we do not. Ultimately, scansion reminds us that we never know
how much time we have in life, and, thus, adds a dimension of anxiety
regarding mortality into the therapeutic mix that may be utilised and
worked through to advantageous purposes. The variable-length session also reiterates that the analytic venture is different from our everyday affairs, where time is scheduled by the hour. This is another way
in which Lacan, ever the questioner, takes the radical spirit of analysis
seriously. Lacan continually puts analytic technique and doctrine into
question. He questions what a fifty-minute hour does rather than just
accept it. The unconscious, as far as we know, still does not work on a
fifty-minute hour.[19]

While I concur with Lacan's ideas regarding scansion, my use of
scansion in sessions was limited to fifteen minutes, more or less, during the traditional fifty-minute hour because of the expectations of the
clinic where I worked. However, I found even a limited use of scansion to be very helpful. This indicates that while scansion is integral to
Lacanian technique, it is not a diehard requirement. Clinicians who cannot practice "scanding"[20] because of the demands of their work setting
can still benefit from integrating Lacan's teachings into their practices.[21]

Readers may also notice that I use a particular vocabulary of therapist and client rather than doctor and patient or the traditional Lacanian
analyst and analysand (a term described below). "Client" was the terminology that my clinical psychology training encouraged (with the
exception of my clinical supervisor Dr. Bruce Fink); and besides the
hospital where I worked, where "patient" was used, every clinic or
counselling centre I have worked at has used the term "client". These
days, the term "client" provides a shortcut with other clinicians. Many
of the people I converse with would not understand if I were to ask, for
example, whether an analysand had arrived for a session. However,
if it were not for the complication of communication, I would gladly
use the term "analysand" because I like what it represents. In 1967,
Lacan switched from using the more traditional term patient to using
analysand (see Lacan, 1968, p. 18). This term implies that the one being

analysed is actually the person doing the bulk of the work, that she or he is an active rather than a passive party.[22] While I do use the term client, I conceptualise the role of the person I am referencing in terms of the meaning that accompanies the term analysand, for I adhere to the idea that the true responsibility for doing the therapeutic work ultimately lies with the client.

I thus offer a way to utilise Lacanian theory and technique in practice that might not always fit into an orthodox idea of Lacanian analysis. That said, the cases indicate what therapeutic criteria are presupposed and entailed in the work of someone self-identified as Lacanian.

The cases, a preview

In the following case studies, I highlight the role a Lacanian orientation played in the interactions, formulations, and results, from initial meetings to terminations. Concepts examined include the Lacanian diagnostic system, the role of symptoms, desire, language, fantasy, lack and loss, the ethics involved in Lacanian work, and a host of others, all of which are grounded in concrete clinical material. *Ultimately, the case studies illuminate specific and universal themes of human suffering and how we can attenuate that suffering by speaking.*

Psychoanalysis has been called "depth psychology" in the sense that we explore "deep" into the psyche. Whether this label is a misnomer or not, when we speak psychoanalytically we talk about our dreams, literally and figuratively, our fears, and fantasies—sexual and masturbatory—in other words, things not discussed in "polite" conversation. Such are the things of analytic work and talk therapy, and such are the things included in these cases. We talk of that which we tend to repress, that which is "forgotten". And as Freud teaches us, what is repressed concerns what our ego, our public sense of self, does not wish to own, which usually has to do with sex and aggression—Eros and Thanatos. It seems to be how we are made in conjunction with how our civilised society operates.

Each of the five cases illuminates components of Lacanian theory and is a weaving together of clinical material and theoretical exposition. The articulation of hysteria and obsessional neurosis is an overarching theme, but other than that, Lacanian concepts and formulas emerge organically and as necessary to advance the case discussion and understanding.

In chapter one, I delve into the Lacanian diagnostic schema and begin with the topic of diagnosis, as it is often foremost on the clinician's mind during preliminary meetings and is an important jumping off point.[23] Moreover, the Lacanian diagnostic schema is one of *the* factors that make the Lacanian orientation unique. The first case study, "Needling the virgin: navigating the pathways of hysterical desire", illustrates a number of the defining characteristics of hysteria, particularly the hysteric's question as Lacan formulates it, "Who am I? A man or a woman?" and often more specifically, "What is it to be a woman?" (Lacan, 1993, p. 171). And the status of the hysteric's desire, particularly the notion that *the hysteric desires via a string of identifications*, is demonstrated.

Mona's presenting complaint was that her romantic relationships caused her considerable pain. Was she choosing the wrong men and doing the wrong things when it came to affairs of the heart? She questioned whether she was a woman capable of being loved. We also see fluctuations in what Mona desires, particularly regarding partners, children, money, and careers, and what seems like a preoccupation with other women. Lacan's formulation that hysteric structure involves reaching an object of desire via an identification with another person, helps sort out the complexity and at first seemingly nonsensical and confusing form of Mona's intricate relationships with various men and their female friends and lovers. We see how Mona desires *via* her romantic partners.[24] Lacan's notion that "Man's desire is the Other's desire" (2006, p. 628/525) also proves pivotal in sorting through and explicitly articulating Mona's previously implicit or unconscious desires. Both Freud's case of Dora (1963), the quintessential hysteric in the psychoanalytic literature, and Lacan's commentary on Dora (1994) assist my conceptualisation of the case.

Lacan's theory on how the signifying chain[25] sets the preconditions for a person's desire and how unconscious desire is set into play and displayed in the signifying chain was invaluable in all the cases. For example, in the first case, it encouraged us to hear and connect the repeating signifiers such as "fight", "big", "needling", and "getting a rise out of", to name but a few, at work in Mona's discourse. This allowed us to isolate, via her speech, the repetition of a specific symbolic constellation regarding Mona's romantic relationships, a constellation that was originally unconscious. For as Lacan states, we need to become aware of the "symbolic constellation dwelling in the subject's unconscious" (1988a,

p. 54). In listening to and acknowledging the repetition of signifiers, we tied together the string of "big" men who were "hard on" Mona and "turned their back to [her]" and towards other (saintly) women. Explicitly articulating this unconscious dynamic, which was a triangular circuit of desire, provided Mona with the *choice* of whether or not to continue to participate in and even create this underlying relational model or to choose alternative ways of positioning herself within her romantic relationships. The specifics of the chain of signifiers also lead us to decipher meaning in Mona's many somatic symptoms and connect her physical distress to her mental turmoil.

The second case, "The male in the coffin: a case study of an obsessional", illuminates some of the defining characteristics of obsessional neurotic structure, including an exploration of the obsessional's question, "Am I dead or alive?" (Lacan, 1993, p. 180), as it shows itself in the concrete circumstances of the case. The obsessional's relations to the Other as well as his strategy with respect to being are explored. And the roles of the symbolic matrix, death, time, guilt, the anal drive, and anal eroticism and fixation are discussed in the clinical context.

Max's presenting problem was that he was depressed, unmotivated, and unsatisfied with his life. He also had trouble climaxing and experienced severe intestinal problems. Max felt exhausted because he "couldn't stop thinking"; he was "too much in [his] head". Lacan's recommendation that we situate the client's symptoms within the larger symbolic matrix, because what is at stake in analysis is "to recognise the subject's position in the symbolic order" (1988a, p. 67), proved fruitful. Encouraging Max to fill out this symbolic matrix via his speech undoubtedly led to a greater understanding of how his symptoms related to the larger concerns and questions in his life. We connect Max's withholding to the larger matrix of the pre-conditions of his birth and to his relationship to the Other. Lacanian theory, which shows how symptoms are tied to the Other's discourse, makes it possible to arrive at a greater understanding of Max's symptoms. Indeed, his father's discourse, which included the repetition of phrases such as "you're a pain in the ass", "you're a piece of shit", and "it's all in your head", can be viewed as the very wording of Max's symptoms. Connecting the Other's discourse and the signifying chain to Max's symptomatology lent sense to Max's otherwise enigmatic cognitions and behaviours. We also focus on the defence of withholding from the Other as a means towards separation and independence, as well as

Max's attempts to annul the Other's presence in his life and to retain his sense of self.

Max's symptoms of not climaxing, constipation, and perpetual thinking made more sense when they were connected to Max's own "*elimination*" and his desire to simultaneously *retain* his sense of self and to *hold back* or stave off death. A focus on the existential given of death anxiety (never to be underestimated) is fleshed out in relation to the obsessional mode or form of the neurotic's question, particularly as it manifested in Max's symptoms, dreams, ego identifications, and our therapeutic relationship.

Why was Max's existence so inextricably tied to death? Within his family, we uncover a "symbolic debt" in the form of a death of which no one spoke; the repressed in the form of a family secret returns in Max's being. I encouraged Max to narrate the constellation that presided over his birth and played a significant, albeit unconscious, role in his troubles. Lacan's theory that symptoms can be understood as "a reformulation, or even an insistence, of [the neurotic's] question" (1993, p. 170) was indispensable to my understanding of Max's predicament, suffering, and tendency towards withholding and inaction. Finally, I relay a dream, a gift from Max's unconscious, which compactly highlights the themes of the therapy, including a fear of loss and the connection between death and castration. While the importance of death was first and foremost forced upon me by Max's actual discourse in our sessions, my understanding of the case was certainly furthered by Lacan's formulation of obsessional neurosis.

The third case is "Speaking of throwing up the id: symbolically situating symptoms". Lisa came to therapy on the verge of quitting her doctoral program. She had been depressed most of her life, but the case traces a particular symptom, a phobic response to and fear of vomit and vomiting and elaborate avoidance strategies—a reverse bulimia of sorts—in relation to Lisa's anamnesis (her family story).

The case illustrates the Lacanian concept of the symptom as a metaphor, and of finding meaning in a seemingly nonsensical symptom, rather than setting out to eradicate it immediately. For "throw up" was not merely relegated to either a substance or an act, it proved a signifier of Lisa's desire that had been repressed from her consciousness. The symptom began as a mystery to Lisa, an incomprehensible signifier, but by articulating and connecting the physiological function to the scenes and signifiers of her history, a wealth of material was brought into the therapy room and subsequently worked through. Lisa's symptom indexed the entire cast of characters from her nuclear family matrix and the unconscious dynamics and relationships between them, as well as Lisa's relationship to loss and the Other's desire. This specific symptom also stood for and shed light on how Lisa confronted sexuality with both revulsion and repulsion; in other words, it pointed to her unconsciously adopted stance towards sexuality. Working with this symptom was key to unlocking a treasure trove of repressed material and helped relieve Lisa's depression.

"The case of the poisoned salami: doubts, dreams, guilt, and love" examines the characteristic obsessional symptoms of rumination and indecision, in light of one young man's troubled libidinal relations with others, and his tendency towards a splitting of love and desire, which is quite common to obsessional neurotic structure and is clinically important to comprehend.

Edon's indecision was manifest in the question of whether or not to break up with his girlfriend, and this dilemma caused him considerable mental and physical fatigue. He turned the decision about whom to love and desire into his symptom. In this and other ways, the case exemplifies the obsessional's tendency to ruminate about the important and great existential issues in life such as love and death.

Edon's troubled libidinal relations affected his romantic, sexual, and family relations. The case describes the labyrinth of the obsessional's sexual relations and stance, particularly in relation to the role of prohibition and what Lacan terms the paternal function. It does so by describing the phenomenological particulars and specificities of the case, and offers a different angle into obsessional neurosis than described in Max's case.

Edon experienced considerable guilt over sex, masturbation, and pornography usage. Living in fear that he would be punished for thoughts and acts of erotic desire, he found himself in a tough, classically obsessional spot. The case is a portrait of the obsessional's struggle between his desires and the reactions against them. We witness first the desire for sexual pleasure, then the prohibition of that pleasure, in a veritable seesaw between satisfaction and prohibition, and the successive, diphasic way in which it finds expression.

Anything and everything to do with Edon's sexual desire was tainted, and everything he touched with what I dub his "poisoned phallus" became tainted in its turn, as it were. Where did this strange but only too common obsessional feature of his sexuality originate? As we shall see, it arose from his history, particularly his relationship with his father. Each of the cases exemplifies how *people's sexual being in the world bears the marks of their history*, albeit in unique ways. For Edon, his phallic inheritance, we might say, is marked by a sense of deficiency and illegitimacy, and hence everything he touches turns not to gold but to something rotten, and he found himself at the sexual impasse he was in when he came to see me for consultations.

Edon "sacrificed" his lust and desire, but he also got off on the sacrificial stance. What Edon had entered therapy bitterly complaining about, he also, at another level, derived enjoyment from, and began to articulate as much. He spoke about how on some level, he enjoyed that he was not enjoying, achieving a secondary satisfaction, a pleasure in forfeiting his means of pleasure. This paradoxical phenomenon of obtaining satisfaction by ceding one's desires was described by Freud (in *Civilization and its Discontents*, 1930a); Lacan gave this human oddity the name of jouissance, which can be understood as a particular way of deriving satisfaction from sacrifice, which is why it is often understood as deriving pleasure from pain. Edon "sacrificed" his lust and desire, as the case lays out in some detail. Indeed, the myriad and very particular forms of jouissance are traced in all five cases, as are the always keenly specific unconscious preconditions for loving someone.

Another aspect that is illuminated by the case of Edon is the role of the obsessional's aggressiveness, which is marked both by self-punishment and by the aspiration to destroy the very thing (the Other) on which his desire depends. It is often a repressed aggression. In the specifics of Edon's case *we see a cycle of aggression, followed by guilt, and then a reaction formation of altruism, quite common in the obsessional's dynamic.*

Finally, dream analysis provides an important gateway to the unconscious, and allowed Edon to speak about his symbolic relationship to his father. A series of "father" dreams as they relate to phallic inheritance are discussed in detail. Edon's associations to these nightly interruptions proved fruitful in connecting the dots about the failure at the level of the father that may have resulted in the transmission of this poisoned phallus, which is epitomised in one particular dream, but also permeates all the way through his relations with others and ramifies through other aspects of his way of being in the world.

Edon's case highlights the concept of the symptom as located *between a desire and a self-reproach*. His symptoms are quite different from Lisa's, in the previous case. Whereas the hysteric effects a compromise between two competing desires in the one symptom (often via conversion), as we will see in Lisa's case, the obsessional tends to express the two tendencies sequentially, one after the other. Edon's case really brings this distinction to the fore.

In the final case study, "Family ties that bind: The *wait*ress, lack, and loss," we explore Lily's difficulties in getting out of the life she was leading, even as she saw that her life was in a rut. Lily's symptomatic fixation on a life with her father was such that there was no room for another man and no way for her to leave the parental home or find a career outside the family business. Lily was strongly committed to her family, she was the glue that held things together, but, as we shall see, there was a fair chance she would never escape the whirlpool (or sinkhole) of the family structure that was constantly pulling her back and down. Here we find a scenario that maps particularly well onto Freud's cases in the *Studies on Hysteria*: the girl who stays behind, "wedded" to the family, its constant support, much to her own psychic and physical detriment. It is a role Lily dutifully fulfils—even as her neurosis is a protest against her fate. Lily's case illustrates how we find the same existential dilemmas that confronted Freud's patients in the nineteenth century, just in a different temporal and cultural context. *Lest we think that hysteria and obsessional neurosis, as Freud encountered and described them, have disappeared, this and the other cases in this book should make us think again.*

In speaking about familial roles, Lily continually pointed to sexual difference and castration, via her utterances, without exactly putting her finger on it. Lily peppered her speech with phrases like the following: "I experience loss after loss and nothing will make up for it", "I've never known anything but loss", "I have no rod", "I am broken", and "My life is a complete loss".

Lily connects much of her sense of loss and lack to her father. Love for her father is clearly present, but so is a seething anger. She wrestles with a strong love/hate split for her father, which mostly manifested in animosity towards him. And she employs this split to undermine him. Lily's repressed love for her father reared its head in resentment towards him. Outlined is the concept of *"revendication"*, holding a pervading grievance arising from a past-perceived injustice, and a subsequent demand for restoration. Lily exemplifies *the hysteric demand for the restoration of what, to her eyes, is rightfully hers.*

Further illuminated is how the structure of Lily's desire was such that she wanted to be the being necessary to fill the Other's lack, but also leave it unfulfilled, and how this structure of desire caused Lily substantial pain, psychically and physically via many somatic symptoms. She was experiencing an enjoyment crisis. A discussion ensues about what Lily needs, including the notion of separation from the Other's desire.

I also link the structure of Lily's desire to her symptom formation and the fundamental fantasy, explicating how Lily unconsciously answered her existential question of being with the response: I am a servant to my father, which provided her with *a sense of being*, for better *and* for worse. All of this comes through her speech. The question of what is so fundamental about Lacan's concept of the fundamental fantasy—taken up as an underlying unconscious working explanatory principle—and how it differs from regular dreams and daydreams is explored, and the case details how the fundamental fantasy can be formulated or constructed and worked with in therapy. We see how Lily's desire was at once caught up in and weighed down by the articulated fantasy. On the one hand, the fundamental fantasy lends her a sense of being, on the other, it fixates and ossifies her desire.

I also explain how Lily's want-to-be-the-phallus relates to her history and her family's dynamic. Concepts like the "want-to-be", *manque-à-être* (see Lacan, 2006, p. 826/700), are hard to grasp outside of their clinical context. Indeed, two of the cases of hysteria point to the differential treatment of boys and girls within the family and how the women felt they were lacking and wanted to be seen as more powerful, able, and valued than they perceived they were on the basis of their gender and experience (a common theme in hysteric structure). With Lily, we also connected her sense of loss to the opening of the all-consuming family business. She lost her childhood and her sense of being loved; she wanted-to-be-loved.

The concluding chapter takes up an interesting question: is there such a thing as a complete analysis or a complete therapeutic process and if so, what constitutes a proper end of analysis and how do these relate to the goals or aims of analytic work? To be sure, different approaches to therapy and different psychoanalytic schools provide and work from different answers to this question. In fact, Freud's and Lacan's answers differ somewhat from each other, as is discussed in the conclusion.

Finally, Lacan provides numerous formulations for what constitutes a proper "end" of analysis at various stages of his work. Are these variant conceptualisations actually different aims or are they rather alternative ways of conceptualising and speaking about the same thing? And how do these aims relate, if at all, to happiness? These topics are taken up in the book's conclusion.

The unconscious still exists

While it would seem that over the years the import of Freud's views has waned in the mental health field, there is something most valuable to be found in this tradition. And Lacan is a way into Freud that is both very interesting and useful. It is a more *traditional way* of working with psychic suffering, one that emphasises speech, listening, and the unconscious. One might make an analogy with yoga. To be sure, yoga (hatha yoga—the physical system of yoga) is a much more ancient practice, but like psychoanalysis, there are various schools and approaches; however, all have in common the use of asanas and breath work. Likewise all psychoanalytic schools (at least in theory) hold that working with the unconscious is paramount and one works differently—therapeutically—when presuming a profound effect from the unconscious. Not many people would say that the more classical yoga approaches, those that hold closer to ancient practices, are silly to do so. For there is often wisdom in tradition, and newer is not necessarily better. Lacanian therapy is likewise a more classical form of talk therapy and mental health treatment.

To stretch my analogy, one yoga class might add modern elements, a funky song, for example, to motivate us to do the difficult postures, but the asanas and structure of the class, the move from one asana to another, is still *based on* the classical series, but with a modern twist. Lacan, if you will, is a return to the classics of Freud, with a modern twist. Some might question how modern, given that he passed away in 1981 (this to me does not seem that long ago, but to the eighteen-year-olds I teach, who were not yet born at that time, it may seem ancient, indeed). But it would be unwise to discard ideas and methodologies because they are older. And we are in need of treatment methods that highlight speech and language as essential to our personhood, our suffering, our healing and growth. In this spirit, I present Lacanian cases with modern twists. The context, the background, and the forms of expression are contemporary, but the problems, the structures, and the existential dilemmas, are quite classic.

Notes

1. On a broader scale, the expansion and impact of technology, particularly connective technologies and social media (texting, Facebook, and Tweeting), serves to keep us from actually speaking with each other in person. See Turkle (2011) on the role of technology and how it affects our attention, relationships, our experiences of intimacy and solitude, and self-identity in the age of computers, the internet, and robots. Sherry Turkle, a trained clinical psychologist and MIT professor, has been studying the interface of people and computers since the 1970s. Her latest book, *Alone Together*, tellingly has the subtitle "Why we expect more from technology and less from each other." Turkle also wrote an excellent book in 1978, *Psychoanalytic Politics: Jacques Lacan and Freud's French Revolution*.

2. iPatients as in iPhones, iPads, etc.; see Verghese (2008) on the losses entailed in the medical profession's shift from personal contact with patients to "learning" about patients via their computer data files, charts, and lab reports.

3. From a Lacanian perspective we might think of the "i" in "iPatients" as standing for imaginary patients; we are seeing a false whole image, rather than the real or even the symbolic person. We come to a static image of a person, they are given a *DSM-5* diagnosis, and the nuances of the person's actual experience—bodily and in real time—are lost.

4. Dr. Glen Winthrow related a story to me that really hit the nail on the proverbial head. He was watching another doctor interview a patient whilst entering data into a computer. The presiding doctor asked the patient how her home life was, and the elderly woman replied, "Okay", which the doctor entered into the computer as he went onto the next question. Dr. Winthrow, looking on, observed one solitary tear roll down the patient's cheek as she uttered, "Okay". The doctor interviewing, eyes on the screen, missed it.

5. On how the wide-spread use of psychiatric medications for youth and adults shape long term outcomes (past six weeks) and may be doing people's brains, and thus people's lives, more harm than good, see science and medical writer, Robert Whitaker's *Anatomy of an Epidemic: Magic Bullet, Psychiatric Drugs, and the Astonishing Rise of Mental Illness in America* (2010). Another very interesting read is *Beyond Therapy: Biotechnology and the Pursuit of Happiness*, which discusses in detail how "We can produce through drugs the subjective experience of

contentment and well-being in the absence of the goods that normally engender them. In some cases—as with traumatic memories or a pervasive and crippling sense of anxiety and despair—the new drugs can help return a person to the world and enable him to take responsibility for his life. But in many other cases, the growing power to manage our mental lives pharmacologically threatens our happiness by estranging us not only from the world but also from the sentiments, passions, and qualities of mind and character that enable us to live in it well" (2003, p. 266).

6. Alan Schwartz, in a front page article of the Sunday *New York Times*, entitled "Drowned in a stream of prescriptions" (February 2nd, 2013), powerfully and eloquently discusses the overuse of prescriptions for diagnoses such as A.D.H.D and the trend of young people becoming dangerously, sometimes fatally, addicted to these psychotropic drugs.

7. The term "talking cure" was first coined by "Anna. O," the pseudonym Josef Breuer gave Bertha Pappenheim (1859–1936) in his famous case study (Breuer, 1895d, p. 46). Breuer's encouragement of Anna O. to verbally discuss her life brought about symptom relief, much to Breuer's own surprise.

8. On the importance of the signifier in the formations of the unconscious, see Baldwin, "Reading 'On an ex post facto'" in *Reading the Écrits: A Guide to Lacan's Work* (forthcoming).

9. On the dearth of available clinically explicit and relevant literature on Lacan, see Fink (1997), Malone (2000), and M. J. Miller (2011).

10. All references to the *Écrits* will be from the 2006 edition and will list the original 1966 French pagination first and the English 2006 page number second.

11. See Freud (1895d, p. 148). After Freud, numerous authors have taken up this phrase. For a discussion of the process of symptoms "joining in the conversation" as an intricate part of the talking cure as exhibited in Freud's case study of Elisabeth von R., the case from which the phrase stems, see Parker (2003). On the role of the symptom joining in the conversation specifically in the Hispanic community, see Gherovici (2003).

12. Phobia is discussed in Fink (1997), Nobus (2000), and Baldwin, Malone, & Svolos (2011). For those interested in further understanding the psychotic diagnostic category, I recommend Lacan's "On a Question Prior to Any Possible Treatment of Psychosis" (in Lacan, 2006), as well as Vanheule (2011), Grigg (2008 & 2013), Leader (2011), Svolos (2001), and Fink (1997, 2005, & 2007). On the subjective structure of perversion, see Dor (2001), Nobus & Downing (2006), Fink (2003), and Swales (2012).

13. For a critical examination of diagnoses and the *DSM-5*, from a Lacanian standpoint, see Vanheule (2014).

14. On case study methodology and author subjectivity see Spinelli (1997), who implores us to remember that, although since Freud, case studies have been standard methodology for practitioners to "demonstrate the efficacy of their chosen approach," case studies are "highly selective 'fictions' usually told from the perspective of one, highly biased, participant in a shared experience whose 'meaning' is open-ended and likely to change significantly over time" (pp. 2–3).

15. Lacan questions the very notion of a "standard" psychoanalytic treatment in "Variations on the standard treatment" (in Lacan, 2006).

16. Lacan states rather humorously that "a psychoanalysis, whether standard or not, is the treatment one expects from a psychoanalyst" (2006, p. 329/274), and I am not, strictly speaking, a psychoanalyst. While in the United States, federal or state law does not protect the title "psychoanalyst," there is a common understanding among clinicians in the U.S., that "psychoanalysts" have been trained in a psychoanalytic institute post-licensure. This is a much-debated issue and continues to be called into question. This is not necessarily the case in other countries where a psychoanalyst is a mental health practitioner (like myself) who is trained in psychoanalysis.

17. On Lacanian psychotherapy, see M. J. Miller (2011).

18. Freud mentions that in some cases "fixing a time-limit for analysis" (1937c, p. 217) is helpful. He states, however, that the benefits of a time-limit may be costly. Freud says, "It is effective provided that one hits the right time for it. *But it cannot guarantee to accomplish the task completely.* On the contrary, we may be sure that, while part of the material will become accessible under the pressure of the threat, another part will be kept back and thus become buried, as it were, and lost to our therapeutic efforts" (1937c, p. 218). Freud makes it clear that if we wish to enact a more thorough end of analysis "our road will not lead us to, or by way of, a shortening of its duration" (1937c, p. 224). I personally find the pressure to shorten our process displeasing, but, unfortunately, necessary to discuss.

19. In recounting his experience of his own analysis with Lacan, Stuart Schneiderman describes the effects of what he refers to as the "short session". Schneiderman remembers, "The combined pressure of the shortness of the sessions and the unpredictability of their stops creates a condition that greatly enhances one's tendencies to free-associate. When things come to mind they are spoken almost immediately, with spontaneity, for there is no time to mull them over, to find the nicest formulation. The analysand is encouraged, rather unsubtly, to get to the point, not to procrastinate or beat around the bush or even to prepare the analyst to hear disagreeable comments. Almost by definition the

ego can never be the master of the short session" (1983, pp. 133–134). The variable-length session also encourages "a free association that took place between sessions, in both senses of the word between" (1983, p. 136), and a coming to terms with not being in complete control. Schneiderman states, "Lacan was evidently not bothered by the fact that a short session could never permit the patient to think things over, to enclose things within the net of consciousness. For him psychoanalysis was the enemy of all that" (1983, p. 15).

20. Fink prefers the verb "scanding", rather than "scanning", because "scanning", "the accepted verb form, has rather different connotations which could lead to considerable confusion here: looking over rapidly, quickly running through a list, taking ultrathin pictures of the body with a scanner, or 'feeding' text and images in digital form into a computer. All of the latter should be clearly distinguished from Lacan's idea of cutting, punctuating, or interrupting something (usually the analysand's discourse or the analytic session)" (1995, p. 187, n22). In agreement with Fink, I employ "scanding" as the appropriate translation.

21. Indeed, Lacan's use of the variable-length session fuels much of the controversy surrounding Lacan. It was part of the reason he was excluded from the International Psycho-Analytical Association (IPA). On Lacan's excommunication from the IPA and a history of the psychoanalytic community's response to Lacan, see Roudinesco (1990).

22. Fink discusses the term "analysand" (*analysant* in the French) as derived from the gerund of the verb to analyse (1997, p. 9). One could also say that Lacan is making a substantive use of the present participle form of *analyser*. *Analysant* literally means "analysing," or "analysing one". It is mostly working as a verbal adjective (participle) describing the action of the subject. The English word analysand cannot fully capture Lacan's meaning, because it can easily be taken by readers in the sense of a Latin *gerundive*, which actually has a passive meaning (compare Latin gerundive of *porto*: *portandus*, which means "being carried", or often, "having to be carried" or "needing to be carried"). And that is the meaning that Lacan was expressly trying to avoid.

23. As Freud states, "A decision on the diagnosis and the form of therapy to be adopted has to be made before any thorough knowledge of the case has been arrived at" (Freud & Breuer, 1895d, p. 256).

24. As Fink states, "The hysteric does not so much desire her partner as desire *via* her partner" (1997, p. 166).

25. This term and other Lacanian vocabulary, which appear in this introduction, are glossed and discussed in the successive chapters as they arise and where appropriate.

CHAPTER ONE

Needling the virgin: navigating the pathways of hysterical desire

In each of these five case studies, I have chosen a few aspects of therapeutic work, from amongst the myriad, to bring to the fore. In this case, I focus on the role of speech in recognising a person's (Lacan would say subject's) desire, and how that desire relates to the Other's desire, maps onto ego identifications, and is embedded in the workings of the signifying chain. I also explicate Lacan's formulation of "the hysteric's question". And if only fragments or possibly none of those opening sentences made sense, the case itself will hopefully shed much light. I often tell my students that when working with Lacanian theory, we must take a breath and remain calm in the face of uncertainty. Lacan's teachings remind us to dwell in the realm of unknowing, to listen, and to follow the signifiers. The following case also offers an example of working with a client with hysterical structure. First a brief discussion of Lacan's specific diagnostic scheme is in order.

Diagnostic distinctions, Lacanian style

A main feature that distinguishes a Lacanian approach from other therapeutic models is the adopted diagnostic system. Clinicians use diagnostic categories as short cuts to reference a client's problems, symptoms, style, and pervasive relational patterns. These categories orient clinicians regarding treatment recommendations. Currently, the majority of mental health professionals in the United States rely on the *DSM* model.[1] Lacan's diagnostic schema, however, is not your regular *DSM*, and the difference in systems can make dialogue between clinicians of varying schools more difficult. We are utilising distinct vocabularies; the translation barriers of English and French are repeated in the *DSM* versus the Lacanian diagnostic divergence. In an effort to further conversation between practitioners across theoretical orientations, Lacanians must elucidate our diagnostic system in a manner that resonates with other mental health professionals.

There are a number of excellent theoretical accounts of Lacan's diagnostic schema available in English (see Fink, 1997 & 2005; Grigg, 2008; Guéguen, 2013; J. -A. Miller, 1996a; Nobus, 2000; and Soler, 1996). For present purposes I will draw upon the five case studies presented here to illuminate two of the categories, also known as subjective structures, that fall under the neurosis category: hysteria and obsessional neurosis, of which a very brief elaboration is in order.

Lacan's diagnostic schema is based upon the works of Freud, as well as various classical European psychiatrists including Kraepelin and Clérambault. Unlike the *DSM*, with its ever-burgeoning diagnostic classifications, the Lacanian schema has only three main categories: neurosis, perversion, and psychosis. From a Lacanian approach, the clinician must work on situating the subject by distinguishing between structural categories. One of the first questions the clinician asks herself is whether the client has a neurotic, perverse, or psychotic structure. This distinction is particularly important because one works quite differently with neurotic patients than with psychotic ones.[2] One certainly does not want to trigger a psychotic break in a client with psychotic structure, which is possible if one is not careful.

If a client is believed to have neurotic structure, then one determines more specifically whether he or she falls under the hysteric, obsessional, or phobic type. These categories are not comprised of a variety pack of symptoms as the *DSM*'s are. While people with shared structures are likely to exhibit similar symptoms, these alone do not guarantee structure. One must decipher how the symptoms relate to psychic structure. A main task in describing a Lacanian approach is articulating how to recognise structural differences between diagnostic categories, what they can actually look like in practice, and how we work differently depending upon the diagnosis.

Differentiating between hysteric and obsessional structure, Lacan poses that both are concerned with the question of their being. However, obsessionals are more concerned with the question of existence, "What am I as a living being?" or "To be or not to be?" Whereas the hysteric's question concerns her sexual being, "What is it to be a woman?"[3] Those somewhat acquainted with Lacan may have heard that the hysteric's question is "Who am I? A man or a woman?" and still may not have understood it. People who have heard of this formulation have asked me, "But what does that actually *mean*?" I find that fully understanding these questions, in relation to the two structures, is possible only in relation to actual human/clinical experience.

In this chapter, I explore the diagnostic category of hysteria and emphasise the hysteric's question. Certainly, a client does not (usually) embark upon therapy articulating, "I want to know what it is to be a woman". Rather, the neurotic's question is a "secret and muzzled question" (Lacan, 1993, p. 174). One asks her or his question via symptoms, parapraxes, and relationships to others and the world. Lacan deciphered and distilled these questions from Freud's texts and clinical phenomena. Indeed, one of Lacan's leading contributions is his formulation of these questions in relation to neurotic structure.

In the following, I discuss how Lacan's formulations of hysteria guided my clinical work with a client whom I shall refer to with the pseudonym Mona. I chose this name, in part, because the sound "Mona" simultaneously captures a reference to both sexuality and suffering. It evokes the sense of pleasure and pain related to sexuality. It also connotes a complaint. Indeed, this client bemoaned her circumstances, particularly in the sexual relationship arena, and blamed the Other—an important term we will return to below—for her misery. Also, the meaning of Mona's actual given name implied sadness and had a sexual connotation, and thus while the name I have bestowed upon her is fake for the sake of confidentiality, it also remains true. Readers may also notice that the signifier Mona shares phonetic similarities with the name "Dora", who was Freud's hysteric *par excellence*, and we will have occasion to discuss Dora later in this chapter.

To be sure, there is always something in a name. A child's given name is a signifier *par excellence* of the parents' desires. As a therapist, I make a point to explore a client's given name and why a particular name was bestowed—the story around the name. Names often play an integral role in situating a person, unconsciously and consciously, within a family and the larger social environment.

The case: the other, the signifying chain, and coming attractions

Early in our work together, it became clear that Mona fit into the hysteric category rather neatly. My first clue was what Mona talked about most—she spent the majority of her sessions discussing her relationships with men. Whereas the hysteric tends to fill up her[4] analytic sessions speaking about her relationship to the Other and where she fits into the Other's desire, the obsessional, as we shall see in Chapters Two and Four, endeavours to eliminate the Other from his discourse and speak about theories, the world, or himself divorced from the Other, as much as possible. One thing was clear—Mona's discourse was intent on questioning the Other's desire.

Lacan explicitly distinguishes between the "other" and the "Other" with a capital O (in French it is *"autre"* and *"Autre"*, hence the symbol *A* for Other and *a* for the other in Lacanian algebra). The "other", also known as "the little other", "small other", or *semblable*, refers to other people, people who are like you or me, often with whom one competes, in the form of ego rivalries.[5] The "Other", also known as "the big Other" takes on many forms—the Other as language, the Other of speech, of law, of desire, and the Other of the unconscious, to name a few. Perhaps it is easiest to think of the difference between "other" and "Other" in terms of a position that stands in relation to the person. Whereas I can point to an "other", for example, a sibling or friend, and say she is so and so and is like me or not like me, the "Other" is abstract; it is actually not a person at all but a locus, a place, that is present in any relationship I have with another person and mediates the relationship between us. The Other holds a locus or position, which may be, for example, of demand, desire, or power. One example is the notion of "Big Brother", which we interpret as a group of people who have desires and power over us, but we have trouble pinning "them" down. We can also make a comparison with a game of chess where the relationship I have to the other player is mediated by the rules of the game. There is always an imaginary component in any game—of bluff, intimidation, rivalry, and seduction—but ultimately, in a game like chess, the rules of the game determine how the players relate. Similarly, the Other always mediates one's relationship to others, though obviously in a much more complex manner. If we take sexual relations as an example, we can say that Oedipal issues will mediate access to a sexual partner. Indeed, psychoanalysis has shown that the Oedipus complex is close to being the bedrock of the Other.

Mona's position in relation to the Other proved to be representative of the hysteric's position. What also unfolded in our work together was how Mona's romantic relationships served as supports for her desire, which also proved to be characteristic of an hysteric logic of desire. Mona's neurotic strategy can be most clearly elucidated if we look in turn at her relationships with five significant men in her life. Each relationship formed *a triangular circuit of desire*, which contained the imperative presence of another woman. These relationships provided the material out of which Mona formulated the hysteric's question "Am I a man or a woman?" via complex identificatory processes that are characteristic of hysteric structure. We will also see how Mona embodied the hysteric's question with her very being, including her somatic (i.e., conversion) symptoms, which are characteristic of, although not definitive of, hysteric structure. In addition to the case material, I utilise both Freud's case of Dora (1963), who in analytic literature represents a classic case of hysteria, and Lacan's commentary on the Dora case (1994), to shed light on the logic of hysteric desire.

With respect to the way in which the Other is present in the life of a subject, Lacan invokes what he calls the "insistence of the symbolic chain" (1994, p. 135).[6] Lacan seems to use the terms "symbolic chain" and "signifying chain" somewhat interchangeably. For some reason, the former was used more in his earlier work, and the latter in his later work. If we bear in mind Lacan's remark in *Seminar III* that "discourse [...] is a signifying temporal chain" (1993, p. 176/155), then the signifying chain appears to be an amalgam of the symbolic chain and the chain of discourse, and, of course, discourse is tied to the symbolic and to the unconscious. Lacan states, "The symbolic order subsists as such outside the subject, as distinct from, determining, his existence" (1993, pp. 111/96–97). The symbolic chain or signifying chain at once "determines" the person's existence, but is also separate from and goes beyond the person. It touches upon the larger social and symbolic matrix and context in which an individual is embedded. Language is a perfect example. This chain precedes a person's birth and continues after her death. When Lacan says, "the unconscious is fundamentally structured, woven, chained, and meshed by language" (1993, p. 135/119), he provides another image of the signifying chain. This signifying or symbolic chain also embodies the implicit rules by which a subject lives her life. For as Lacan explains, "Once you have entered the play of symbols, you are always forced to act according to a rule" (1993, p. 63/51). A main aim of Lacanian analytic work is to explicitly articulate this implicit chain and the rules governing the client's life, unbeknownst to the client and to put these into words. Paying very close attention to and highlighting a client's words, illuminates this chain, this mesh, this web that holds and moves one along in ways of which she or he is unaware.

Both the signifying chain and the hysteric logic of desire can be viewed more concretely via a discussion of Mona's relationships to five important men in her life. Thus, I turn to Mona's narratives of John, Luke, Matthew, Mark, and last but not least, her father.

The presenting problem

When Mona commenced therapy with me, she was in her late-twenties and in graduate school. Mona usually attended therapy once a week, but when she felt either acutely distressed or especially interested in her own discourse, particularly when she associated to dreams, she came more often—twice or three times a week. I recommended she maintain two sessions a week, but she often resisted and refused to comply with my desire. We can detect in her fluctuations in the number of weekly sessions a propensity to keep the Other's desire both alive and unsatisfied, which will be discussed below. After fourteen months of sessions, Mona took "a break" during the summer, for three months, and said this was due to scheduling problems. She was working full time and finishing a degree. However, we had also reached a place in our work where we were discussing Mona's own involvement and role in orchestrating relationships in certain ways that will be fleshed out below, and which threatened her "comfortable" way of being with others. Her "break" can be viewed as an evasion of assuming responsibility and as avoiding knowledge of it, even though, at some level, it was also an admission. On yet another level, she may have also felt that I was too forcefully pushing her own role and responsibility in what she had deemed to be the other's fault, and her break may have been this message to me. Or her desire for a "break" could have signified that I was simply barking up the wrong tree, getting things wrong; although I did not recognise any particular evidence for this (that does not mean it was not the case).

Importantly, I phoned Mona after the summer break and invited her to return to therapy. My inviting her to return was premised on Lacan's theory of "the analyst's desire", which, as Lacan states, is what ultimately operates in psychoanalysis.[7] This desire must be open and enigmatic, a placeholder for the client's desire as opposed to a specific desire for the client to do x or be y. However, there is one desire that must be manifested. As Fink states, "If there is a desire in therapy that serves as a motor force, it is the analyst's, not the patient's" (1997, p. 4). The analyst holds a desire for the work to continue, most importantly for the client to speak and then say even more. This is an area that distinguishes a Lacanian approach from many others. While many therapeutic schools place the responsibility for the drive or eagerness to engage in the analytic work in the client's hands, and thus leave it up to the client as to whether or not to attend or continue sessions, Lacan claims this is naïve. The passion for ignorance and the satisfaction and enjoyment one obtains from symptoms and resistance in general is a given. The analyst must "hold the place" of *a desire to continue the work, to say ever more,* and I adopted this position when I called Mona and invited her to continue to talk with me.

Mona initially began therapy because she was "distraught" over her love life. A string of relationships with men had gone awry. A man she had recently *"fallen* for" had abruptly "broken it off". This word, "fallen", uttered in our first session, was particularly apt. Mona was raised in a Catholic family for which sex before marriage was taboo, and this was principally true for females. Mona interpreted that her family did not mind if her brothers had sex before marriage, even though they too were raised Catholic, and she, understandably, took this to be a double standard. That Mona had sex with men out of wedlock made her a "fallen woman" according to the religious context in which she was embedded. The cultural context of Mona's Catholic upbringing proved integral to understanding her symptoms and neurotic condition, her suffering and pleasure. Throughout my work with Mona, I found that punctuating her signifiers and questioning their origins and meanings often led us to discuss her Catholic upbringing and the cultural context of her symptoms.

The phrase "broke it off" was likewise seminal, for Mona's relationship to the phallus and lack thereof, as will come into relief, played a significant role in her suffering. The wording of her presenting problem, uttered in that first session, that "a man [she] had fallen for had broken it off", was very significant and meaningful. But it would take time and much more speech to understand how this phrase was situated in the larger context of Mona's psychic life.

In our first session, Mona also questioned, "what was wrong with [her]?" such that her beloved would leave her. The latest break up had caused a narcissistic trauma. She specifically questioned her choice of prospective partners. Was she choosing the wrong man? Why did the men in her life *make her* suffer and miserable? Mona looked to me to answer these questions. She began therapy with a request to know why these men behaved so badly, thinking I might hold the answer. In other words, Mona began our work with a self-pitying, "poor me" complaint. She presented herself as ignorant of what *she* was "doing wrong" regarding her romantic relationships.

Following Plato and others, Lacan discusses "three fundamental passions": love, hate, and ignorance (1988a, p. 271). That "the subject who comes into analysis places himself, as such, in the position as somehow in ignorance" (1988a, p. 271) and simultaneously places the analyst in the position as the one who knows something (the "subject supposed to know" or "*le sujet supposé savoir*", see Lacan, 1978, pp. 230–243) is a fundamental condition of Lacanian analytic work. Indeed, this ignorance slowly becomes subjectified—that is, worked through as well as owned, when the client assumes responsibility on multiple levels. Through the analytic or therapeutic process, through speaking, the client takes more responsibility for her role in the inter-human dialectic of which she is a part, as will become evident in this case.

Mona also complained, in our first session, that since the recent break up, she had "lost [her] fight". Her words: "I lost my fight". I found this phrase curious. She had not "lost *the* fight", but rather had "lost *her* fight". In losing her romantic partner, she lost her fight. When asked, Mona explained that she intended this phrase to mean that she could no longer concentrate on schoolwork or much of anything. She felt disconcertingly tired and not her usual spirited self; she thus described depressive phenomena. But as we shall see, rather than focus on the depressive states per se, focusing on and working with Mona's (unconscious) desire, which Lacan—following Freud—reminds us to do, came to affect and even relieve these phenomena. Going back to the wording of her presenting problem, we shall see that this phrase, "to lose [her] *fight*", was part of the signifying chain that constituted Mona's desire. For Mona, fighting had to do with desiring.

Mona's questioning of her status as a scorned single female, whose lover had run off and no longer seemed to want her, gave rise to a substantial amount of recognised angst. But it also seemed to provide a detectable degree of unrecognised or misrecognised pleasure. Mona was particularly angry that her friends and family told her to "get over it" or "move on". She said they did not understand how *"important this rejection"* was to her; she wanted to be allowed to talk about her dilemma. She reported that her friends and relatives were getting "bored" hearing (over and over again) about her problems. Thus, she came to therapy to tell *me* about it. And indeed therapy, in one sense, *provided a substitute pleasure*; it was a place where Mona could explore her questions and yearnings with someone who would listen and was supposed to know something, and who in this case was another woman, which takes on importance, as we shall see.

The story of John and the virgin

In addition to voicing her complaints about others, in our first session Mona told me that up until the time she finished college, she had thought herself "too selfish" to have children. She would have time for a lover or a husband, but not children. Money, time, and a lover/husband were the objects[8] she desired. But Mona said this original "mind-set" had radically changed three years ago when she became involved with John, a man who wanted to have a big family. He told her of this desire, and she reacted by adopting it. Through her relationship with him, she also began to want a "big Italian family", and told John of her newfound ambition. According to Mona, John, upon hearing about her change of heart, then promptly joined the Seminary to become a Catholic priest! Mona was understandably distraught and angry over John's actions, but she said that as a result of her relationship with John she kept her new position and shifted her concentration from focusing on work and money to having children. She clung to her newfound identification of herself as a mother and fantasised about finding a man to father her children and moving to Italy—the land of "big, warm families". In this way, she retained her identification with John and adopted his object of desire as her own even after he had abandoned her. She described the "irony" in the fact that her mother had always wanted Mona to be a "traditional wife and mother", but Mona had previously positioned herself against her mother's desire. Mona marvelled that it took "falling in love with a man" whose desire was for children, for Mona herself to want them. In this way, *Mona desired what the Other desired*. Lacan is renowned for his statement, "Man's desire is the Other's desire" (2006, p. 628/525, also 1978, p. 235). As we will see, Mona, as an hysteric, exemplifies this position by continually adopting the other's (and Other's) object of desire as her own via a series of identifications.

Mona's narrative about John epitomised how Mona's desire formed around a man who rejected and left her for the Virgin Mary (in this instance both literally and figuratively). The man Mona desired turned away from her and towards a saint. As will be shown, this very tale, which Mona told in our early therapy sessions, contained many of the key points in the symbolic or signifying chain that carried Mona along and set the preconditions for her desire, unbeknownst to Mona or myself. The tale was a shard, with a fractal quality, of the entire matrix that repeats.[9] At the time of the telling, I did not know this; I merely paid attention to what Mona presented, to her words. But I kept an ear out for similar patterns and substitutability (a key aspect of Lacanian listening), which eventually appeared in Mona's discourse. In other words, as Lacan suggests, I "set out in search of unconscious desire" (1978, p. 235) as it appeared in her speech. This unconscious desire was indeed located in the signifying chain, as Lacan tells us it will be.[10] Thus, I listened for how Mona's desire was constituted in and by both the Other's desire and discourse.

Luke: all good things come in threes

Mona spoke of another pattern: she fought with all her boyfriends. Fighting, she articulated over time, fuelled her passion. She mainly fought about other women, some she described as "virginal," others as "sexual deviants," and what became clear was that there needed to be a third party in play for Mona to be involved with a man; this allowed her to orchestrate and fit into the circuit of desire.

For example, Mona described her very first lover, Luke, as "a bastard" who "pushed [her] buttons", got her all "fired up", and "made life hell". Mona met Luke on a high school trip and described a school bus ride during which Luke "needled" her about drinking too much at a recent social gathering and told her *ad nauseum* about his girlfriend. Mona was hooked. For the next six years, on and off, Mona and Luke fought over other women and often ended their *heated* arguments in bed. Mona said their "best sex" always followed a fight about another woman. Late night squabbles with Luke kept Mona energised, made her feel alive—indeed she said they "got [her] through college", (and may have been the most interesting part).

Mona also befriended Luke's other women and "learned from them". She admired one of Luke's ex-girlfriends, Julie, in particular. Mona's friendship with Julie revolved around Luke. She said befriending Julie really *"helped with* Luke and was therapeutic". Eventually Julie wanted Luke completely out of her life, which Mona (unconsciously) could not tolerate and therefore ended her friendship with Julie. What *I* heard in Mona's discourse was the following: If Julie no longer helped Mona navigate the path to Luke's desire, then what use was she? For that matter, what good was Luke on his own, *sans* the other woman? Shortly after Julie left Luke, Mona put an end to her own relationship with him. For Mona, without consciously recognising it as such, removing one character from the circuit of desire was intolerable, for then the whole circuit collapsed.

Why did Mona, even if she did not consciously realise it, *not* want to sustain a one-on-one relationship with Luke? Because through the pathways of desire, Mona identified with Luke and adopted his object of desire, Julie, and in turn used Julie to help formulate the question, "What causes Luke's desire?" For Mona longed to be the cause of his desire, even as she found an answer to what it was to be desired by a man in the man's desire for another woman. Lacan puts it very well when he says, "For each of the partners in [a] relationship, both the subject and the Other, it is not enough to be subjects of need or objects of love—[each] must hold the place of the cause of desire" for the other (2006, p. 692/581). Mona set out, albeit unconsciously, to figure out what it was to be this cause and how to become it; one could say it was her cause.

Of course, Mona did not present the situation in these terms; rather, she discussed the cast of characters and how she related to them, including how badly she suffered and how the people involved—in this case Julie and Luke—*put her*, she felt, in awkward positions.

However, over many months of speaking, we began to notice that the portrait and discourse repeated, and repeated. Other women took Julie's place and then Mona was able to sustain an on-again off-again relationship with Luke. According to Mona, the best sex she and Luke ever had came after Luke showed Mona a photograph of his ex-fiancée. Mona had never seen her image and was very curious. Luke, as Mona rightly remarked, "Knew how to play". When Mona's desire waned, he introduced another woman into the circuit. Luke then became engaged to a woman who did not believe in sex before marriage; she was an "Italian, Catholic virgin". Mona wondered aloud what Luke saw in this saintly woman. In one therapy session, Mona went through a list of characteristics, provided by Luke, and compared herself to the supposed cause of his desire. By choosing other women—culminating in a saint/virgin—and by "needling" Mona, Luke remained in the picture. The question that burned for us was what made this scenario, which tirelessly repeated, so frustrating yet also so very attractive to Mona?

Matthew: getting a rise as proof of love

The signifying chain insisted. The demise of Mona's two-month affair with Matthew, a man she thought was "the One," was what initially brought Mona into therapy. She called it the "last straw on the camel's back". Mona had hoped to keep Matthew's desire coming, so to speak, and wanted to know what "mistakes" she had made and if there was something undesirable about or wrong with her. She (rightly) expressed concern that if she did not understand what had occurred, the pattern would repeat—men would keep "turning their backs *to*" her. I questioned, "Turning their backs *to* you?", for I thought the expression was "turn your back *on*" someone. The "to" insertion pointed to an image of a man turning his back to Mona and turning toward another woman. In associating to the slip, Mona said she suspected that Matthew was having an affair and had left her for another (more satisfying) woman. For, when Mona went to his house to speak with him about the break up, he would not let her in to his house. He turned his back to her and shut the door. Mona *imagined* he was returning to a woman who awaited him inside.

Mona's relationship with Matthew was marked from the start by the presence of other women. She met him at a party where she watched him lick whipped cream off another woman's body. While this act had "repulsed" Mona's friends, it had secretly turned Mona on. Matthew had more than a few things going for him. Mona said she thought he was "the One". I asked Mona what made someone "the One?" First, she said Matthew was *"big"*. Also, his past girlfriend had died and, therefore, knowing what we know, was a perpetual other woman, with a martyr quality no less. Mona unconsciously interpreted Matthew's desire as extending beyond her to this other woman who was, according to Mona's Catholic belief system, in heaven. This scenario of a man's desire extending beyond Mona to a saintly other woman did not cease to appear in Mona's discourse, rather it *insisted*. This relationship could be diagrammed as follows:

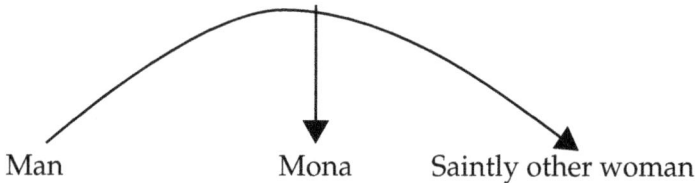

Man   Mona   Saintly other woman

The man was Matthew and the saintly other woman was the deceased girlfriend. In the preceding relationships, the men were Luke and John, and the saintly other women were the virginal fiancée and the Virgin Mary. In the three relationships, Mona interpreted that the men argued with or "needled" her while they desired beyond her.

A few months into their relationship, Matthew accepted a job out of town, but not before Mona told him she thought she was pregnant. Matthew promptly left the state without saying goodbye. Mona was not pregnant; she informed Matthew of this in writing but received no reply.[11] His stance towards her, one of seeming cruelty, seemed to only enhance his status. For despite the fact that she suspected him of having an affair, and that he coldly refused to let her into his house to talk things over before he left town after she told him she was pregnant, Mona *continued* to speak of Matthew as "the One", and even as "such a good guy". It seemed that for Mona, a "good guy" and "the One" correlated with being both "big" and "abusive" (her words for Matthew). I asked Mona who else in her life was "big and abusive"? She replied, her father, and added that her father and Matthew shared other similarities—both were also "not formally educated" and looked like "lumberjacks".

Through a series of projections,[12] Mona had unconsciously (and then through talking in therapy, consciously) identified Matthew with her father. This was reinforced in one of Mona's dreams. By speaking about her dreams, Mona connected arguing with Matthew to fighting with her father and to the circuit of desire. Mona dreamt that Matthew called her and when she picked up the phone he yelled at her for not trusting him. Mona found the dream upsetting and spoke of her fear that Matthew was angry with her; she said that she did *not* want him to be angry with her. I brought up how in dreams, and waking life for that matter, a fear can also represent a wish (I did not explicitly reference Freud, but of course recognising the unconscious wish inherent to a fear is classic Freud). Mona was very taken aback. Why would she *want* him to yell at her? She wanted him *not* to be mad! Didn't I get it? But following this intervention, Mona said that perhaps she did wish Matthew *would* yell at her, because that would at least show he cared one way or the other, that he thought of her even. He had left town "without so much as a fight". They could have at least had a fight; she had *"lost [her] fight"*, the fight she wished she had. The phrase, the very one she uttered in our first session to describe her depressive phenomena, returned.

I asked Mona to say more. Mona associated her wish/fear with the fact that throughout her childhood and teenage years, her father often yelled at her. They often argued. "About?" I asked; usually about Mona's siblings and mother. Mona said during those *"heated* arguments", she felt closer to her father—at least they were interacting. At least he was paying attention to her. At least Luke, like her father, had the decency to care enough to be mad, to fight and engage with her. Mona said, "The worst thing is indifference." Fighting signified to Mona that she was worth fighting about, over, even for. In this way, *fighting was a sign or proof of love.* As long as the other was not "indifferent", she would be all right.

Moreover, as Mona described with Luke, arguing turned her on. Indeed, Mona would bring her libidinal ideations into the therapeutic conversation by first discussing her arguments and indignation. *Whenever she pointed to or brought up her anger, her desire and sexual feelings were not far behind.*

Mark and hysterical questions

After her relationship with Matthew ended, roughly nine months into our work together, Mona became involved with Mark. This relationship, *overdetermined* as it was, epitomised how her desire was created and sustained in and by the signifying chain, and provided the material with which Mona formulated the hysteric's question. When Mona met Mark, he had just ended a six-year relationship with Suzy and was dating not one but *two* women. Thus, the relationship began with Mark having to give up two women for Mona, double trouble. This was another pattern. *Mona's lovers had to give something up as a proof of love.*[13] And in so doing, in giving something up, their lack was revealed. Desire is coextensive with lack in that one cannot desire what one already has. *To keep the Other's desire alive, the hysteric attempts to keep a lack in place—to keep the Other lacking.* This lack in the Other came to the fore when the men Mona was involved with had to give up someone they desired. This was a precondition for commencing the relationship.

This pattern repeated. Some months into their relationship, Mark told Mona that he had been having an affair with another woman, but he added that the sex was "not so hot". Mona came to therapy distraught and yet exuded a detectable degree of pleasure; a jouissance[14] seeped through as she spoke of her "horrible" newfound circumstances. Mona seemed at once upset, irate, but also very animated and excited, heated, as she cried and asked through tears, "why me?" throughout the session.

In the next session, Mona said her relationship with Mark had "greatly improved". I encouraged her to elaborate by repeating, "Improved?" Mona said the relationship was better than it was before the affair. It took the affair (Mark turning to another woman) and repenting, feeling badly (like her father did on specific occasions), and then making a show of giving up this other woman (revealing a lack), for Mona *to feel loved and loving* toward Mark. Mona said that ultimately she was glad the affair had happened. It put her in "a better position" regarding Mark. How? For one, Mark's giving up the affair served as a proof of love and also as a reinstatement of Mark's lack—he lost an object that he desired. And by needling or arguing with Mark about his affair, Mona pointed to his lack.

In a similar vein, Mona described how Mark occasionally drank too much and could not sustain an erection; he then blamed her. Mark "went soft" and then was *"hard"* on her. One night, when unable to perform intercourse, he told Mona, "Our sex life would be better if you lost weight." Mona was hurt and angry. He apologised the next day and Mona said in our next session, "The sex has been better ever since." She added, "It's funny, but it took a comment like that to make things better."

What was it about this incident and comment that improved things? First, Mark's occasional impotence highlighted his lack of desire (the sex could be better and thus was lacking a certain something). Mona could also interpret Mark's comment to mean that he desired something else (a thinner woman was one of Mona's interpretations), which meant that his desire was unsatisfied and thus *sustained*.

It was important for Mona's desire to sustain desire, to highlight (if not create) the lack in the Other. The signifier of the Other's desire extraordinaire is the phallus; the phallus is also the signifier of lack. Mona imbued the Other, in this case Mark, with the phallus. He held power and had phallic attributes. When Mark uttered the "sex would be better if you lost weight" comment, he indexed both a desire and a lack of satisfaction. He also made a comment that we came to understand as reminiscent of her father's verbal abuse. It was familiar to Mona.

Mona had unconsciously identified Mark with her father, just as she had done with Matthew. Both Mark and her father were big men, not formally educated, and had a tendency to upbraid Mona, although Mark did so less frequently and usually while in bed. Mark and Mona's father turned out to have another trait in common. Neither was fond of children. Mark wanted to spend his time and money on having the "good things in life", material possessions and travel adventures, not on children. Mona said she understood this "mind-set" as she herself once held it (before her relationship with John), and re-found it through speaking with Mark and encountering *his* desire. Faced with decisions regarding her future and particularly whether or not to have children, Mona struggled to locate her *own* desire, which seesawed between identifications with different men.

Additionally, in Mona's eyes, both Mark and her father had another woman, a love beyond Mona, and the other woman served as an object of fascination. Not long into the relationship, Mona found herself wondering about Mark's ex-girlfriend, Suzy. Mark had told Mona that sex with Suzy was fantastic and deviant, and had kept him with her for several years. Mona often fantasised about Mark and Suzy having acrobatic, "deviant" sex. While having sex with Mark, Mona fantasised about Suzy being in the room, and wondered how she compared to Suzy. Mona thought, "What would Suzy do now?" These thoughts put Suzy in Mona's place, put Suzy in the bed as the cause of Mark's jouissance, as the cause of the transgressive, "deviant", painful pleasure that he got off on. Why did Mona do this? For one, in conjuring up

Suzy, Mona could be the cause of Mark's desire and yet avoid being the cause of his jouissance. During one session, Mona excitedly proclaimed, "I want to know what makes sex with Suzy so great!" The slip was revealing; she said "makes" rather than "made" (and at least in theory, Mark and Suzy were no longer lovers). Mona orchestrated things in such a way that she could fantasise that the sex was enjoyable for Mark because he was, in a way, (still) having sex with Suzy instead of Mona. This scenario exemplified how through all of the hysterical shenanigans, the hysteric tries to avoid being the cause of the Other's jouissance. But why? Fink articulates, "The hysteric is someone who finds the Other's sexual satisfaction distasteful, and attempts to avoid being the object the Other gets off on. She refuses to be *the cause of his jouissance*" (1997, p. 127). Mona did not want to be the object that Mark got off on. Rather, she wanted him to desire and love her, but not find sexual satisfaction through her, not be entirely fulfilled by her.[15] She wanted to be the object that caused his desire, but not the object that satisfied it *completely*. Thus Mona's fantasies of the other woman, in this case Suzy, provided an escape route; Mona escaped fully satisfying the Other. *Lacan's formalisation of hysteric structure hinges on the hysteric's propensity to orchestrate her romantic relationships around this escape route and around sustaining an unsatisfied desire in both herself and her partner—even as she complains about her lot.* Lacan formulates hysteric desire precisely as a "desire to have an unsatisfied desire" (2006, p. 621/620).[16]

Another of Lacan's formulations of hysteric desire is that because it is wrapped up in the symbolic chain, it repeats, whether we like it or not. The Lacanian analyst and theoretician, Jacques-Alain Miller, states,

> Love is metonymic. There is a connection between the fundamental object and object x, object x borrowing certain features from the fundamental object. [...] Love actually manifests that the subject is bogged down in a choice that is always the same. (1994, p. 10, translation modified)[17]

What was Mona's forced choice, or in what net was Mona ensnared? I mentioned that the tale Mona told in her first session was fractal-like and, like a crystal or snowflake, evinced the whole structure in miniature form. Mona's choice seemed caught up in the model of a man turned toward another woman, and often involved a virgin. So where did the virgin fit in with Mark? For, given the tendency toward repetition, the automatism in the symbolic, I kept an ear out for this aspect, just in case. And, to be sure, it surfaced; only this time, we heard a variation on a theme. Interestingly, the virgin in play was Mona.

Mona claimed that at the beginning of their relationship, Mark viewed her as virginal and pure. For the first three months of their relationship, they did not have sexual intercourse, which for Mona was a substantial waiting period. Mark told Mona he thought she was "so good, [she] would burn up if he touched [her]". The "burning up" could again be understood in terms of the Catholic context. Mona found the role of the virginal object of desire confusing. She said she had usually been a "swinging from the chandeliers kind of girl", who just the year before had considered a career as a dominatrix where she could play the abuser, stepping into her father's shoes, and at the same time punish men. But with Mark she played the role of the "good girl", which she thought was what he wanted her to be or do. By imagining that Mark desired something that she was not, and could thus not desire her completely, *she kept both of their desires unsatisfied.*

To fully understand both *the substitutability and metonymic aspect of the signifying chain in play*, we must turn to Mona's original matrix—that is, the role she adopted within her nuclear family, which she unconsciously repeated in her later relationships.

The father: the original matrix of our dominatrix

How does the above relate to the original matrix? The original matrix concerns Mona's position within her family of origin, particularly in relation to her mother and father, but also to her siblings. In particular, Mona had a brother (another "big man") two years her junior, with whom she also identified. For example, she called him a "player", which she also called both Luke and herself on occasion. Mona often angrily discussed the unequal treatment that was given to both her brothers, such as different chores, car privileges, and what was expected and allowed in terms of their sexuality. In this sense, the phallus was linked not only to the father but also to the brothers, and social privileges and power accompanied it. Mona was not allowed, for example, to drive her father's car, but her brothers were. Indeed, her parents gifted cars to both brothers when they were in high school. Mona was given a car much later, as a reward for graduating from college. For Mona the car symbolised her strife and the inequality between men and women.

In the interim when Mona did not come to therapy, when she took "a break", she got into a car accident. The car she had been given, which was a phallic object for her in that it represented what she did not have as a young woman and what she later received for her academic achievements, was destroyed. Mona described how it was very difficult for her to grapple with this accident; she felt "a great loss", "depressed again", and said a substantial amount of her energy went towards mourning this loss during her time off from our therapy.

Regarding her parents, Mona described her father as bitter, negative, snobby, particularly concerned with money and material possessions, and "emotionally and verbally abusive" to her and the family. Mona recalled her father telling her when she was twelve years old, "I wish you were never born. You cost too much money!" He told her not to have children, because "when you have kids, you end up with no money, no time, and no respect". This sentiment was later echoed in Mark's stance toward children. In this way, Mona's occasional "mindset" of "selfishly" not desiring children formed a basis of identification with her father. Lacan states, "When her question takes shape in the form of hysteria it's very easy for the woman to raise it by taking the shortest path, namely identification with the father" (1993, p. 178). Mona's father told her that rather than become a mother, she should become a successful lawyer and make money. Thus, we can see in Mona's desire to renounce motherhood and become professionally and monetarily successful that she identified with her father and adopted his desire for money as her own. Indeed, she considered becoming a lawyer. Her first ideal of the successful, wealthy, independent person was linked to an identification with her father, whereas the second, the nurturing maternal ideal, was linked at once to her love, John, but also to her mother, who Mona said "really played up the traditional role of the mother". Thus, we see a shifting of identifications and objects of desire, but the structure of selecting an object of desire via identification with another person, particularly a man, remained strongly intact. The identificatory process and object relations were characteristic of hysteric structure. Mona struggled between two main identifications— one with her father, a man, and the other with her mother, a woman. However, Mona did not like to explicitly and directly address her identifications with her father. She insisted in her speech that she "struggle[d] *not* to be like him" and yet surprised herself in session after session with the ways in which her identifications with and attachments to him impacted her ways of being.

Mona remembered recoiling at age seven, when her grandmother told Mona she was "just like her father". Mona replied, "But I hate him. I'd be glad if he died. Then mom would be happier." When I asked her to elaborate, Mona said her father criticised and harped on her mother so her mother would be better off without him. We can read this, in one way, as Mona taking care of her mother. Mona took her mother as a love object, and in this way adopted her father's object of desire. She wanted her father and mother to split up so that she and her mother could live more happily. Even here we can detect an identification with the father, who at times indicated he wanted the kids out of the picture so that he and his wife could just enjoy life in peace. Or we could read the inverse, something Freud repeatedly reminds us to do: Mona wanted her mother to leave her father, and then her father (and Mona) would be happier. For in the same session, Mona remarked, "I wished my Mom would leave (pause) him (pause). She would have been happier." The pause that came after "wished mom would leave" was a pregnant one. If mom left, Mona would have had dad to herself. Mona also described how she argued with her father over allowing her mother to work outside of the home, which he opposed and Mona wanted. Mona said she "fought with Dad in order *to get Mom* out of the house and *away from Dad*". This statement has a number of meanings and must be read on multiple staves of the score.

Mona's speech pointed to a repressed desire for her father. In this sense Mona had not fully resolved her Oedipal attachment to her father. And what we know about neurotics, what is key, is that the repressed returns, and returns via speech. We could construct from the verbal links, which tied her speech about her lovers to her speech about her father, that at some point the situation with her father also turned Mona on. One might object here that this is just what you would expect from a Freudian, that all Freudians end up commenting on women's repressed desire for the father. Perhaps because of this, we must stick closely to Mona's own words. For this repressed desire spoke loudly and was expressed in the sexual connotations of the expressions and words, the very signifiers, that Mona used to describe her communications and

NEEDLING THE VIRGIN   21

relations with her father. Mona recalled that her father often called her a "smart ass" and "ball buster". Although Mona associated that these terms related to her argumentative style, there is clearly a sexual content as well. Similarly and strikingly, Mona called her father a *"prick"* and said he was always *"hard on"* her, that he *"hammered"* and *"needled"* her (as in harassed her, but I also heard as in poked with a rod-like instrument, prodding and piercing), and that he was always *"riding"* her. She referred to her father as *crotchety*, as in cantankerous, but one also hears in this the word *crotch*, as in the place between the legs where the sexual organ is. Indeed, phallic imagery very often arose when Mona spoke of her father. She often repeated, "he is *so big"*, and spoke about her pleasure from *"getting a rise* out of him". These were the phrases that most readily came to Mona's mind as she spoke of her father and their relationship. The signifiers, the sounds of the words, conjured up multiple meanings, too many of them too sexual to ignore. She was using one signifier and pointing to multiple things. And the connections between the words and phrases spoke volumes, although Mona did not consciously realise all that she was saying. When she used these terms, and in my punctuating them, highlighting and saying them back to her, she was eventually able to hear the manifold meanings inherent to the terms, particularly the repressed sexuality (*a sexuality that is at once repressed but also very much on the surface of speech*), and thus through paying attention to these signifiers we can work with the repressed, which is key to working with neurotics. For Lacan, the words we choose out of all the possibilities available really matter and tell us something valuable about the unconscious, if we listen.[18]

On the one hand, Mona strongly insisted upon her hatred of her father, yet verbal bridges between him and her chosen objects of desire—the string of *"big"* men who were *hard on* her, verbally abusive, and turned toward other women—peppered her speech. In this matrix, to get a man mad is *"to get a rise* out of him". The list of verbal bridges went on. For example, Mona used the same phrase to describe both Luke and her father. She said both men were "prick[s], and made life a living hell". In the therapy, I punctuated these words, repeating them back to Mona, and thereby pointed to the insistence and metonymy of the signifying chain. In this way, *my role was as a repository for her signifiers*. And as I heard them, I asked, "Who else did they apply to?" a question that indicated they might be verbal bridges. Through this work Mona began to recognise that she was saying more than she thought she was saying and began to make connections between her speech about her lovers and her speech about her father. Moreover, she began to recognise repeating patterns regarding her desire and started to hear the multifaceted meanings inherent to her own speech.

Then there was the question of whom her father loved. Mona described her mother as saintly, devoted to others, especially her children, and a devout Catholic who did not believe in sex before marriage. Thus, Mona's father was turned toward the saintly, virginal woman, Mona's mother. Mona turned to her mother as a symbol or placeholder of Woman and as the cause of her father's desire. Moreover, while Mona's father loved a woman beyond Mona (the mother), he fought with Mona. Thus, we see here the foundation of the now familiar constellation.

Mona said that her mother was the only person to whom her father was affectionate; however, he also fought with the mother, often about money and also about having children. When Mona was eleven, her mother became pregnant again. According to Mona, her father wanted to abort the unborn child but her mother would not hear of this, as her religion deemed such an act sinful. The child was born with health defects. Mona secretly thought the child was born unhealthy as God's way of punishing her father, when asked why he would be punished she replied for being so "terrible" about the pregnancy. She spoke about how dreadful he was to want to abort a child, but we can also hear other possibilities in Mona's description of the trauma. The father giving the mother a baby was traumatic for Mona. He needed to be punished. This may have played a role in the seeming fixation at the Oedipal stage.

While Mona's father fought with her mother, Mona said she was the only one who really *"got a rise out of him"*. By accepting her father's verbal abuse, Mona put herself in the place of her mother. And yet we also see that Mona identified with her father. For example, she used to tell her parents that one day she too would have someone who dotes on her like her mother doted on her father. As a young girl, she would tell them, "One day I am going to have a doting wife" as opposed to "I am going to be a doting wife". In her identifications, she was positioned somewhere between them. We can diagram the relationships as follows:

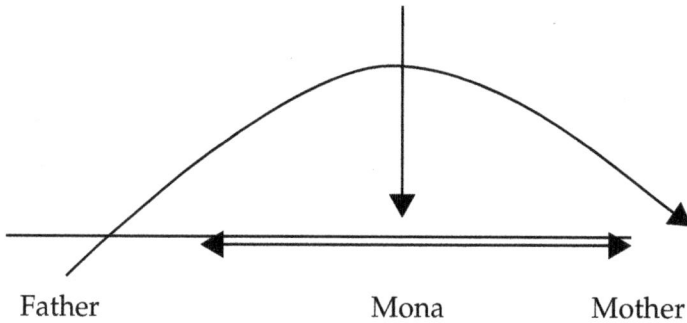

Father   Mona   Mother

This constellation became explicit in our work. At first, Mona said her father was distinct in his position because "he was the only one [she] really fought with". After hearing herself speak in sessions, she added Luke, her first lover, to this list. She said, "Those two are the only ones [about whom] I can say: I hated them", at which point, I added, "or can say, loved". In uttering this phrase, I attempted to bring into the conversation—into the explicit articulation of the symbolic chain— what had not been properly symbolised, which was a repressed love for the father. This would add the missing dimension to the anger that was expressed. Mona heard this intervention and was silent. After a pause, she said, "Yes, love".

By mapping her discourse about her romantic partners onto her family history and tracing her role in her relationships, the matrix of the preconditions of her desire came into relief, which in turn would ultimately bring Mona more relief from her fixated subjective position and suffering.

Employing Dora to explore the hysteric's question

Now that we have a portrait of the case, we can use Freud's study of Dora to tie some theoretical threads together here. In *Seminar IV, La Relation d'Objet* (1994), Lacan discusses the Dora case. Dora represents a characteristic hysteric, and I will utilise Lacan's discussion there to sharpen my case conceptualisation. Lacan's commentary also served as a warning about what *not* to do with my client, Mona.

Lacan argues that Freud failed with Dora because he did not trust in the workings of the symbolic chain, which, according to Lacan, is the very thing upon which the analyst should base her interventions. In other words, symbolic repetition must be understood in its full glory.

What Lacan calls the "insistence of the symbolic chain" (1994, p. 135) is, by definition, not known by the subject. In other words, the subject does not recognise it as such, but is swept along by this symbolic chain. Lacan charts how this insistence manifests itself in Dora's symptoms, dreams, and the therapeutic relationship.

Freud (1963) tells Dora that she will not admit to and resists her love for her father's friend, Herr K., in part because she refuses to give up her Oedipal attachments to her father. This is how Freud reads Dora's symptoms and dreams. Then, in a footnote, Freud tells us that he failed to see the importance of Dora's homosexual attachment to Frau K. (1963, p. 142, fn. 2). Lacan takes up *how* Frau K. was an object of great interest for Dora in terms of hysteric structure and Dora's position within the now infamous quartet made up of Dora, her father, Herr K., and his wife, Frau K. In formulating what he gleans from Freud's text, Lacan views this quartet somewhat differently than Freud.[19] He claims that throughout the case, "you can read in it […] the greatest ambiguity concerning the real object of Dora's desire" (1994, p. 138). Indeed, it would have been important for Freud to stay with this ambiguity. Rather, the interpretations he makes to Dora jump the gun, so to speak, in identifying the object of her desire.

Likewise, we can view the cast of characters in Mona's case in terms of the overall constellation and Mona's position within it, and we can recognise the ambiguity of the object of her desire. Did Mona desire the men in her life, their women, her father, or her mother? And, perhaps more importantly, who desired *in* Mona? That is, via which identifications was she desiring? Rather than fixate on her objects of desire, we can take up *how* these people interested Mona via the roles they occupied in the circuit. Lacan states,

> In order to know how to respond to the subject in analysis, the method is to first determine where his ego is situated—the ego that Freud himself defined as formed by a verbal nucleus—in other words, to figure out through whom and for whom the subject asks *his question*. As long as this is not known, we risk misconstruing the desire that must be recognised there and the object to whom this desire is addressed.
>
> The hysteric captivates this object in a subtle intrigue and her ego is in the third person by means of whom the subject enjoys the object who incarnates her question. (2006, pp. 303–304/250)

For example, Lacan tells us that Herr K. is important not as an object of desire per se but in terms of the role he plays regarding Dora's bond with Frau K. He is important "as a libidinal link" and as an "intermediary" (1994, p. 138). Herr K. is a middleman, so to speak. Likewise, we can see that the men in Mona's life were important and ask "how?"

We saw earlier that Mona tended to identify with the multiple men in her life and adopt their objects of desire, often other women, as her own objects of fascination. Mona's desire was for the same thing as the Other's desire. Hence Mona's remarkable interest in Luke's, Matthew's, and particularly Mark's other women. Lacan relays,

> The hysteric is someone who loves by proxy, and you find this in a lot of cases—the hysteric is someone whose object is homosexual—the hysteric approaches this homosexual object through an identification with someone of the opposite sex. (1994, p. 138)

Mona did indeed love by proxy. Her desire was dependent on the Other's desire. In a simple schema we can see a triangulation characteristic of hysteria. The love triangle that Mona set up could be diagrammed as follows:

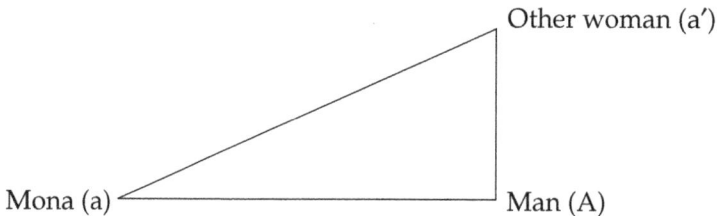

In the diagram, the *a* stands for the ego, the *a'* (a prime) stands for another ego like myself (myself being the original *a*), and the A stands for the Other. We can plug in the various characters. With Luke, the place of the other woman shifted often (first Julie, then his virginal fiancée, and so on), but the structure remained. With each man, the names changed but the circuit of desire, the triangulation, remained the same. Ultimately, we can see that the original matrix is such that Mona's father took the place of the Other *par excellence*, A, and her mother stood for *a'*, the saintly other woman whom the father desired and whom Mona both identified with as an object of her father's desire and took as an object of her "own" desire via an identification with her father.

Returning to the case of Dora, Lacan asks why Dora's attachment to Frau K. was so important. We can ask the same of Mona. Why was her attachment to Mark's other women, for example, so important? To be sure, the other women were important, on the one hand, because they were the objects desired by the men with whom Mona identified. In this way, Mona's desire was for the Other's desire. But these other women were not important solely because they were the Other's objects of desire. Lacan says that as the object of the Other's desire, Dora turns to Frau K. to answer a question. That question is, "What is it that my father loves about Frau K.?"; Lacan adds, "The whole situation is set up as if Dora had posed [this] question" (1994, p. 141) and indicates that what actually made Frau K. important to Dora was that she offered a possible answer to the riddle of what caused her father's desire.

Furthermore, Lacan reminds us that the hysteric is consumed by the question of womanhood. Frau K. held the role of Woman, with a capital W, for Dora.[20] This is what Freud failed to comprehend. Dora's question is the hysteric's question: "Am I a man or a woman?" and more specifically, "What is a Woman?" And Frau K. embodies this function as such. Thus, Dora's father and Herr K. are important not merely as Oedipal fixations, but in that it is through Dora's identification with them that she is shown the way to Frau K., and in turn is shown the way to understanding her own being as a sexual person, as a woman.

The *structure* is the same with Mona. It was through her identifications with the men in her life, from her father through Mark, that she was shown the way to the women who held the place of the question. In terms of Dora's identification possibilities, Lacan says, "There are as many potential crystallisations of her ego as you have men" (1994, p. 138). It is Likewise with Mona. We can diagram Mona's scenario, which she used to ask, "What is a Woman?" and "How can another woman be loved?" in the following way:[21]

Suzy ——————————— Mark
the question   *with whom Mona identifies*

Mona ————————
                Father
                remains the Other par excellence

Suzy occupied the place of the question and Mark occupied that of the man with whom Mona identified and through whom she arrived at Suzy. The other woman needed to be situated for Mona to find her place within the circuit. This place can be viewed as "the form of a question" (Lacan, 1994, p. 146). We saw that various men and women held the two upper positions in the schema. In *Seminar III*, Lacan says that the neurotic's "symptoms have the value of being a formulation, a reformulation, or even an insistence, of this question", and that situations and other people are the "material the subject uses to express his question" (1993, pp. 170–171). We can thus view the scenario as material with which Mona formulated the question characteristic of the hysteric, "What is a Woman?" or "How can another woman be loved?"

The question was asked in myriad ways. The role of the analyst is not to look for the answers, per se, but rather to grasp the relevant question (and how it is being asked) and bring it to the fore.[22] Indeed, Mona incarnated this very question. For example, with Matthew, Mona experienced a hysterical pregnancy of sorts, raising the hysteric question that Lacan phrases in *Seminar III* as, "Am I or am I not someone capable of procreating?" (1993, p. 170). Lacan states, "This question is obviously located at the level of the Other, insofar as integration into sexuality is tied to symbolic recognition" (1993, p. 170). This question was directed to Matthew in the role of the Other.

Somatisations of the question

Mona and Dora are by no means extraordinary. Every woman grapples with the question of what it means to be a woman. *One* answer or definition that our society tends to provide is that to be a woman is to be a mother. Mona probed this potential answer, querying whether motherhood was for her. This was also evident at an unconscious level via her somatic symptoms. Hysterics are known for their conversion symptoms, although one cannot define hysteric structure simply by these symptoms. In Mona's case, she experienced three main somatic symptoms, all of which related to the "fantasy of pregnancy and procreation" (Lacan, 1993, p. 168). In *Seminar III*, Lacan examines Joseph Eisler's case of a tram conductor. The conductor's symptoms were "characterised by an increase in pain in his lower rib, a pain that started out from this point and drove the subject into a state of increasing discomfort" (1993, p. 169). Lacan suggests that in this case of traumatic hysteria, the conductor's symptomatology is "caught up in the question that arises—*Am I or am I not someone capable of procreating?*" (1993, p. 170). Correspondingly, we can recognise how this question was inscribed in both Mona's symptoms and structure.

For example, for a period of time, Mona complained that she bled every time after having sex with Mark. She saw a gynaecologist, who could not explain the bleeding. This occurred around the time we were discussing Mark's desire not to have children. This was when Mona brought up the fact that her father did not want children at all and almost aborted her younger sister. Mona's bleeding seemed related to the question of whether she would be a mother and the discourse that surrounded this question. After discussing her desires more fully with me, the bleeding stopped.

Another of Mona's physical symptoms was distracting and limiting lower back pain. Again, lower back pain can be related to being pregnant. I asked Mona when she first noticed this pain. Mona traced the origin of these lower back pains to when she was twelve years old and had to run while she "carried [her] youngest sister" through the woods (the story goes that they were running away from a wild animal)—"carrying a child" being a maternal gesture on multiple levels—including of course, a term for pregnancy. While running while carrying a child (and her father's child at that—her younger sister), Mona sprained her back, which resulted in "bed rest," another potential feature of pregnancy. The back pains then continued on and off for years, and in light of the case we can see how her back *joined in the conversation*.

Perhaps most unusual, dramatic, and symbolic was that for the previous three Christmases in a row, Mona had passed kidney stones. It is often said that passing kidney stones resembles giving birth. During this time Mona was sexually active and the question of procreating was on her mind. Her physical symptoms—the bleeding, the back pains from "carrying a child", and the passing of objects through her body during a time that celebrates the birth of a baby (this also can be read as representing the Virgin Mary, though in a rather complicated way)—were all somatic material for expressing the hysteric's question. Thus, we see the hysteric's question played out on multiple staves of the score, in Mona's words, body, and being.

The signification of the phallus, in this case

Mona questioned why the men she loved left her—"Was there something wrong with [her]?" She described herself and her body as "inadequate". Mona had recognised that her parents treated her brothers differently than they treated her. Because her brothers were male, they were given special driving and going out privileges. They were also allowed to date and be sexual in ways that were forbidden to Mona and her sisters. Mona had felt she lacked that which made her brothers privileged. This angered her and indeed sparked many arguments with her father. She wanted to be loved and treated equally, regardless of her gender.

In speaking about Mark, Mona said, "I can't change who I am. But what if Mark (although you could substitute any other of the five men as well) can't accept me for who I am?" In this sense, Mona wanted to be loved for what she did not have. In "The signification of the phallus", Lacan discusses how the "subject [...] wants to be loved for himself" and, moreover, sends a message to the Other, "love me for what I do not have", including the phallus (2006, pp. 693/581–582).[23]

In many ways, Mona constituted her lovers as the phallus; they signified the phallus for her. However, she also brought forth their lack. How are we to understand this? J. -A. Miller states,

> To love the other is to constitute him as the phallus, but to want to be loved by him—that is, to want the beloved to be a lover—is to castrate him. Lacan has analysed the love life of the woman in the following way: she constitutes a man as phallus while secretly castrating him [...]. In the lover's relationship to the beloved, the lover's essential purpose is to bring out the lack in the beloved. This is the very formulation of hysteria. What is the basis of this operation? Quite simply, it is the demand for love. The demand for love, inasmuch as it is the demand to be loved, is the demand that the Other reveal his lack. (1994, p. 12, translation modified)

We saw the ways in which Mona brought forth this lack, how she brought a big man down, so to speak. She fought with and teased the men in her life, cheated on them sexually (this last aspect was originally left out of her narrative but later was brought to light through speech), and then yelled at them for cheating on her. Thus, in addition to the "automaton of love", the way in which the signifying chain persists, "the implication of castration in love", in relation to a demand to be loved, was also brought into view in this case (J. -A. Miller, 1994, p. 11).

The reader might ask why analysts, particularly Lacanians, often resort in their explanations to the role of the phallus. In this case, I am speaking about the hysteric's desire, which is tied up with the Other's desire. And the phallus is "the signifier of the Other's desire" (Lacan, 2006, p. 694/582). In our culture, the phallus is still the desired object extraordinaire. Additionally, J. -A. Miller clarifies that "in order for the subject to be situated in his or her proper place in the symbolic order, the subject must refer to a phallic signification" (1996a, p. 246). That is, in our culture, as far as symbolisation is concerned, it is easier to grab a hold of the phallus, so to speak. Thus, it was important to recognise where Mona stood in relation to the phallus, the phallus as a mark of castration, in order to understand her place in the symbolic order.

We have seen how Mona presented her love life to me as the material by which she formed the hysteric's question in its many forms. However, another question remains. How did this question, Mona's psychic structure, and the constellation of her desire play out in *our* relationship—mine and Mona's? For Lacan reminds us that the insistence of the signifying chain manifested itself in Dora's relationship to Freud. How did the signifying chain I have detailed above manifest itself in my relationship with Mona? Let us turn to the transference and counter-transference.

The transference and counter-transference: begging the question

Lacan claims the transference "essentially occurs at the level of symbolic articulation" and is useful in therapy as it relates to the insistence of the symbolic chain (1994, p. 135). In various ways, I detected where Mona positioned me in terms of the signifying chain and how the transference concerned a repetition of the unconscious matrices discussed above.

For example, Mona often positioned me in the role of the other woman. Mona said, "I see you, and then I fight with him". In this way, I was yet another woman who fuelled both her anger at and desire for her partner. She came to therapy and discussed her frustration with her partner, and left impassioned or infuriated. This also provided a substitute satisfaction, where her symptoms and structure which themselves once provided a substitute satisfaction, were failing; it made things "more interesting" for Mona. Thus, she placed me in the position of the third, who helped her navigate her relation to the Other.

And, not surprisingly (given hysteric structure), Mona attempted to position me in the role of the woman who could *answer* the question, "What is a woman?" or "How can a woman be loved?" She positioned me as someone who knows and could show her the way. How did I manoeuvre in my allotted position? And how did my situating Mona in the hysteric category affect my work within the transference? Unlike my work with people with obsessional psychic structure, which I will discuss in other chapters, I did not need to bring my Otherness into the room. Rather, *knowing how the hysteric studies the Other's desire in search of answers to the question of her own desire, I attempted to keep my desire enigmatic, neither here nor there, so as not to further alienate her desire.*

I situated myself in the place of the question but *not* the answer. And I encouraged Mona to question and examine her discourse and, therefore, her own desire. One must not just provide an answer, "you are this" or "you desire x". For that would have merely perpetuated the alienation of Mona's desire in relation to the Other's desire, in this case, my own. Rather, as the analyst and author Colette Soler states, "When the subject presents her demand to the analyst, the analyst responds with a question of his or her own, namely, 'What do you want?' That is why I say 'What do you want?' is the answer" (1996, p. 265). You have to make the hysteric work. Thus, I continued to ask Mona about what *she* wanted. In so doing, I found Lacan's formulation of hysteric structure a helpful guide.

And what about the counter-transference? Lacan's treatment of the Dora case reminds us that Freud got hung up on the love objects (Herr K., her father, and ultimately himself) and missed their import in the identification process, which as it turns out, was *more important* in terms of the overarching structure. The lesson to be learned is to see the structure at play and to bring this to the fore in the therapy. I aimed at this with Mona. This made room for Mona to glimpse a dynamic that repeated and not just complain about her suffering and pleasure, but see and articulate the role she played in this game, and how she orchestrated the situation, for better and sometimes for worse. It allowed us to focus less on the specifics of *whom* she desired at any moment and the nitty-gritty of her relational concerns (for this would have led to an interminable analysis for sure), but *how* she desired and *via* whom. We looked at her relationship within the broader context of her psychical structure.

Why did Freud fail with Dora in the manner described by Lacan? Lacan argues that it was due to Freud's own counter-transference. First, Freud had a tendency to work less well with women as attractive as he found Dora. Second, Freud identified with Dora's father and that played a role in his interpretations and conceptualisations. And third, we know that the question "What does a woman want?" haunted Freud (and many a man and woman) until the end of his days. As usual, Lacan detects a structural element. Lacan states,

> The Freudian topography of the ego shows us how a hysteric, or an obsessional, uses his or her ego in order to raise the question, that is precisely in order *not to raise it*. [...] The neurotic is in a position of symmetry, he is the question that we ask ourselves, and it's indeed because it affects us just as much as him that we have the greatest repugnance to formulating it more precisely. (1994, p. 174, italics added)

Lacan draws our attention to the fact that *the neurotic's question may be threatening to us*, and as clinicians we may have a vested interest in not recognising or working with it (or in quickly answering it).

I would be remiss to deny or repress how this question played a role in Mona's life. However, my counter-transference was also in danger of getting in the way. At the time of our work together, I was only slightly older than Mona and I too, at that time, was thinking about children and careers and how the two intersected and related to identity. There was a risk that Mona and I would remain stuck on the imaginary level and get caught up in imaginary relations and identifications.[24] The topics that Mona discussed—Am I capable of procreating? Who am I as a sexual and desirable being and what is my position regarding work and child rearing?—hit close to home; they resonated with me on a personal level more than some of the other topics, like withholding in relation to life and death, which came to the fore in my work with the obsessional client who I will discuss in the next chapter. In supervision, which Lacan cleverly calls "super-audition" (2013, p. 8), I discussed *my own* feelings about careers, children, and romantic partnerships, so as to keep those out of the way when working with Mona. I had to be careful to not allow my own desires, experiences, and beliefs (part of the counter-transference) to seep out and impact the therapy. Mona could easily have picked up on and even adopted or thwarted my own desires, via an identification with me, if I was not careful. In other words, I had to work to keep my desire enigmatic. Rather than work from my own personality and desires, I attempted to position myself in the role of the dummy, as Lacan recommends in "The direction of the treatment" (in Lacan, 2006), where he uses the metaphor of playing bridge to explain that the analyst must position herself in a place which encourages the subject (the analysand) to guess what is in her own hand unbeknownst even to herself. The analyst situates herself via her position as a listener. In holding the position of the so-called dummy, I encouraged Mona to guess what cards were held in her own unconscious.

In conclusion: any answers?

Mona ended our work before it was what we might call "complete",[25] when she moved to a different state to pursue further graduate schooling in a different program.[26] She decided to continue along a career path, not as a lawyer or educator as she imagined when she first came to see me for consultations, but as a counsellor, which she said was something she always *desired* to do but before therapy never thought she "had it in [her]".[27] She was moving with Mark and they were discussing the possibility of marriage and of having a child. Mona explained that she was "on the fence" about how important having children was for her, but now she was figuring this out "for [her] self", and here we can hear that she was less fettered by the Other's desire. About her relationship with Mark, Mona said it was "not perfect". In other words, *it left something to be desired*, but it "would do—at least for now". She described how both she and Mark were both lacking in certain areas, but could both love each other regardless (or, we might add, because of this!). Indeed, Mona seemed more accepting of her position and to have experienced an acknowledgement of and even shift in her means of obtaining satisfaction. By speaking she gained more freedom regarding whom and how she could desire; her desires and ways of desiring, were more conscious and less fixated than in the past.

Whereas Mona began our work complaining that she found herself, more often than not, in jealous rages and distractingly anxious about whether her partner desired her, Mona concluded our work with more understanding of and less anxiety surrounding the part she played in her relational patterns. Mona reached a greater recognition of her desire, which is one of Lacan's earliest formulations of an analytic goal.[28] Moreover, Mona had the experience of formulating her desire, in words, for me to hear. Lacan states, "It is only once it is formulated, named in the presence of the other, that desire, whatever it is, is recognised in the full sense of the term" (1988a, p. 183). And once it has been formulated for the other, it has likely shifted. In *Seminar II*, Lacan states,

> The subject should come to recognise and to name his desire; that is the efficacious action of analysis. But it isn't a question of recognising something which would be entirely given […]. In naming it, the subject creates, brings forth, a new presence in the world. (1988b, pp. 228–229)

In other words, the client's desire is constituted and *reconstituted* in and through the therapeutic process. It was through the therapy that Mona came to recognise her role in the orchestration of desire, and in so doing she simultaneously experienced shifts in this very desire.

Mona articulated some of what had previously remained enigmatic, including the unconscious preconditions of a man's charms. J. -A. Miller states,

> Analysis allows a subject to determine what makes him fall in love and makes him desire. […] At the centre of Freud's work on the psychology of love life is the determination, in almost mathematical formulas, of certain subjects' condition of love—for example, a man who can only desire someone else's wife. This requirement can take different forms: he may only be able to desire a faithful married woman, or an unfaithful woman who can easily become attached to "any x" who is a man. This causes the subject to suffer the effects of jealousy, but analysis reveals that it is part and parcel of the woman's charm, determining the unconscious status of her charm. (1994, p. 8, translation modified)

Mona, to a degree, determined what made her fall in love. She still suffered, but it was a different suffering, for she came to understand her role in it. She no longer blindly blamed the Other, but rather saw more clearly how she got off on a certain unsatisfied, heated desire. And for the time being, that was satisfying enough for her. She was able to work and love a bit more freely and easily.

In my work with Mona, I punctuated the structure in play. I tried not to focus exclusively on her object choice and miss the bigger picture, which included the role of the men in her life as *middlemen*. I came to view Mona's relationships, in part, as products of her psychic structure. Lacan's critique of Freud's folly was helpful in this regard. Lacan reminds us that Freud in working with Dora "is too centred on the question of the object, that is, in that he doesn't bring out the fundamental subjective *duplicité* implicated in it. He asks himself what Dora desires, before asking himself who desires in Dora" (1993, p. 174).[29] I explored with Mona *who* desired within her; we examined how her desires stemmed from various identifications with various men and her adoption of their objects of desire as her own. In so doing, we undertook a venture—via speech—*to further free Mona's desire from the Other's desire.* I aimed to direct the treatment to foster more separation of Mona's desire from the Other's desire. This is often a worthy analytic aim with hysterics, and we will see a similar pattern emerge regarding this goal, with the cases in this book that discuss work with those with hysteric structure.

I also punctuated the unrecognised pleasure at stake in the constellation that Mona maintained and thereby highlighted that what was originally couched as anxiety in the presenting problem, could also be seen as enjoyment and satisfying. In this way, we also highlighted Mona's jouissance.

Looking back, I would say the dialectical process was under way. Fink discusses Lacan's term "dialectization" as

> [An] exchange of demand for desire, this giving up of fixation for movement [...]. The patient, when this shift occurs, enters the dialectical process of analysis—"dialectical" in the sense that the patient becomes free to say, "well yes, I want that; on second thought, I don't really; come to think of it, what I really want is ..." The patient no longer feels he or she has to be consistent; he or she can assert a wish during one session, contradict it during the second, reassert it with slight changes during the third and so on. (1997, p. 26)

Fink goes on to say that with dialectization, *"desire is set in motion, set free of the fixation inherent in demand"* (1997, p. 26). The term also refers to questioning and confronting the contradictions and gaps within our narratives, and is related to the Greek philosophers such as Plato and Socrates who brought their interlocutors to question their own responses.

Through our work, *through talking*, Mona proceeded to dialectise her desire. Speaking helped un-stick the unconscious circuitry of her desire, providing her more room to move, particularly in, but not limited to, her romantic relationships. And this process substantially affected her symptoms—her physical complaints lessened or disappeared altogether, as did, her depressive phenomena.

Notes

1. The "DSM model" is based upon the diagnostic system that is outlined in the American Psychiatric Association's *Diagnostic and Statistical Manual of Mental Disorders*, currently in its 5th edition (2013). The publication of the 5th edition of the *DSM* has sparked much dialogue about its usefulness and validity. On the history of and critical evaluation of the *DSM-5*, from a Lacanian and phenomenological perspective, see Vanheule (2014).

2. Again, much could be said about these categories, but perhaps most importantly, Lacan makes the case that the three categories—neurosis, perversion, and psychosis—correspond to three central psychical mechanisms: repression, disavowal (or denial), and foreclosure, respectively. And one works very differently with someone who has undergone repression versus foreclosure. Central diagnostic clues can be found in the nature of the client's relationship with the therapist (including the transference) as well as the client's relationship to her own speech (Lacan, 2002, pp. 279–284/68–71; Nobus, 2000, pp. 6–11). And because analytic work is via speech, and speech works differently when it is speech that returns from the repressed, for example, versus speech that comes from a place of foreclosure, clients will, and in response clinicians should, speak differently in treatment.

3. Lacan takes up these structural questions in numerous texts. These particular formulations are found in *Seminar III* (1993), see pp. 180, 168, and 192–193 specifically.

4. I refer to the hysteric in this chapter as female, in part for convenience, but also because the majority of hysterics are female. However, there certainly are male hysterics and, for that matter, female obsessionals. Lacan states, "There are many more women hysterics than men hysterics—this is a fact of clinical experience—because the path to the

woman's symbolic realisation is more complicated. Becoming a woman and wondering what a woman is, are two essentially different things" (1993, p. 200/178). Lacan states, "In masculine hysteria the situation is certainly much more complex" (1993, p. 200/178). This complexity, for one, involves the different paths taken in the Oedipal complex by males and females. This discussion about male versus female hysteria would lead us too far astray from the case material. I direct the interested reader to Nasio (1997, pp. 113–117), and to Dor (1997, pp. 83–101).

5. On the little other, see, for example, Lacan (1988b, p. 321), and on the big Other, see Lacan (2006, p. 628/525).

6. Citations for Lacan's *Le Séminaire, Livre IV: La Relation d'Object* (1994) reference the French pagination. The translations of *Seminar IV* are my own. Lacan's commentary on Dora is peppered throughout his writings; his most extensive commentaries can be found in *Seminar IV* (1994), *Seminar III* (1993), and "Presentation on transference" (in Lacan, 2006).

7. See for example, Lacan (1996, p. 419).

8. Lacan adopts the psychoanalytic term "object". The psychoanalytic community does not restrict the use of the term "object" to inanimate things but rather extends it to persons or things, partial or whole, such as "the object of my desire" (on the history of this term in psychoanalysis, see Laplanche & Pontalis, 1988, pp. 273–276). As with many of Lacan's concepts, the object takes on many meanings throughout his work. The role of the object in Lacan's theory is, to be sure, dense and sometimes confusing. Here we find a parallel process between theory and praxis: we try to decipher the multi-faceted roles of the object in both the therapy and the theory.

9. A "fractal" quality refers to the mathematician Mandelbrot's concept that seemingly random or non-uniform phenomena, such as crystals, snowflakes, or eroded coastlines, in which similar patterns recur at progressively smaller scales, can actually be modeled via what are defined as geometrical figures, and that each part of the phenomenon repeats the statistical character of the whole such that a very specific pattern replicates itself.

10. In *Seminar XI*, Lacan states, "Analytic experience shows us that it is in seeing a whole chain come into play at the level of the Other's desire that the subject's desire is constituted" (1978, p. 235, translation modified).

11. Both Matthew and Luke eventually *turned around* and pronounced their love for Mona, who replied, in both cases, that it was "too late". At the time that they proclaimed their love, a man turned toward Mona was simply not attractive to her, did not stimulate her desire. What was attractive was a man turned toward another woman, or as will be

discussed below, an unsatisfied desire, which is a common pattern of desiring in hysteria. However, this fixed paradigm of desire shifted by the end of the therapy.

12. This is one way in which Lacan describes love, as a series of projections, based on the original love objects, onto the other. We can see in this case how Mona's "the Ones" were based on projections of both her father and the original familial situation in which she found herself as a child and young girl.

13. On the demand for a proof of love, see Lacan (2002, pp. 691/266–277).

14. Translating the French word jouissance and grasping its meaning is not simple. *HarperCollins Dictionary* translates jouissance as pleasure, enjoyment, delight, sensual pleasure, orgasm, and climax. The verb *jouir* is conjugated as to enjoy and to climax, but also in conjunction, for example, with *douleur*, as to suffer agonies. Fink defines jouissance as "a pleasure that is excessive, leading to a sense of being overwhelmed or disgusted, yet simultaneously providing a source of fascination" (1995, p. xii). It is a primal or primordial experience of pleasure and pain. A general definition of jouissance that I find useful in clinical work, is of a satisfaction entailed by suffering, that odd mixture of pleasure and pain, and that which we often characterise as most foreign to us. It is what one "gets off on". Jouissance comes in many forms and takes on a variety of functions—in our everyday lives as well as theoretically and clinically. It also takes on many adjectives. Lacan speaks of phallic jouissance, clitoral jouissance, other jouissance, the Other's jouissance, morbid jouissance, masturbatory jouissance, conscious jouissance, imaginary jouissance, avaricious jouissance, renounced jouissance, and surplus jouissance, to name a few. Then there is the supreme jouissance that flourishes before triangulation, before the instating of the symbolic via the Name-of-the-Father. This is the jouissance that is renounced and sacrificed in order for entrance into the symbolic order to occur. And there is the jouissance we are left with post-paternal-function-instatement. In Lacan's later works he differentiates between phallic jouissance and other jouissance. The former ties into the realm of the symbolic; it is mediated by language and is analysable. The other jouissance, the "better" one and the one limited to those with feminine structure, is beyond the speaking subject and unanalysable. The point is that there is a germinating heterogeneity of jouissance.

15. Lacan differentiates between love, desire, and jouissance. His theory on the discrete qualities of the three allows us to better comprehend the quagmire and complexity of relationships, as is exemplified in these five cases. See Lacan (2001, Chapter Eight).

16. Lacan extracts this formulation from Freud's case of the butcher's witty wife in *The Interpretation of Dreams* as well as from clinical phenomena (see Lacan, 2002, pp. 620–630/246–253). Lacan utilises the dream of the butcher's wife to illustrate hysterical desire, including the role of identifications and triangulation. For excellent expositions of Lacan's reading of the butcher's wife as related to hysterical desire, see Fink (1997), and Soler (1996).

17. I am using a translation of Miller's (1994) "Labyrinths of love" that is courtesy of Bruce Fink. However, I will refer to the page numbers as they were published in *Lacanian Ink*.

18. Fink speaks of the unconscious as "written in the subject without the subject being conscious of it. This unknown knowledge is locked into the connection between signifiers—it consists in this very connection" (2004, p. 109).

19. The Dora case, and all of the commentaries it has inspired (for example, for critiques from feminist theory see Bernheimer & Kahane, 1990), serve to illustrate how case studies have the potential to go beyond the theoretical intentions of their authors and are thus very useful for the transmission of theory and practice.

20. On Woman with a capital W as an essence that does not exist, see Lacan (1998b, p. 13/7).

21. This schema mimics the one Lacan creates to explain the circuit of desire in the Dora case (see Lacan, 1994, p. 143). It is based on Lacan's L schema. In "On a question prior to any possible treatment of psychosis" (in Lacan, 2006), Lacan lays out the L schema and discusses the four corners. This schema serves to explain how the "question of the subject's existence arises for him … as an articulated question—'What am I there?'—about his sex and his contingency in being: namely, that on the one hand he is a man or a woman, and on the other, that he might not be, the two conjugating their mystery and knotting it in symbols of procreation and death" (2006, p. 549/459).

22. In this way, the analyst must be like the good *Jeopardy* game show contestant who must conceptualise and formulate her responses/answers in the form of a question.

23. In *Seminar IV* (1994), Chapters Seven and Eight, Lacan discusses Freud's case of the "young homosexual woman" in terms of how the subject— in this case the young woman—wants the Other to love her for what she does not have.

24. For an interesting discussion on how the transference relationship can be mired in the imaginary dimension, and how the imaginary in the counter-transference can negatively affect a treatment, see Grigg's (2013) account of Ruth Mack Brunswick's work with the Wolf Man after

Freud. This is also yet another example of how case material can be used in the conversation and dissemination of analytic ideas.

25. See the concluding chapter for a discussion on the concept of complete analyses.

26. At the time of this work, well over a decade ago, I did not engage in phone sessions or telecommunication systems, like Skype sessions, with clients. Nowadays, it is much more common to continue working with clients via such telecommunication technologies if they move locations.

27. One might be suspicious of this career move, and worry that identification with the therapist is at play here. As the work ended before it was complete, we cannot be sure how much this was Mona's own desire, based on her experiences, including that the therapeutic work was interesting, and how much was identification. To be sure, one of the risks of premature termination is that the patient is left with a strong identification with the analyst that itself needs to be analysed. As Freud remarks, "nothing is destroyed in *effigie*" (1912b, p. 108).

28. Lacan states that a goal of analysis is the "recognition of desire" (1988a, p. 183).

29. Russell Grigg, in his translation of Lacan's *Seminar III* (1993), translates *duplicité* as "duality" in order to avoid Lacan's notion of the duplicity of the signifier and the signified. I have left the original French word because neither duality nor duplicity truly seem to suffice.

CHAPTER TWO

The male in the coffin: a case study of an obsessional

Max began therapy with me when he was in his late twenties. For over a year, he attended once a week sessions sporadically—he had a problem with regularity. When he left therapy, without warning or contact, I felt our work was unfinished.[1] Yet the case still amply illustrates certain aspects of obsessional structure.

The contrast between hysteria and obsessional neurosis can be put in stark terms. With Mona we had focused on the question of her desire as a hysteric, whereas here with Max what comes to the fore is something like the *absence* of desire. This is not really true, not for an obsessional any more than for any living, breathing human being. But the obsessional would like to think it so, and thus the fundamental question for him (or her, though they are mainly men) comes down to this: "Am I dead or alive?" When working with obsessionals, sentiments of death, time, guilt, and anal eroticism tend to rear their heads in related patterns. Let's explore, then, how Max's speech brought these concepts to the fore and how Lacanian theory informed my work with him.

"A man out of time":[2] the presenting problem

Max's main complaint was that he was not where he should be at this point in his life (indeed, he was never in the right place at the right time). Spatial and temporal metaphors peppered his speech. He saw himself as a "big kid", who at twenty-seven "should be further along in life". As he slumped on the couch, clutching a bottle of mountain dew, wearing baggy jeans and a baseball cap, he told me in our first session that he had *"no idea how a twenty-seven-year-old [was] supposed to act"*. We will better understand the multi-layered significance of the wording of his presenting problem soon. Max also complained of a "lack of direction", particularly in romantic relationships and work. We will see that via these spatial and temporal metaphors that peppered his presenting statements, Max spoke what he did not know he knew; he spoke his unconscious.

Max worked in a restaurant, which he found unsatisfying, and occasionally painted signs and murals for businesses around town as an outlet for his true passion—art. A visual artist at heart, Max could not envision a future for himself and said he could "not picture" himself at age forty. He also complained that he was unmotivated; he spent his days smoking pot and playing video games, and generally had trouble taking action in most realms of his life. He thought of himself as an artist but did not make the time to draw, to create. Rather, he described sitting around "waiting for things to happen". He felt very depressed, slept a lot, and said he wanted to "sort through [his] head".

Max also wanted to renew his anti-anxiety prescription, the medication his general practitioner had prescribed a year prior to our therapy. Max had experienced the medication as "somewhat helpful" up to a point, and wished to have more. At the clinic where I saw Max, in order to see a psychiatrist, a client must also see a clinic therapist. Hence, the main motivation for Max's decision to enter therapy and talk was to gain access to medication; speaking to another person was something he would put up with in order to get the drugs. Such a scenario is not unusual for the obsessional. People with obsessional structure tend to rely less on the Other. Whereas the hysteric, as was displayed in the previous chapter, is verbally consumed by the Other, particularly by the question of what the Other wants, the obsessional would prefer that the Other just go away or at least have the decency to be silent. Hence, obsessionals are less likely than hysterics to seek out treatment from an Other—another person who supposedly has something to offer.[3] However, mid-way through the process of the therapy, following a "hysterisation" of sorts, Max decided to use therapy alone as a means of symptom relief and went off the very medication he began therapy to acquire. By hysterisation, I refer to the process that needs to take place for an obsessional, indeed for any client, to engage in analytic work. The client, obsessional or not, needs to open up or recognise the Other and the Other's desire and in this way become more like the hysteric. Indeed, Max did begin to engage with me as an Other; although, as we will see, ultimately his desire to be independent from an Other may have been the reason that led him to leave therapy.

During the course of therapy, prominent symptoms, which were not articulated in the presenting problem, came to light. I will discuss some of them below. These symptoms centred around excreting, sex, and thinking.

Excrement, sex, thought, and withholding

First, withholding proved to be a common theme in Max's life. This tendency to hold back manifested itself in a myriad of Max's behaviours and speech acts, in and out of therapy. Max expressed that he "won't give it" to the Other who demands, be it his mother, the women in his life who request sexual relations, or teachers or employers who require certain things of him (therapists included). For example, angered and insulted by a remark made by his mother that his younger brother John was her last hope for getting the grandchildren she desired, Max told her, "Now I will wait to have children until after you are dead". This remark, uttered in our session, points to how his "waiting", his sense of the "right time" to do things, and his own desire, are intimately connected to the Other and to death. Similarly, Max left art school when he realised teachers wanted him to paint in certain ways at certain times, and he stopped painting murals when he experienced a loss of artistic control because of a boss' demands. Thus his stance towards family and work, at the time that he came to me for consultations, were a direct response to the Other's demands.

Not surprisingly, this tendency toward withholding manifested itself in the therapeutic relationship. Max often said he had nothing to say or repeated an intellectual or political spiel, which I had to repeatedly interrupt if our session time was not to be entirely filled up by his discussions on topics such as the state of the local club scene or the possibility of time travel (which was of course a favourite).

A prominent example of withholding was revealed roughly six months into the therapy when Max told me he had suffered from severe intestinal problems for as far back as he could remember. He said that, as a child, he "did not know when to go to the bathroom" and thus suffered extreme constipation. Max's anamnesis—his narrated recollection of past events—contained many stories of his parents interfering with his toilet habits, such as checking the state of the toilet for evidence of a bowel movement, which Max reported continued to occur until he left home at age eighteen! (By age eighteen, such behaviour on the part of his parents, indeed, constituted "the wrong time").

Max explained that he would not go to the bathroom until excretion would be extremely painful, in part, and because he was *scared to go* (one must notice the language). The extreme withholding of his faeces led his mother to give him enemas and even to hospitalisations because medical attention was required. The medical establishment diagnosed him at a young age with Hirshprungs Disease, where the colon is viewed as missing the necessary ganglia cells for the muscles to work properly. While he had a medical diagnosis ready to hand, Max said no medical treatment had actually helped him or provided relief, so my tendency was, as I will explain, to view his intestinal problems, which continued to bother him throughout his life and during the therapy, as psychosomatic symptoms.[4] I also viewed these symptoms in relation to the larger symbolic matrix.

What do I mean by the symbolic matrix? By this I refer to the network, the symbolic context, in which we understand a person to be embedded. The symbolic matrix determines both what is and is not allowed to be said, done, or even experienced. Just as a word is only understood within the matrix of a particular language and culture (day is only day in relation to night and the concept of a calendar, for example), so a person's thoughts, desires, actions, and words, are only fully meaningful in relation to the larger matrix of which he or she is a part. We are born into a pre-existing system of language, relationships, history, into an entire world. This matrix determines our position in relation to others and ourselves, before we arrive on the scene and after we take our leave. It is a task in Lacanian-oriented therapy to make this matrix, which is implicit, more explicit. *We are to decipher the rules of the symbolic matrix, for these are the rules the client is following, usually unbeknownst to himself.*

Part of this symbolic matrix required that Max not only withhold his faeces, but also withhold his ejaculate. Thus another symptom, which was withheld from our discourse for quite some time, was that Max had trouble climaxing—both with a woman and via masturbation. Although he presented himself as something of a ladies' man, ten months down the therapeutic road, he told me that he rarely climaxed and if he did, it took him many hours to come. Once again, he did not come at the "right time". He often refused to make love to a woman who told him she wanted him, then and there. He said that seeing women naked and having a woman "ask for it", then and now, and expect something from him turned him off. In this sense, he would rather the Other play dead than demand he act on or in time.

Max was attracted to a woman if her desire was enigmatic with regards to him. For example, he spoke of his love for a woman named Wendy and how he just could not figure out what she wanted from him. One thing he did know Wendy wanted was for him to choke her during sexual intercourse; she was into asphyxiation practices. This sexual ritual linked sex with death in a rather explicit manner. At first this disturbed Max, but later he came to enjoy it. He rather got off on the idea that the Other's desire was to die and thus go away.

Wendy also told Max that she could not bear children. On having children and being a progenitor, Max expressed ambivalence and conflict. On the one hand, he said that having children was the only reason he could see to be on this earth; he particularly wanted a son. On the other hand, the only woman he expressed a desire for could not have children, and therefore by being with her, Max could blame her for the inability to bear children and thus avoid the question. However, he said the reason he did *not* want to marry her was that she could not have children, and yet she was the focus of his romantic attention. Hence, the only relationship Max chose to be in was one that, based on his own beliefs, he believed must come to an end. In this sense, his relationship to his desire was set up to be *impossible*, which Lacan tells us is characteristic of the obsessional's stance towards desire. Finally, following what Max had pre-ordained as the inevitable demise of their relationship, Max said, "I can't let go of her and of the past". He said he felt "weighed down" by their past, like he could "not move past it". The not letting go, not moving, and feeling weighed down can also be heard in terms of the *anal metaphor that captured Max's being*, which we will turn to shortly.

Max said, "I don't like being forced." He felt pressured by one woman, who spoke of sex, and he told me, "I don't like having that hanging over me—the pressure; it's not natural. I knew she wanted to have sex with me that night. I didn't want it to be like that. I never came." Max offered many reasons for why he held back his ejaculate during intercourse. For one, he often felt guilty about something and the guilt "stopped" him. Second, he said it was a "power trip", by withholding his come, he explained, he made the woman he was with question herself and her desirability. Third, he said, "Most girls just don't deserve it."[5]

We can see a strong connection between not letting go of what he has and not giving the other/Other what, as he interprets it, she or he wants from him. With women, this concerned his climaxing, but we can trace this back to withholding his stool from his parents, who would wait for the treasured stool. Max considered both of these symptoms, the intestinal trouble and difficulty climaxing, as a hindrance to his being. He complained about both for hours in therapy. In other words, not coming was a real "pain in the ass". But both symptoms were an intricate part of his psychic structure.

At one point in the therapy, the two symptoms were connected in Max's speech by the word "television", which formed a *verbal bridge*— a signifier that connects one aspect of his history to another. In one session, Max discussed how when we was a child, his parents placed a television in the bathroom and made him sit on the toilet and watch TV until he finally had a bowel movement. In another session, Max remarked that while making love with a woman he was "in [his] head", and had spent most of the time thinking about television. He said he was bored and unable to climax so he thought of TV—"It was like I was watching TV while we were having sex". It is not unusual for the obsessional to continue thinking while having sex. Sexual intercourse poses the threat of submersion in the Other and the loss of being, and the obsessional often attempts to nullify the Other and avoid non-being by continuously thinking. As long as Max thought of TV, he was safe. Thinking of other things while having sex was a way to remain in control and remain alive. Continuous thoughts thus seem to be the obsessional's version of safe sex! *For the struggle was against death*— even the *petite mort* of orgasm. The word "television" was a verbal bridge and his parents were verbally implicated in the fact that *Max could neither come nor go.*

Problematically, for Max's life, neither coming nor going connected with retreating into inaction, illness, and thinking, and proved to be tied to his parents' discourse. On being a sickly child, Max said, "I think my dad believed that my problems were brought on by me—like I made myself sick. I didn't ... don't ... want to be sick. Dad thought I wanted attention and said it was all in my head." I repeated *"all in your head?"* about four times. Max did not respond and characteristically annulled my presence in the room.

By thinking of TV, Max was able to annul the Other's presence. He often negated our work by denying any memory of it, and thereby annihilated myself as an Other in his life. He would forget our sessions, literally, by not showing up. Or if he showed up, he would proudly pronounce that he could not remember anything about what we had spoken about in last week's session and also had nothing to say. Rather than speak to me, he would remain silent, thinking.

Thinking was his greatest pleasure, but also a curse. Max spoke about being too much in his head. He said his "great ideas" provided a retreat from a world in which he felt under-appreciated and that he "[got] off on" his own thoughts. However, he found himself unmotivated to actually do anything about them—everything seemed to stop at thought. He also complained that sometimes he "couldn't stop thinking" and said he thought so much that he exhausted himself and felt separated from his body, as if he were only a mind, only a head. Max said he also used thinking as a way to feel in control; he said people and things surrounding you can "control a lot, but they can't control your thoughts". That his father told him, "It's all in your head", was important. But Max replied, as he so often did, "Whatever he said, I didn't really care. I didn't really listen." Max did not want to think that the Other's discourse was powerful or affected him. He would negate such possibilities. Of course if we take out the "not", as Freud reminds us to do, Max "did *really* care" and "did *really* listen". When I shared this Freudian trick with Max, remarking that if we just removed the "not" for a moment, he began to think about the words he recalled his father saying a bit differently.

Max associated that his father also often repeated another phrase: that Max was a "real pain in the ass". The father's discourse that Max was "a pain in the ass" and that it was "all in his head" can be viewed as the very wording of some of Max's symptoms, and *the signifiers intimately connected with his somatisations*. Yet Max described the hurtful things his father said and did with little to no emotion and thus separated thought from affect, which is another characteristic of obsessional structure. Max cut himself off from the hurt and anger. However, to be sure, *something* in Max listened *and the Other's words, in this case his father's, provided signifiers of his existence that carried him along*. These phrases made up a signifying chain in which Max was too securely and unconsciously embedded. How might we better understand this signifying chain—that is, Max's symptoms of holding back, first his faeces and then his ejaculate, and his retreat into a world of thoughts? Let us turn to Lacan.

In *Seminar VIII, Le Transfert*, Lacan ties the three stages of the libido—oral, anal, and genital—to what he calls "the demands or requirements of the subject as we broach them in our interpretations" (2001, p. 242).[6] I will focus on what Lacan says about the "anal libido" stage, as it is most pertinent to the case and often to obsessional structure.[7] I apply this aspect of Lacan's theory because it sheds light on the clinical material that arose when working with Max and helped guide both my conceptualisation of the case and my work with Max. It also helped me further grasp Freud's concept of the connection between obsessional neurosis and the anal drive.

Lacan asks, "What sort of demand is made in the anal stage?" and answers, "the demand to hold it, to hold in excrement, insofar as it no doubt founds something: the desire to evacuate" (2001, p. 245). He goes further and states, "evacuation is also demanded at a certain point by the educating parent. The subject is demanded to give something that satisfies the expectation of the educator, in this case, the mother" (2001, p. 245). Lacan calls that which is demanded and is given the "excremental gift" (2001, p. 245). There is a gift demanded of the subject by the Other, which is to be given in the other's time, *when the other says so*. In this sense, Lacan says, "it is in the anal relationship that the other as such becomes truly dominant" (2001, p. 247). Thus, on the one hand, we can see how Max manipulated and played with the Other's demand. He withheld his gift and thereby refused the Other's schedule while he was simultaneously consumed by the Other's demand. However, Max's refusal of the Other's schedule merely demonstrated that he was severely caught up in or trapped in the Other's time. Max's time never comes, so to speak. Lacan discusses how Hamlet is caught in the Other's timetable or schedule, "*à l'heure de l'Autre*" (1983, p. 14), and the Other's desire, and demand, and thus cannot take action or make his own move. Max was also trapped and unable to act, and he made himself sick over it. He withheld to the extreme; he could neither come nor go—his time was eclipsed by the Other. Max was, in this sense, always already eliminated.

Thus, we can also read Max's symptoms on the basis of elimination. Lacan says we can situate the "fundamental relationship of the subject as desire with the most disagreeable object" (2001, p. 246), with the turd. The turd is *one* example of what Lacan refers to as object *a*, the cause of desire,[8] in this case the cause of the parents' desire. Max's parents wanted Max to excrete the excremental gift. Perhaps Max identified with object *a*, the turd, and saw himself in object *a*? Was he not, as his father said, "a pain in the ass?" The big turd that his parents wanted and looked for in the toilet, the big turd, which he was afraid would hurt him as it had in the past, was himself. It was where he found his place—down the toilet. As I indicated in the previous chapter, Lacan states that, "for each of the partners in the relationship, both the subject and the Other, it is not enough to be subjects of need or objects of love—they must hold the place of the cause of desire" (2006, p. 691/580). In this way Max came into being in the place of the turd. Furthermore, in this sense, if he did not have his faeces, if he relinquished his faeces, he had no self. To withhold the excrement was to retain his self. We can read the retention of his ejaculate, his "vital fluids", in the same vein. To be sure, both relate to potency and the possibility of impregnation.

Excrement and the ejaculate are linked; they are tied beyond demand, to sexuality and desire.[9] For desire too is symbolised by the turd. Lacan says it is "what is flushed away in the process. Desire, literally, goes down the tubes" (2001, p. 246). Did Max see a part of himself as being flushed away, and thus hold on for dear life in an attempt to avoid a loss of desire and ultimately death? Lacan says the obsessional neurotic "bases the entirety of his fantasy on his own evacuation" (2001, p. 248). This word elimination (*élimination*) is a verbal bridge for my conceptualisation of the case. We can see the question of elimination in terms of identifying with the "little excremental *a*" (2001, p. 248) and with the question of Max's own elimination, that is, his own death. Not letting go of his faeces, not climaxing, and continually thinking can be understood as ways of staving off death. This brings us to Max's relation to time and death.

Birth, time, death, and the "do nothing"

In his spare time, Max read about the cosmos, alien life, altered states of consciousness, and "doubted our place in the universe". He questioned whether he lived only in one time and space as he experienced it or if there were multiple realities and space-time continuums working simultaneously. In this way, Max could view himself as living outside of the boundaries of time and space—these were things Max ruminated on. He also often wondered about the origins of life and spoke specifically of being born at the wrong time and place.

For example, Max thought he should have been born to Native Americans when they "ruled the land" and wished he were the child of his paternal great grandfather who was Cherokee. Max thought a Cherokee father—indeed, Cherokee culture in general—would better suit his spiritual and existential interests. Max's own father was fascinated by sports and war, both of which Max had little talent for or interest in. In this way and others, Max was born to the wrong father— a living one. Lacan states, "The Father the neurotic wishes for is clearly the dead Father—that is plain to see" (2006, p. 824/698).

Max said he was born to the wrong parents, the wrong culture, at the wrong time, even in the wrong town. He recalled that his parents divorced immediately after he was born, but then reunited. Max learned of this event when he was ten years old, and his father said he would divorce Max's mother *again* if Max did not behave, as if the initial divorce was Max's fault. It is likely that the circumstances of his parents' divorce during the months following his birth, which constitutes part of his symbolic matrix, contributed to Max's thoughts that he was born at the wrong time.

Max also described living in his parents' house as "crappy", a descriptor that neatly follows the anal theme that drove his speech and inactions. He described how his parents were "poor" during the time when he was growing up and that the family's lower socio-economic status led to stressful family relations. However, Max's parents later earned more money and then spoiled his younger brother, John, who is ten years Max's junior. His younger brother, according to Max, was "born at a better time". John had the advantages of his parents being older, wealthier, more "mellow", and of having already dealt with Max. Max also said that, in general, his parents preferred his brother.

I often heard Max say, "I wasn't the child they wanted", and when I asked "How so?" he would answer in terms of not being popular, not being into sports or war, like his "macho" father was, and often being ill. He said that if he died, his parents would be all right—they would still have his younger brother. Max said, "My parents were looking for things I did wrong. Maybe I wasn't what they expected. I didn't do things like a normal kid. My brother was the normal one." He continued, "I kept my hair short the way my mother liked it and ate my food. But they were still angry with me for, like, keeping to myself[10] and staying in my room."

Max often said that, on the one hand, he was not like his parents and, on the other hand, he feared ending up just "like his father". He spoke of rebelling against his parents. Yet as an adult he mimicked his father's life, as Max described it. Following the description Max gave of his father to a tee, Max also was unhappy, did not have a job he liked, and slept most of the day. Max claimed that he lived his life in opposition to his parents' lifestyle, yet unconsciously he mimicked their behaviour.

Max wondered what his parents wanted him to be, for he did not seem to be it. Rather, through his father's eyes, Max saw himself as "a piece of shit", a phrase his father used on occasion. Max was often in trouble with his father, who Max described as violent, "full of rage", and "trained to kill" as a Green Beret in Vietnam. Max believed that when he was sixteen, his father tried to kill him—for being late, no less. Max said his father choked him until he was unconscious, because he was an hour late for dinner. Max thought he was going to die. His mother yelled until his father let go. Before leaving the house that day, Max looked back and told his father that if he ever touched John (his younger brother), Max would kill him. I asked Max why he put his brother in the role of the one who should not be beaten or killed; I was curious as to why the brother was Max's potential reason for killing his father.[11] Max replied that he had no regard for himself, what was his own life worth? Besides, he said, unlike himself, his brother was an "innocent kid". "Innocent?" I punctuated. But Max hit a wall of language. He could not say why or "in what way" his brother was innocent, but Max was not. Comments such as these could only be better understood in relation to the preconditions of Max's birth, the part of the symbolic matrix to which I will now turn.

It was not until a year into our therapy that Max disclosed that his parents had borne a child before Max was born. This first born son, named John, died soon after childbirth. John was named after his father, as is Max's younger brother. As far as the father's name was concerned, Max got passed over. The event of the birth and death of a "first born"—a signifier Max had used to refer to himself in relation to his mother—was revealed when I enquired into Max's name and why Max's younger brother, rather than Max, was his father's namesake. When I asked Max to say more about John's death, he found it difficult to speak. Max said the incident of the first son's birth and death was very rarely talked about by anyone in the family, including Max, although he remembered once seeing the gravesite. It was as if the family attempted to deny the death, and yet Max unconsciously kept it very much alive.

After a very long pause, I asked Max what crossed his mind. Max told me that he had always been convinced that his parents did not really want a second child. As proof, he pointed to his younger brother being ten years Max's junior. Max hypothesised and interpreted that had his parents actually *wanted* two children they would not have waited as long between Max and John. Additionally, Max heard his parents say that his younger brother's conception was an "accident". Thus, according to Max's (albeit rather strange) logic, since his parents did not want a second child, if the first had not died, Max would never have been born. He articulated that he had always thought that he was alive strictly *because* his older brother had died.

This scenario helps explain Max's oft repeated ideas that he was "not the son [his parents] wanted", he was not "first with them", his own life was not important, and ultimately that he was "guilty". He was *guilty of surviving and living in the place of another*. According to Max's logic, without his brother's death, Max would not exist. His very existence was premised on death. We thus find a significant component of the symbolic matrix, that is a "symbolic debt", and what Lacan has called "the forced subjectification of the obsessional debt" and "the fateful constellation that presided over the subject's very birth, the unfillable gap constituted by the symbolic debt against which his neurosis is a protest" (2006, p. 303/249). Furthermore, we see that Max pays for this debt with his very being.

Just as Max did not feel "first" with his parents, he said he could not imagine how he could be a woman's *"first* choice" or a *"prize in* somebody's eyes". Max spoke of not seeing himself reflected in the other's eye as desirable; he was *"not the right man for a woman"*. This relates back to his mother. Max did not feel he was "the prize in [his] mother's eye". He was not that which was won; he was not the *right one*; he was not the first. Rather, *there was a brother* and a father who *came first*. So who was Max? Would it matter to his mother if he died? Max asked himself this question, and his reply was, "no".

Max felt his life was somewhat "worthless". He often complained about not getting the recognition from people that he deserved. In these moments, when he questioned his behaviour and whether he was a "good catch", or could be "the sparkle in someone's eyes", he showed hysterical traits. At times Max seemed engaged in the therapeutic process, hystericised, in that there was a space opened up for the Other. But when sessions were missed, this space was often closed again.

Max spoke of "dying for love" and how he "would take a bullet for another". He said, "I have no regard for myself. If it was between me or my brother, I more likely would want myself to die." He did not index which brother; thus I heard both as implicit in his speech. He spoke of his brother as innocent whereas Max was guilty. We never reached exactly what Max was guilty for, although we touched upon one answer, the fantasy that it was so that he could live that his brother had died. Max also told me that he thought it was because he was born that his mother did not go to college and have a better career. He thought both his parents worked in jobs they hated and seemed unsatisfied in order to feed the family. Perhaps this was why Max followed so closely in their footsteps by working in unsatisfying jobs, albeit in the guise of a protest. Perhaps Max assuaged his guilt of being the cause of their suffering by sacrificing himself—flushing his own life down the toilet, so to speak.

We can also read his holding back as a way to gain the attention of the Other. His parents were wrapped up in the timing of his bowels; his mother gave him enemas and both parents accompanied him to the hospital. Even if Max did not like the attention given to his bowels, it was still attention, it was being cared for and about. We can also question the role that his illness played in keeping his parents together? Did Max use his illness to ensure his parents had something in common? Or did he use his illness as a way to escape his father's expectations? Max said his father wanted him to be a sports star, but Max could not play sports *because* he was a sickly child. We can wonder if Max's illness also gave him a reason not to satisfy his father's desire.

The structure is that of a life premised on the death of another. This premise also sheds light on why Max withheld both his excrement and his sperm. Perhaps Max did not climax in order *not* to begin a new cycle of life, which by his logic was reliant on another's death. To give life is to bring death. We can see a connection here between his pattern of withholding his excrement and the cycle of life and death. In *Seminar III*, Lacan states that in the symbolic nothing explains, "why some being must die for others to be born", but that "there is an essential relationship between sexual reproduction and the appearance of death" (1993, p. 179). We must never underestimate the anxiety surrounding death and what we will do *or not do* to avoid it.

To be or not to be? that is the question

Death was a favourite topic of Max's. He often said, "Death is the most important thing to me." He also said the same thing about thinking, "Thinking is the most important thing to me." Thus, this verbal bridge suggests that his continual thinking was tied to thwarting death. However, I do not want to *limit* the scope of the relationship between thinking and death by utilising the word "thwarting"; Max was also fascinated by death—*he was pushed and pulled by death*. During one session, he said, "It all comes down to the big question—when and how am I going to die?"[12] Lacan reminds us that neurosis takes the form of a question; he states, "The question of death is another mode of the neurotic creation of the question—the obsessional mode" (1993, p. 180). According to Lacan's formulation, the obsessional's question, which is certainly the one Max posed, is "Am I alive or Am I dead?" And, as Lacan says, the client's "symptoms have the value of being a formulation, a reformulation, or even an insistence, of this question" (1993, p. 170). Lacan states, "This, and not the disturbance of some oral, anal or even genital relation, is the determining factor in a neurosis. [...] The issue here is a question that arises for the subject at the level of the signifier, of the *to be or not to be*, at the level of his being" (1993, p. 168). This question was manifested in Max's symptoms, dreams, and the therapeutic relationship. However, an important point to recall is that the symptoms themselves do not necessarily indicate an obsessional structure. Rather, as demonstrated, they manifest themselves in relation to the structure. The question comes first, and the symptoms might be viewed as answers. Max looked for other answers as well. Ego identifications are also attempts to come to terms with questions of being.

Indeed, the question of his status as a being also manifested itself in his ego identifications. The question is directed to an Other and we must ask by means of whom and for whom the subject asks his question? Here we find an identification with the dead brother. For Max presented himself as dead too—as a dead man, a doppelganger, a double to his deceased brother—in his inaction. Perhaps this inaction was a strategy to escape blame and guilt. His younger brother was allowed to have a life, whereas Max got skipped over. This was indeed how Max said he felt: passed over and overlooked.

Max found himself unable to act and lacking motivation. He complained bitterly that he had not done anything with his life—he had not finished college, he did not have a "real job" or a family of his own, and his art supplies more often than not remained hidden in the closet. Max said he hated when he felt his time was wasted, and yet he often did just that—waste time. He wasted time in our sessions by repeating moral rants; he sat around all night playing video games, only to sleep away the day, and wasted time in dead end jobs and impossible relationships. In our first session he told me, "I am waiting for something to happen, but I really don't know what that is yet … a change in my life." He said jokingly, "I need to get a life." This then popular phrase was eerily apropos on many levels; it also pointed to the socio-cultural demands for productivity, financial success, and finished products. In the face of these cultural expectations, Max felt that his life was "going nowhere fast".

Inaction connects to the anal stage. Lacan says the "anal demand is characterised by a complete reversal of initiative, to the Other's advantage" (2001, p. 260). This "reversal of initiative" is linked to Max's relation to time and death. For the obsessional it is always the time of the Other, "*l'heure de l'Autre*", and thus the obsessional need do nothing. Max did nothing. He waited. It was not his time; in this case, it was the time of the dead br(O)ther. Max is like Hamlet, the man who Lacan says is "constantly suspended in the time of the Other" and "who has lost the way of his desire" (1977a, p. 12). And because it is "not the hour of the Other", Max, like Hamlet, "suspends his action" (1977a, p. 18). Moreover, Lacan states, "For Hamlet, there is […] only one hour, the hour of his destruction" (1977a, p. 25). What does Max await? The time of his own death and, Lacan adds, "the death of the master". What does "the death of the master" mean?

Lacan is referencing Hegel's master/slave dialectic. In the *Écrits*, Lacan states,

> It is the master's death that [the obsessional] awaits. [...] This is the intersubjective reason for both the doubt and procrastination that are obsessional character traits. [...] He is in the anticipated moment of the master's death, at which time he will begin to live; but in the meantime he identifies with the master as dead and is thus already dead himself. (2006, p. 314/97)[13]

In *Seminar I*, Lacan tells us "there is no other master than the absolute master, death" (1988a, p. 287). He continues,

> What is the obsessional waiting for? The death of the master. What use does this waiting have for him? It is interposed between him and death. When the master is dead, everything will begin. You re-encounter this structure in all its guises. (1988a, p. 286)

Lacan points out that this is a means of not confronting death; the obsessional "does not assume, in the Heideggerian sense, his 'being-for-death'" (1988a, p. 286).[14] By playing dead, Max is able to avoid both death—for he *already* is, via his identification, dead—and the responsibility to the Other that is inscribed in living. We arrive at a responsibility to the Other. Via his own speech, Max began to recognise the central role his dead brother played and would continue to play in his life if not addressed and worked through. Thus, Max began the journey of the "realisation of his history in its relation to a future" (Lacan, 2006, p. 303/249). Max was enslaved by his structure, but via free association was starting to articulate the unconscious ties that bound him and how they might be loosened.

In speaking about Freud's exemplary work with the Rat Man, Lacan explains that where Freud succeeds is in bringing the Rat Man "to rediscover in [his] story what had happened in his life, prior to his birth and after, that created a 'symbolic debt' that he had been preoccupied with paying with his very existence" (2006, p. 303/249). In a Lacanian approach, bringing the symbolic matrix to the fore is a vital component of the therapeutic work.

The fertile castration dream

Lacan tells us that the obsessional,

> [H]as no greater fear, in the end, than of what he imagines he aspires to: to act freely and to live in the state of nature, if I may put it thus. Natural tasks are not his thing, nor is anything else that leaves him master of his own ship, so to speak, along with God—namely, functions where he has extreme responsibility, pure responsibility, the responsibility one has toward the Other in which what I am articulating is inscribed. (2001, p. 306)

In many ways it comes down to the existential given and anxiety of accepting our immense freedom and a fear of our relationship and responsibility to the Other. How did this ultimately play out in the therapy? Max stopped coming after he brought me an interesting dream, which hit upon the discourse of castration. He gave a parting gift—the dream—to the Other, myself, and then relinquished responsibility; I view this dream as a nodal point of the therapy. Here is the dream:

> I and others were kidnapped on a bus by security guards. I escaped through a window and saved Wendy as well. I told a policeman what took place and the policeman arrested the kidnappers.

Max continued:

> I had a gun at some point; they had taken it away from me. I was wondering about not having my gun. I was looking around at the security officers. They were not frightening; they were ready to help out. They all had brown uniforms and holsters, but no weapons, just a towel. I pulled out one of their towels and in the bottom of the holster were big silver dollars. One of the security guards had a sub-machine gun. I asked to have my gun back. He handed me both, his and mine. I gave the Uzi to the cop, and cleared my gun chamber, *making sure it wouldn't go off*. Then I woke up.

I invited Max to associate to the dream, which he did for a number of sessions. In thinking back to his relation to the gun, Max added,

> I wanted the gun back. *I didn't want my gun to be used. Then I would have been responsible. I would be responsible if someone used my gun.*

So it can't be used. I cleared the chamber and made sure the safety was on. *If it went off somebody could get hurt; somebody could die. And I like things from the beginning to be set to zero.* I cleared it to reload it myself. Get to my starting point. I had to check the gun so it wouldn't go off.

Max focused his associations on the gun as both a symbol of death—a gun could take a life—and a symbol of power. The dream material and the accompanying associations point to various forms of the phallus, like the gun (Max's and the guard's "Uzi"!) and the money (the silver coins)—signifiers of power and what is desired by society—and to Max's relationship to the phallus *qua* signifier. In the dream, Max remembered a time when he knew or believed he had the phallus, and then a subsequent time when he felt he lost it, when it had been removed from him: "I had a gun at some point; they had taken it away from me. I was wondering about not having my gun." The dream gave voice to how Max was wondering about losing that which he needed to feel powerful, recognised, and desired by others and society.

Via his dream associations, Max said about both the guns and the money, "It's good to have it but not to use it". About the silver coins, he said,

> Money gives stability. I don't want to have it, but I need it. It is evil and it makes people do stupid things. I don't want to have it, but I'd love to be extremely wealthy because once you have wealth you don't need money anymore. Rich people get stuff for free. *If you have it, you wouldn't have to use it.* If you have it, you can control what's going on with it.

Max desired to have the phallus but not to use it, to feel confident enough in his knowledge of possessing it that he did not have to show it off (or ever *make it go off*). In his waking life, Max waited and did nothing. If he did not use it, if he did not come, then he did not run the risk of getting someone pregnant. And recall in his schema the first child has to die for the other to live. By not coming, Max avoided starting the cycle of death, or the circumstances (ejaculating/pregnancy) that lead to that situation. We can see that there is more at stake here than simply the refusal to satisfy the Other, or a power play, which were the reasons Max offered for not climaxing while having intercourse with women.

This was a matter of life and death. We can also see this dynamic in Max's reluctance to let go of his faeces. The family history that predated Max profoundly affected him; he preferred *"things from the beginning to be set to zero"*, which of course, they never are.

To return to the specifics of the dream, there was the sense that Max's penis was not his own, and that it could become detached and taken away from him. Indeed, at one point he realised he no longer had it, but that he needed it. The fear of castration, of the possibility of loss, was well articulated in the dream. The security guards, representing the authoritative male (his father, and/or perhaps me), are also revealed not to have the phallus. The towel in the dream covers over a lack. Recognising this lack in the Other is at once "scary" but ultimately necessary and even empowering. Max asked the authoritative Other, the security guard/cop, if he could have his gun back. Indeed, he could—to Max's surprise (his own and the Other's). During his associations, Max said, "It was weird that there was no struggle; they were happy to comply." The dream pointed to anxiety around castration but also to the possibility of overcoming it, of coming to terms with one's own lack and the lack in the Other, something which Max had been unable to do in his waking life, but was doing in his dreams.

Max's dream and his associations pointed to the work we had been doing in the therapy: it related to the discourse of making sure nothing risky goes off, that nothing happens, so no one gets hurt, including Max himself (and possibly me). Whereas Max often annulled my presence and our work (by not coming to sessions or saying he could remember nothing from our last session), he presented a dream that impressively and compactly highlighted the therapy's underlying main themes.

Although I did not know it at the time, these dream associations comprised our last sessions. Max gave the gift, but never came again.

In conclusion: it's all about the Other

How might I make sense of Max's premature termination? Perhaps a transferential crisis occurred and did not get worked through. Possibly Max experienced a reproduction of the situation with his parents during toilet training and beyond—feeling that I was demanding that he excrete a gift during the time allotted in our sessions, in a sense, on my time. He gave me gifts, his words and ultimately the fertile dream, and perhaps I was supposed to be satisfied with them, with the "little excremental *a*", and leave him alone. Perhaps in giving up object *a*, in excreting a gift in therapy, he lost his desire, which was eclipsed by the Other, myself. *Did he fear the loss of his own being, his desire, or perhaps the opportunity for a rebirth of sorts, and thus stopped coming?* It is possible; for as Lacan reminds us, the obsessional believes he is doing "everything for the other person" (2001, p. 245), but at the expense of his own desire. This is one interpretation of the transferential crises. An alternative and rather optimistic possibility would be that in presenting and working with the fertile dream, Max experienced a certain triumph or success in relation to the task of working through castration. Perhaps in asking for his "gun" and getting it from the Other, he experienced a shift. Unfortunately, because he did not return, I cannot know. Certainly, in this case, the problem of desire was left unresolved and, I must admit, half the time *I* did not know if I was coming or going.

Notes

1. For a discussion on what might constitute a complete analysis from a Lacanian perspective—that is, various analytic goals and endings—see the conclusion of this book.
2. This case reminded me of Elvis Costello's wonderful lyrics from his song "Man Out of Time" (1982): "He's got a mind like a sewer and a heart like a fridge. He stands to be insulted and he pays for the privilege. To murder my love is a crime, but will you still love a man out of time?"
3. As mentioned in the last chapter, there tends to be a correspondence between being male and having obsessional structure and being female and having hysteric structure, which explains, to some degree, why males are less likely to begin and remain in therapy than females. Of course, societal pressures and standards also play a role in this inequality.
4. Nowadays, we are more and more likely to see obsessional structure present with psychosomatic symptoms reminiscent of hysteria. Fink states, "It seems that obsessionals are increasingly succumbing to physical ailments that are 'stress related'—which is nothing but a modern medical buzzword for psychosomatic—and that are just as *telling* in the choice of the part of the body affected as the hysteric's psychosomatic symptoms ever were" (1997, p. 115). Regarding the chosen areas for somatisation, Fink observes the obsessional's "predilection for the digestive and excretory tracts" (1997, p. 115).

5. In these discussions of how Max withheld his ejaculate during intercourse, one is reminded of Lacan's question, "How do neurotics make love? That is the question with which people began" (1998b, p. 80/86), and the myriad answers to it.

6. The following citations for *Le Séminaire de Jacques Lacan, Livre VIII: Le Transfert* correspond to the French pages. The translation is courtesy of the translation by Bruce Fink (forthcoming).

7. Soler reminds us that "Freud links obsession with the anal drive and hysteria with the oral drive. But in his definitive conclusion, it is not possible to identify one kind of neurosis with one kind of drive—it is a matter of frequency" (1996, p. 252).

8. The notion of object *a* (*objet a* or *objet petit a* in French), is another example of Lacanian algebra. It goes through an extensive theoretical elaboration in Lacan's theory and is loaded with meaning. Lacan presents numerous formulations regarding object *a*. Bruce Fink provides the following as possible representations for object *a*: "the other, *agalma*, the golden number, the Freudian Thing, the real, the anomaly, the cause of desire, surplus jouissance, the materiality of language, the analyst's desire, logical consistency, the Other's desire, semblance/sham, the lost object, and so on and so forth" (1995, p. 84). For our purposes in this case study, the most important definition of object *a* is the cause of desire, often that which is perceived to be the cause of the Other's desire. That said, various conceptions of object *a* will come to light through the context of the different cases presented in this book.

9. In *Seminar III*, Lacan discusses the analyst Joseph Eisler's case of the Hungarian tram conductor to discuss how "elements of the libido [...] are inscribed not only in the symptoms but also in the structure" (1993, p. 169). Lacan states, "One mentions his anal preoccupations, for example. But what does the interest he brings to his excrement revolve around? Around the question of whether in his excrement there may be fruit seeds still capable of growing if they're buried in the ground" (1993, p. 171).

10. This could also be related to his parents being angry that Max kept his faeces to himself. Later in life Max generally kept to himself. In his late twenties, his friends also remarked upon his tendency to "keep to himself".

11. In light of this death threat against the father, we may also hypothesise a lingering desire to kill his father. When Max's father suffered heart failure during our therapy, Max said "*not* that I wish him ill, but ... I did*n't* wish him harm ... but I knew it wasn't his time." This pointed to a possible repressed death wish for the father, surfacing in the negation, "I *don't* wish him harm", where a fear, like in a dream, can

represent a wish. Freud, in *Totem and Taboo* (1912–1913), reminds us that a fear of death, for oneself or another, can result from a desire or wish that another or oneself would die.

12. Max held the belief that his death would be due to internal, as opposed to external, causes. He felt the Other was dangerous, but not as dangerous as his own body! One day, Max complained of a pain in his loins and his own anger at himself for falling prey to such pain. He called the boy and man who succumbed to bodily weakness, also read as bodily enjoyment, a "wuss", and said he tried to control this part of himself with logic and thinking, but sometimes failed. He worried that his body would lead to his own demise.

13. See Leclaire (1980, pp. 106–107) on how the obsessional speaks of the refusal of the possibility of his own death, in that the obsessional lives as though he was already dead.

14. Lacan elucidates, "The master, let us get it straight, has a much more abrupt relation to death. The master in the pure state is in a desperate position in this respect, because he has nothing but his own death to wait for, since he expects nothing from the death of his slave, except a little inconvenience. On the other hand, the slave has a great deal to expect from the master's death. Beyond the death of the master, he really will be obliged to confront death, as every fully realised being has to, and to assume, in the Heideggerian sense, his being-for-death. Now precisely, the obsessional does not assume his being-for-death, he has been reprieved. That is what has to be shown him. That is the function of the image of the master as such" (1988a, pp. 286–287).

CHAPTER THREE

Speaking of throwing up the id:
symbolically situating symptoms

I worked with a woman I shall call Lisa once a week for a year. Lisa was a student specialising in cell reproduction research and was nearing the end of her graduate school career. She was what we call ABD, all-but-dissertation, however, rather than dissertating, she was suffering from a major depressive episode and was contemplating quitting even though she was at the tail end of the doctoral program. Her advisor, an older man, suggested she might be depressed and, rather than quit, perhaps she would do better to seek counselling. Lisa was touched by his suggestion. It was a fatherly act of care and attention, representative of acts that she considered to be in too short supply for most of her life. In part because she was so hungry for such acts, she followed his advice and entered therapy.

When I met Lisa she was twenty-eight and suffering from a recurrent depression that consisted of the usual symptoms: low and agitated mood, decreased energy, concentration, motivation, and libido, accompanied by increases in weight, crying, passive suicidal wishes and in feeling anxious, sad, lonely, and overwhelmed. She also stressed that she felt "worthless".

Socially, Lisa maintained acquaintants from her science lab, but had very few close friends at the University. She saw her boyfriend twice a week on average. She thought they made a good match but worried that her rapidly shifting moods and tendency to "end up in a puddle of tears on the floor", as she put it, was threatening the relationship and pushing him away.

As mentioned, she was having real difficulties working. She despised the thought of going into the lab. Instead she often "zoned out" in front of her T.V., for much of the day, which made her feel even worse about herself. Certain days she did not leave her apartment at all. She felt she was failing in love and work and was terribly frustrated that this bout of depression, which had emerged one-year earlier, had struck her. She had experienced six major depressive episodes since she was thirteen; the first one occurred after her parents divorced and her father moved out.

Be that as it may, I am not going to focus on Lisa's depressive symptoms. Instead I will discuss a mysterious symptom that reared its head once the work was well under way—the fact the she was, as Lisa put it, "deathly afraid of throw up". Six months into our work, Lisa presented a fear of "throw up" and a host of avoidance strategies. However, before I dive into the unravelling of this particular symptom, I will say more about Lisa and her presentation.

Lisa, a tall, overweight, tidy, almost squeaky-clean woman, sat with her arms crossed over her chest. She squinted at me via a sideways glance through her glasses. The look was almost of disgust, as though she was smelling something unpleasant. I did not find her particularly charming (although, in time, I came to be very touched by her own peculiar charm). She was very bright, very guarded, and had little faith in therapy. She had been to the clinic where I worked twice before and, disgruntled with both prior therapists, had terminated therapy after a mere handful of sessions. In her desperation, and because her advisor suggested it, she would try one last time. I told her from the outset that I would be at the University clinic for one more year and could work with her for that duration. Sceptically, she agreed.

Family history: Lisa's anamnesis

Lisa was her parents' first child. When she was born, her father was a scientist in graduate school (Lisa was following his career path). They had little money and lived in a small mid-western town. The family narrative was that Lisa had been a fussy child with many allergies and required a lot of attention. Lisa recounted her mother's comment that she "wondered whether or not [Lisa] would join the human race". The comment stuck, although Lisa did not know what to make of it. Lisa was three when her mother became pregnant again. With the mother's pregnancy and then the sister's arrival, the attention given to Lisa wavered and withered. It was no longer enough. Lisa recollected this event to be very difficult.

When Lisa was thirteen, her mother informed the father that she was a lesbian and wanted a divorce. The father moved out and the girls lived with their mother. Lisa's world spiralled out of control; she said in the small town where she lived, the best thing you could hope to be was "normal". She had desperately tried to fit in, although her intelligence often worked against her, and she believed her mother's sexuality to be a blaring idiosyncrasy and a disaster for her own social life. Lisa went through school, from middle through graduate studies, feeling ostracised. She kept to herself fearing that if she engaged with other people, they would discover "her secret". Lisa said she was tired of feeling "different" and resented that her mother had *"forced [her] to take a different path"*. Indeed, a significant portion of the therapeutic work lay in demarcating further separation between Lisa's and her mother's path and separating blame and responsibility. However, when Lisa came for therapy, she felt her mother's choice had implemented unmovable obstacles.

Lisa was intensely angry with both parents. She recalled a night during the divorce when she overheard her parents arguing in an adjoining room. She heard her father "try to talk [her mother] out of being a lesbian". He said he did not see a problem with the marriage; he felt it was going fine. Lisa recalled that her mother replied that the marriage "was holding her back". Taking in this discourse, Lisa filed away that her mother was at fault for the demise of the marriage.

According to Lisa's narrative, faced with the loss of his wife, Lisa's father, in turn, "abandoned" his daughters. She referred to him as an "absent father". He remarried within a year following the divorce—far too quickly for Lisa's comfort—and dived into his new marriage and his work. He married a graduate student who studied the same field of science that Lisa later chose. Lisa's stepmother did not bring any children to the marriage, nor did they have children together. Regarding her father's love, Lisa felt that after the divorce she took a "back seat" to the stepmother and fiercely disliked her for it.

The divorce was awfully traumatic for Lisa. She said, "They left when I needed them most. They didn't have it in them to help me. They just *disappeared*." Something in Lisa's life disappeared, the love and attention she needed to feel *worthwhile* and secure. She painfully felt the loss of her father's love and anger at her mother for making the wrong choice; indeed she felt both had made wrong choices. Lisa felt that if her mother had chosen her father, then the father would have stayed and chosen Lisa. She unconsciously interpreted that had the mother stayed, Lisa would have had her father's love instead of his refusal. Instead, *Lisa was stuck on this demand and on this irrecoverable loss.*[1] She said she put up a fight; in other words, she addressed her demands for love and recognition to the Other, but her call was not heard and so she stopped asking (at least verbally—for, as we shall see, she demanded with her *being*).

Lisa was likewise stuck on her complaint regarding her father's shortcomings. Lisa heard from the other room that her father was not what her mother wanted; he was inadequate and did not have what it took to satisfy the mother. *The father's lack came to the fore just when Lisa most wanted him to respond to her demand for love* and her discourse became swept up in her father's failing. As we shall see, this lack in the Other was a partial cause of the symptom.

During the course of therapy, Lisa said she wanted to let go of this anger and frustration, but could not do so. Indeed, her jouissance was fixated on the impossibility of making up for that loss. Sadly, by clinging to this jouissance and attaining a strange satisfaction from her position, she did not address her demand for love elsewhere, where it might be better met.

And when I first met Lisa, sublimation was not working, although this shifted over the course of therapy. Recall that Lisa took a profession that mirrored both her father's but also her stepmother's. In so doing she positioned herself on the same plane as the woman chosen by her father. On one level, this was an unconscious answer to Lisa's question of what her father wanted. Through her graduate work, Lisa also connected to her father who was also a scientist. Actually, she felt that work was frequently *all* they connected about. He would often speak to her in his office at school, like a professor to a student. That Lisa's work was not going well was tied to her relationship with her father, which was also failing and which she considered quitting.

One day Lisa slipped while talking about the enzymes she worked with in the lab, saying, "I'm not getting the reaction I want. *He* won't react how I want them to. They're just not reproducing right." "He?" I asked. "I meant they" she replied. By that point in our work, she knew to say more. "My father won't either", she said. She wanted a certain "reaction" from her enzymes and her family but felt a paucity of control regarding both. She described how the most frustrating part of her work was not being able to control the process. She just had to hope that when she called upon her cells in the lab the next morning that overnight they would have done the right thing—what she needed them to do. That said, let us turn to the seemingly nonsensical symptom.

The seemingly nonsensical symptom is spoken

Six months into therapy, Lisa brought up a strange symptom that she had never mentioned prior. She was "deathly afraid of throwing up". She was repulsed by her own and others' vomit. The day prior to our session, a woman in Lisa's lab had thrown up in the only bathroom on their building's floor. Lisa feared she would no longer be able to use that bathroom and was uncomfortable with even entering the lab at all. And while she said the vomit was the last thing she wanted to think about, she could not get it out of her head. She described what happened in detail as soon as she sat down. I asked her if she had been present at the scene and she replied she had not, but she had asked for all the details and then passed them on to me. The exchange was reminiscent of the Rat Man repeating the tale of the cruel captain to Dr. Freud. The initial telling had revolted Lisa and inflicted a punishment in and of itself and she then placed herself in the role of the torturer in relating the tale to me. When I appeared curious rather than horrified, she said she knew it was "crazy", but it was horrendous to her. This was her symptom.

Lisa hated throw up—the act and the object (vomit and throw up being both verb and noun)—and she avoided any place where someone had done it. In elementary, middle, and high school she knew all the "contaminated places", from bathroom stalls to plots of grass on the playground, where children had once vomited, and she did not step foot on them. She refused to use one water-fountain for six years because a child had once thrown up in it; instead she walked to the other end of the school, and yet she was unsure why she did so.

Since she was ten years old, she had thrown up only twice. She resisted doing it and instead performed a ritualistic act. When she had the urge to vomit, she would go to either a couch or a bed—preferably in the dark—and lie on her back, completely still, barely breathing or moving, and not make a sound. Intellectually she knew she would feel better if she purged what was ailing her, but she refused. She preferred to keep it in and keep it down, which, of course, sustained and prolonged the nauseous feelings and the urge to vomit.

The two times she vomited, she had drunk too much alcohol and could not use her usual control mechanisms and ritual to repress it. One of those times, she was with an ex-boyfriend and by the way she described it, it was a rather tender moment. She allowed herself to be sick with him and it felt unusually good. But by and large, throwing up was a prohibited jouissance.

For Lisa, the concept and act of throwing up was hieroglyphic in nature; it remained a pertinent and powerful symbol that had lost its referent—it was a signifier that had lost its signified. Lacan describes the symptom as "the signifier of a signified that has been repressed from the subject's consciousness. A symbol written in the sand of the flesh and on the veil of Maia, it partakes of language by [...] semantic ambiguity [...]. But it is fully functioning speech, for it includes the other's discourse in the secret of its cipher" (2006, p. 281/232). Throw up was not just a substance or an act, *it was a signifier of Lisa's desire* that had been repressed from her consciousness. As Lacan states,

> [In symptoms] speech is driven out of the concrete discourse that orders consciousness, but it finds its medium either in the subject's natural functions—provided a painful organic sensation wedges open the gap between his individual being and his essence, which makes illness what institutes the existence of the subject in the living being—or in the images that, at the border between the *Umwelt* and the *Innenwelt*, organise their relational structuring. (2006, p. 280/232)

And this symptom, which we discovered contained several different wordings, "include[d] the other's discourse in the secret of its cipher" (2006, p. 281/232). Let me explicate how.

Unravelling and unknotting the meanings of the symptom

Needless to say, I encouraged Lisa to explore this symptom via speech, free association in particular. Why throw up? I asked if there was anything in her history that could shed light on this phenomenon. She replied, "No, *nothing.*" However, by this point in our work, she knew that a monosyllabic "no" just would not cut it. We had been connecting the dots of her past and filling in her anamnesis and this symptom stood as *one very big ellipsis.*

Nothing came to mind, *nothing* she could recall, she said; it was just one of those weird things. We sat and she began to talk. It began slowly; then she produced a string of signifiers, a set of events and scenes from her childhood that her discourse chained together. Lisa confirmed the connection of the physiological function to the scenes and signifiers extracted from her history. By the end of her associations over a number of sessions, Lisa was taken aback, and quite taken with herself. Deciphering the message of her symptom (or, put another way, constructing more sense of her symptom in therapy) brought her a certain degree of pleasure and satisfaction. Of course, in both marked and masked ways, which I will discuss, so did the symptom itself.

Lisa began by saying that her fear of vomit made her question whether she could have children because she could not bear the thought of morning sickness. Moreover, infants and children are notorious for throwing up, what would she do, run away from her vomiting child—"just disappear when the child needed [her] most?"—a phrase that echoed what I heard before describing what she perceived her parents had done to her. She asked me, "How am I going to be a pregnant woman? Can I be a pregnant woman?" which we can read as a form of the hysteric's question "am I capable of procreating?" and "am I a man or a woman?" Indeed, this symptom can be read as Lisa's unconscious attempt to grapple with this puzzle; it sustained the hysteric question. But why was the question taken up by this particular signifier—throw up?

I asked her to say more. "You now, when you're pregnant, you're sick", she said, indexing "morning sickness". Met with my silence and interest, she went on. She recalled that her mother told Lisa that she knew she was pregnant with Lisa because she felt so nauseous, so sick. As the story goes, Lisa's mother was at work when her colleagues brought in Chinese food, which Lisa's mother usually enjoyed. But upon smelling the Chinese food, Lisa's mother felt *disgust*, and then threw up. It was at that moment, she said, that she knew she was pregnant. The premise is that to have a child is to make someone sick. The wording could be rephrased as "Lisa made her mother throw up" or "Lisa made her mother sick". Unbeknownst to Lisa, her mother's spoken words, linking her disgust and desire to vomit and to her pregnancy (and ultimately to Lisa's existence—for this was how Lisa located her place in the Other's desire), chained together and helped form Lisa's symptom. In other words, the mother's discourse lent itself to the very wording of the symptom, and something attributable to the maternal Other was imposed onto Lisa. However the symptom did not refer to the mother alone; it referenced an entire cast of characters from Lisa's family matrix.

For example, Lisa knew she was not the only one responsible for her mother's nausea. After all, her father had *something* to do with it. He was "responsible" for impregnating the mother. Thus, the wording could be rephrased as "father made mother sick" or "father makes mother want to throw up" or "father, by giving mother me, makes her sick", even "[Lisa] via the father, makes the other sick". The mother's pregnancy was a signifier of the father's desire, and it made her sick, according to the discourse Lisa carried with her. By not throwing up, Lisa was holding down these signifiers of desire.

The signifier of the father's desire also made Lisa sick in that this desire was met with repulsion. Through this symptom, Lisa confronted sexuality with revulsion. And in this way the symptom is connected to Lisa's "individual manner of confronting sexuality" (Soler, 2003, p. 90). This was evident in her ritualistic act of staving off the throw up. And yet this act simultaneously produced a secondary satisfaction. The symptom as portrayed by Freud, and as Soler states, is an "anomaly of the sexual, more precisely a distorted substitute of the so-called normal sexual satisfaction" (2003, p. 88). Not throwing up was Lisa's substitute satisfaction. For in not throwing up, she holds onto something. The verb to throw up also references getting rid of, or saying "no" to that which is in the stomach, not unlike getting rid of the baby. The retention, which sends her to bed, may also be viewed as a holding on to the baby—which adds another layer of depth to the incredible contradictions potentially inherent to the symptom.

In a reverse bulimia of sorts, Lisa throws up nothing. As Fink reminds us in discussing Lacan's reading of Kris' fresh brains case, the nothing can be an object that keeps desire alive (see Lacan, 1988a, & Fink, 2004, p. 60). By not throwing up, or throwing up nothing, Lisa sustained her desire; moreover, she retained her desire to sustain her desire.[2] By not throwing up, she clung to and protected this one desire that was left to her, particularly because vomiting was a jouissance reserved for others—Lisa's mother, for one, and her younger sister, for another.

For Lisa's sister also had privileged access to this jouissance, which was prohibited to Lisa. Lisa felt the family was a happy threesome until the sister came along. During the pregnancy, Lisa's sister was the cause of the mother's nausea such that the mother could not be as caring and attentive towards Lisa. The loss of her mother's love during the pregnancy was also symbolised for Lisa in another way: Lisa complained that *her pregnant mother's "lap had disappeared"*. Lisa no longer had anywhere to sit; *there was no space for her anymore*. She had lost her place in the family.

And then the horrible sister was born. Lisa said, "I was not pleased; I didn't forgive her for eighteen years." To add insult to injury, her sister had the revolting habit of throwing up (a lot!), which earned her even more attention, much to Lisa's chagrin. Lisa recalled these vomitous scenes. As far as she could tell and remember, she had not consciously recounted these scenes before, but they came to her in rapid succession as she associated to the words "throw up".

For example, Lisa recounted a day when her mother left what she was doing with Lisa to wake the baby and then found the baby in bed with vomit all around. Instead of helping her mother, Lisa ran out of the bedroom screaming. The (likely exhausted) mother yelled at Lisa for being silly and unhelpful. Lisa felt unfairly chastised and shamed, "worthless", and worth less than her (foul) little sister. Another time Lisa could see the bathroom from her own bed and watched as her father held her sister over the toilet as she threw up. The father said "good girl" as he stroked the sister's hair. Lisa said, "I witnessed it. I tried not to listen, but I couldn't not. Why would he tell her she was good when she was being so disgusting? It angered me. Wasn't I good?"

Yet another scene that came to Lisa's mind took place when her parents threw a party for her father's new colleagues. Although Lisa was only four-and-a-half-years-old, she recalled feeling the evening was important to her parents. One of the attendees was a young *"bachelor"* (the term Lisa used), who had little experience with infants. Someone put Lisa's sister in his arms, and the sister promptly threw up on the man. Lisa recalled witnessing the cringe, the expression of horror on the man's face and then the dread coupled with a glimmer of amusement in her father's grimace as he apologised to the bachelor. Lisa's four-and-a-half-year-old self thought, "*I wouldn't do that.* I would never do that." And after that, Lisa rarely did.

While Lisa had not consciously recalled these scenes before, she had embodied these events in the real. She would try to master her own vomit and keep away from others'. She was a girl and then a woman who did not throw up. Her body held it back. This element, which was already there in the real, needed to be symbolised or verbalised so that it could be better integrated into Lisa's psychological life.

Lacan, in speaking about the id, states "the id that's involved in analysis is that of a signifier that's already there in the real, an incomprehensible signifier. It's already there, but it isn't the signifier of some vague, primordial concord that depends on God knows what pre-established harmony" (1994, p. 49).[3] *This previously unspoken, free-floating, signifier was intimately connected to Lisa's history but had lost its link and needed to be restored.* Moreover, the appropriate affect needed to accompany this restoration. Lisa needed to articulate and to feel the hitherto unfelt anxiety, and to experience what was previously intolerable (one might elaborate intolerable to the ego—she was the girl who did *not* throw up on others, who did not make people sick, and who did not get pregnant). She did this in part through her associations. Her symptom—as an uncomprehended signifier, which resided and spoke in the real through Lisa but had not yet been spoken by Lisa—circled around, captured, condensed, and bespoke these childhood scenes, which were related to her unconscious relationship to the desire of the Other—her mother's desire and her father's desire and her desire for her father.

These scenes were attached to the symptom, which contained memories and conflicts condensed into the bodily function of throwing up. The associations moved the symptom further into the symbolic dimension. Working with Lisa's associations helped us recognise how Lisa's symptom was situated within the symbolic matrix. For example, she unconsciously took certain positions via her symptom. These positions were complicated and involved a multitude of scenes, utterances, relationships, thoughts and feelings. Lacan states, "the symptom *is* a metaphor, whether one likes to admit it or not, just as desire *is* metonymy" (2006, p. 528/439). Lisa's symptom contained a specific condensation of signifiers and we can plug in the various characters from her family history and the various scenes. By incorporating the various characters at play and their various positions in the circuit of desire, Lisa's symptom allowed her to find, as Lacan states, "a solution to the impossible by exhausting all possible forms of the impossibilities that are encountered when the solution is put into the form of a signifying equation" (2006, p. 520/432). Her symptom formed a metaphorical chain of possibilities.

To be sure, this signifier was a slippery one. The wording, "father made mother sick" contains a wealth of ambiguity. Because, in this case, to be made sick is both a good and a bad thing—it is to be desired and shunned, wanted and not wanted. On the one hand, to be made sick is to be given the baby. The father gave something (his desire, his sperm, his baby, his phallus, the signifier of desire), which Lisa wanted, to the mother, and not to Lisa. In classical terms, we find a wish for a baby given by the father—a signifier of desire extraordinaire—and a simultaneous repression of that desire. A veritable "you do not make me sick" is performed. We can view the symptom as a *compromise formation* between the two desires.

While on the one hand, the conflict was temporarily solved by not throwing up at all and by elaborate avoidance strategies, on the other hand, her engagement with the symptom, particularly the repetitive thought given to places where the deed had been done as well as the ritualistic act, was an insistence of the conflict. Through the symptom Lisa dwelt on that which she purported she least wanted to think about it, ruminated on that which she claimed she wanted nothing to do with. Her rituals perpetuated relationships and prolonged desire.

However, the symptom also inscribed something that was opposed to the satisfaction that Lisa demanded; *it was a symptom that went against her desire and limited her jouissance. The superego said no.* Throwing up was disgusting; it brought horror and shame. Both mother (through her object choice) and sister (by throwing up on the bachelor) brought shame upon father. For Lisa, vomiting and the pleasure and pain it presupposed and entailed, was prohibited—that revolting thing was not for her.

The refusal is multifaceted. First, it serves to answer the father's failure to respond to her demand for love. "You—father—do *not* make me sick", her symptom said. For, *if you deny me, I will deny you.* Second, the refusal also aligns Lisa with her mother. Lisa's mother turned the father's desire away. The marriage, the man, was not working for her. The mother was lacking because the father was. The father's phallus was enough to make one sick, and Lisa was staying the heck away from it (but, of course, she was also drawn towards it). By not being sick, by refusing the signifier of the father's desire, Lisa's desire was the same as her m(O)ther's desire—that is, it was not for the father. Through this symptom, she unconsciously positioned herself in line with her mother.

And yet, third, we can read "You—father—do *not* make *me* sick" as a way of differentiating herself from her mother's position. This was the position of the stepmother, who was not made sick by the father. After all, "You do *not* make me sick" can also be a compliment, albeit, a suspicious and not so flattering one.

Thus this one symptom inscribed Lisa's complicated, multi-staved relationship to the Other. It knotted it all together, the desire to be made sick or impregnated and the reproach.[4] It invisibly held together the missing links of all the players and the possibilities. At different moments the symptom represented different people—the mother, sister, father, stepmother, the bachelor at the party,[5] Lisa herself, and likely more. In this way "throw-up" was a signifier lacking a univocal sense, rather it held a *condensation of meanings*.

In conclusion: where it was …

How did we work with this symptom? We strove to construct and squeeze more and more sense out of the nonsense, and to glean the meaning of Lisa's desire by tracing its place in the Other's discourse and connecting it to the web of unconscious desires and the symbolic matrix. We did not set out to rapidly and rapaciously exterminate it, the way other treatment approaches might. We did not try to desensitise Lisa to it. I did not make her set foot into that scary bathroom, close her eyes, and get over it. Quite the opposite; we made her more sensitive to its multiple meanings, we got into and under it. What had previously been unspeakable was thrown up and thus thrown into question; it then slowly began to be chewed over and thought through all things considered.

And the symptom did give way. Lisa went back into the notorious bathroom where the colleague had vomited, something in her past she would not and felt she could not have done, and she spoke about coming to terms with vomit, hers and others'. She felt she might be able to handle her own vomit—maybe even morning sickness, even a vomiting baby. She was going to "leave it open", as she put it. Thus, she experienced a little more freedom around the issue. That is not to say that even if this symptom dissipated another metaphor grappling with her loss would not replace it, but in a year of work, once a week, we were able to work with the logic of the unconscious such that it would not direct her life in such mysterious ways. She would allow for the possibility of a new scene to emerge.

As a final aside, Lisa's *actual* symptom did not appear until six months down the track of therapy; it was not her initial complaint. Lisa came for treatment to relieve her depression, which she accomplished, and because she found herself unable to work, specifically unable to finish her dissertation. By the end of our work together, she was well on her way to completing her dissertation, had applied for and attained numerous offers at top universities and accepted one for which she had great hopes. And her boyfriend, whose affection for her she had initially questioned—"would he want to be with [her]?"—was going to join her in these promising endeavours. Lisa felt desirous of and even somewhat triumphant in love and work, and much more "worth" something. And in addition to relieving a depression, which to be sure was no small feat, she accessed an unconscious desire and a will to know more.

Our work was brought to an end prematurely due to both our circumstances. We were both changing work venues and moving geographically, but Lisa decided to continue her work with another analytic therapist in the state where she was relocating, for she was aware of a lack and frustration remaining. She still yearned to see signs of her father's love, although she was no longer as fixated on her demand for it. In our last few sessions, Lisa spoke about our ending. Through tears she spoke of missing her father; *the loss felt especially raw* in light of our impending termination. But she was slowly integrating that loss into her life. Her desire was no longer completely wrapped up in her interpretation that her father's desire was not for her, which she had interpreted to be caused by her mother's desire not being for him, and which had inspired her feelings of worthlessness. Our work with this specific symptom—a phobic response to vomit—furthered Lisa's ability to engage her desire. As a product of her unique history, the symptom made sense, although *not* wholly or fully—for certainly a strangeness remained. Moreover, trying to understand that strangeness set Lisa to work on her unconscious. As though that was where the knowledge lay, for it did. In so doing, she began to take some responsibility for that which had seemed most alien. I do not mean to imply that we reached the Lacanian analytic goal of an identification with the real of the symptom,[6] for that would be highfalutin and incorrect. But where it was, and where it spoke, Lisa came to be and spoke, just a bit more. And she did this through speaking with an Other like no other.

Notes

1. See Chapter 5 for a discussion of the concept of, *"revendication"*, a French term describing the sense of unjust deprivation made upon one by the other and for which the hysteric subsequently demands the restoration of what, to her eyes, is rightfully hers.

2. This formulation is consistent with Lacan's reading of Kris's fresh brain case (discussed in *Seminars I* (1988a), *III* (1993), and in *Écrits* (2006), and with Fink's (2004) exploration of the case). Fresh brains are not just a substance that the patient wants or needs, rather they are a signifier of the patient's desire. Accordingly, vomit is not just a substance, it is a signifier of Lisa's desire.

3. Freud states, "we are 'lived' by unknown and uncontrollable forces" (1923b, p. 23); "Man is lived by the It." Lacan says, "it speaks" (*ça parle*) (1992, p. 206). Treatment then has to do with gaining a knowledge and then an acceptance of a knowledge of "you are this". The "it" that speaks through us, is us (see also, *Seminar I*, 1988a, p. 3, & *Seminar XI*, 1978, p. 44).

4. As Freud states, the symptom aims "either at a sexual satisfaction or at fending it off" (1916–1917, p. 272) or simultaneously of both.

5. Lisa, upon seeing the bachelor's cringe "decided" not to be the one who causes disgust or who brings the father shame. For his was a male's, a bachelor's—that is an available male's—no less, reaction to the act.

6. For a discussion of this formulation of identification with the symptom, see the concluding chapter of this book.

CHAPTER FOUR

The case of the poisoned salami: doubts, dreams, guilt, and love

But in these cases
We still have judgment here; that we but teach
Bloody instructions, which, being taught, return
To plague the inventor: this even-handed justice
Commends the ingredients of our poison'd chalice
To our own lips.

—*Shakespeare*, Macbeth, Act 1, Scene 7

Edon, a bright young man, most tidy in appearance, presented with the most characteristic of obsessional symptoms: he was plagued with doubts and indecision. His inability to decide whether "to break up, or not to break up" with his girlfriend brought him into therapy, but it also revealed a more general stance towards sexuality and libidinal relations—particularly a splitting of love and desire—which is both common in those with obsessional neurotic structure and clinically important to comprehend. Furthermore, this stance, as we shall see, is hallmarked by guilt and shame. In Edon we encounter the labyrinth of the obsessional's romantic and sexual relationships, and we will see how they relate to the question of the nature and transmission

77

of the paternal function, and the consequences these have at the level of the phallus.

Edon's doubts were annoying and exhausting him psychically and physically; they were driving him round the bend. He was so tired that his graduate studies, which usually went very well, were suffering. This was particularly worrisome to Edon and prompted him to enter therapy—it was one thing for him to ache psychologically, but quite another for his work to deteriorate as a consequence. Earning his Ph.D. was a way to make his parents and grandparents back home proud. What would they think if he did poorly? When Edon entered my office at the University clinic, he had never been in therapy before. In the limited time we had together to talk, I did not set out to aggressively alleviate his symptoms, but rather encouraged him to verbalise, to further articulate and bring his experience of them to light, as much as he could in the time we had. In his life, Edon had done *a lot* of thinking, but not a lot of talking. I wanted him to talk, to progressively move more from a thinking being (his very familiar and rather painful existential state), to a speaking being.

Particular aspects of Edon's narrative constituted the over-determined symptoms: doubt and indecision combined with desire, fear, the restrictions and prohibitions Edon placed upon himself, the satisfaction he renounced, and the reasons why he did so. Freud reminds us to *view symptoms as a compromise between a desire and a self-reproach—and nothing captures this more completely than obsessional neurosis*. Whereas the hysteric effects a compromise between two competing desires in the one symptom, the obsessional tends to express the two tendencies sequentially, one after the other. Freud states,

> What regularly occurs in hysteria is that a compromise is arrived at which enables both the opposing tendencies to find expression simultaneously—which kills two birds with one stone; whereas here [in obsessional neurosis] each of the two opposing tendencies finds satisfaction singly, first one and then the other, though naturally an attempt is made to establish some sort of logical connection (often in defiance of all logic) between the antagonists. (1909d, p. 194)

Moreover, with obsessional neurosis we need to distinguish between primary symptoms and the subsequent, secondary symptoms. Primary symptoms such as conscientiousness, shame, and self-distrust appear as what Freud calls a "reaction formation" against the guilt the person feels over some earlier, mostly sexual experiences. This reaction formation is a "successful" form of defence in that the person is well and healthy, at least for a period of time. But the equilibrium can be disturbed, sometimes by life events or sometimes by a change internal to the person, and when the repression fails, rather than the old, repressed memories re-appearing, obsessional ideas and compulsions appear properly for the first time.

Edon's equilibrium was disturbed; and his doubting frenzy was characteristic of his obsessional rumination. Freud speaks of symptoms as:

> [A]cts detrimental, or at least useless, to a subject's life as a whole, often complained of by him as unwelcome and bringing unpleasure or suffering to him. The main damage they do resides in the mental expenditure which they themselves involve and in the further expenditure that becomes necessary for fighting against them. (1916–1917, p. 358)

Edon complained that his doubts were exhausting, unwelcome, causing suffering to him and affecting his relations with others.

In this case, I highlight the symptomatic acts, dreams, fantasies, and pieces of the symbolic matrix that emerged via Edon's signifiers. Edon's associations to his sexual and aggressive fantasies and dreams, in particular, brought out and weaved together some elements of his history that had not been fully articulated, and, most importantly, revealed how his symptoms could be viewed as a partially disguised displacement of this history onto his present moment.

The material presented here includes what Lacan calls:

> [P]henomena in which we had hitherto learned to find the symptom's secret—an immense domain annexed by Freud's genius to man's knowledge that warrants the true title of 'psychoanalytic semantics', including dreams, bungled actions, slips of the tongue, memory disturbances, whims of thought association, and so on. (2006, p. 333/277)

Decades ago Lacan pointed out that working closely with these phenomena had gone out of favour in certain analytic and therapeutic schools. In presenting the kind of material that I focus on in this and the other cases comprising this book, I hope to remind readers that we would do well as clinicians to bring our attention back to them, that such material brings a crucial element to the work because it lies at the heart of the transformative aspects of talk therapy. Moreover, by attending to these phenomena, we also recognise the classic psychical structures inherent to Freud's diagnostic schema, including obsessional neurosis.

Freud's portrait of obsessional neurosis really focused on the profound role of thinking and ruminations. The more contemporary *DSM* diagnosis of OCD, obsessive-compulsive disorder, focuses on behaviours, the compulsion side, both conceptually in terms of diagnostics and in treatments. However, as we will see in the case of Edon, obsessional thoughts not only play a very significant role in obsessional neurosis, but in fact actually *precede* the compulsive behaviour and thus must be addressed first and foremost. Freud discussed how compulsions are defensive rituals people use to ward off the disturbing thoughts, and he reminded us that the obsessions are at the heart of this experience, structurally speaking. We can view the very strong cognitive aspect in this case as a reminder of why we must recognise and work with these obsessions and not just with the manifest behaviour.

In Edon's case, we see a contemporary version of these classic symptoms of obsessional neurosis. The particulars of his case concretise Freud's description of

> [T]he domination of *compulsion* and *doubt* such as we meet with in the mental life of obsessional neurotics. The *doubt* corresponds to the patient's internal perception of his own indecision, which, in consequence of the inhibition of his love by his hatred, takes possession of him in the face of every intended action. The doubt is in reality a doubt of his own love—which ought to be the most certain thing in his whole mind; and it becomes diffused over everything else, and is especially apt to become displaced on to what is most insignificant and trivial. A man who doubts his own love may, or rather *must*, doubt every lesser thing. (1909d, p. 241)

I tried to listen in a way that encouraged Edon to outline some of his story, restore some of the gaps, and fill out the ellipses in his anamnesis. We did not *fully* explain the symptom, in large part because of the defined-term nature of the therapy, although there remains the question of whether one ever *fully* explains a symptom. In the time we were allotted, we did begin to unravel the knot and follow the various threads of Edon's story such that he left with a greater understanding of how his obsessional doubts and troubled libidinal relations connected to his specific life history. Discussing Freud's canonical study of obsessional neurosis in the case of the Rat Man, Lacan states,

> It was by deciphering such material that the subject was able to remember his history along with the outlines of the conflict that determined his symptoms. And the value to be granted in technique to the elimination of symptoms was based on how well the order in his history was restored and the gaps in it were filled. (2006, p. 333/277)

Throughout the process, Edon's symptom, which when he arrived was a major complaint, and seemed most alien and disturbing to him, became more meaningful, more personal for him.

Edon is a good looking, well-groomed, noticeably neat and tidy man, in his twenties. He was born and raised in a country in South-Eastern Europe that was communist from the end of World War II until the early 1990s. Edon lived there during times of hardship; he described an aggressive place, "a battlefield", where he was beaten and bullied on the streets and then, in response, turned into a bully himself. Money was scarce even for his parents who were both highly educated Ph.D.s with, in theory, good jobs. However even with their education level and careers, they did not make enough money and lived in difficult economic conditions. In the socio-political climate of the country, while Edon was growing up, open discourse about sex was unacceptable and actively censored. There was a particularly strong superego at work in this society. One might be tempted to link Edon's symptoms to his country's larger cultural matrix (we certainly see a strongly punitive superego internalisation—particularly around sex), but Edon's symptoms actually have a true specificity that are particular to his own personal and familial history.

The doubt

Edon's presenting problem was that he struggled with disturbing intrusive thoughts and a plaguing doubt, which at the time of our first session had manifested in one particular decision he could not make and for which he wanted an "objective outside opinion" and advice. He was unable to decide whether to break up or stay with his long-term girlfriend, Mindy, and he disliked the misery, the mental and physical fatigue this dilemma was causing him. Thus what looks like a "normal" and important question in life, "should I be with this person or not?", in an obsessional form, was the symptom. Edon turned the decision about whom to love and desire into his symptom.

Edon's speech returns to his romantic partner; it worried and frustrated Edon that he did not know what Mindy wanted from him; he remarked that she was older, she might want more from him than he was ready for, and such struggles manifested in obsessional thoughts. He said, "The ideas in my mind push me and cause pain." Numerous times he said these ideas and doubts made it so that he could not enjoy "everyday life". The obsessional's tendency to ruminate about the important and great existential issues in life such as love and death (as we will see in this case), often prevent the person from actually enjoying the everyday pleasures of life. Such ruminations also resulted in many disruptive somatic symptoms. More often than not, Edon's stomach felt inflamed for which he took many antacids (stomach upsets had also become problematic in other ways, as we shall see), and he suffered from headaches that disturbed his sleep. He was exhausted from the lack of sleep and restless anxiety.

He felt depressed and connected his depression and anxiety to Mindy specifically. Mindy's past bothered him, mainly in the form of his feeling the need to constantly fight off negative thoughts and images of her doing things like drugs and having sex with past boyfriends. Such images returned to him in a manner that felt intrusive and against his will. He described his situation as "fighting against [his] own self". Edon struggled with his love for Mindy because of the internal torment it subjected him to. In fact, his internal life was a permanent struggle between love and hate—with the ambivalence that arose in him whenever he loved a woman. He loved Mindy but also despised aspects of her; or, more accurately, he despised how his thoughts and "visions" of her "sordid and sullied" past plagued him, how, in his own mind, he reacted to the past of the woman he loved.[1] The more he loved her, the more he despised her; and the conflict within him fed upon his mental turmoil.

In the essay "A special type of choice of object made by men", Freud takes up the "'necessary conditions for loving' which govern people's choice of an object" (1910h, p. 165). Edon complained that Mindy's "sordid" past was bothersome, but the insistence of this thought makes us wonder whether there was an unconscious condition that she *have* a sullied past—as if this was a condition of his love, of his way of loving. As it turned out, when he was allowed to speak more fully, Edon's words gave every indication that Mindy's troubled and promiscuous history was indeed a precondition for him to love her.

Edon's response to what he saw as her compromised past was a paradoxical one, illogical even, so characteristic of the obsessional's thinking. He said he did not want to "just quit" by breaking up with her, because he felt she loved and needed him. That he felt she "needed" him to be with her and "protect" her was part of the equation. This is Freud's "rescue-motif": a certain "type" of man can show an urge to rescue a woman, even a command to do so; and so he must choose a woman, another, preferably one whose past might indicate a need for rescue.

Being her rescuer also played into his love/hate attitude towards her. On the one hand, Edon complained that Mindy needed him to be the "good guy who didn't need anything in return", which she had never had because of the string of "bad guys" who had come before Edon. On the other hand, Edon said his own happiness depended on the happiness of others and that he got off on the idea that her happiness depended on him. "I am fine as long as the others are happy", he proclaimed, in a spirit of self-denial that can only be called insincere. Indeed, later in therapy, when he was more able to recognise the conflict within, he allowed himself to speak of the reverse. He said *a part* of him wanted to help Mindy, *but another part* seemed to want her to feel pain and suffer. For example, he would nag her about past boyfriends, drugs, and her state of financial debt. He also hounded her about taking anti-depressants (he thought it pointed to weakness). Rather than solely help and protect her, he also wanted to wound her, although whenever he did, he would subsequently feel guilty. *Thus, we see a cycle of aggression, followed by guilt, and then a reaction formation of altruism, a cycle quite common in the obsessional's dynamic.*[2]

Articulating the obsessional's aggressivity, which is often a repressed aggression, lends a greater appreciation of obsessional structure. It is marked by the desire to destroy the very thing (the Other) on which his desire depends. As Lacan states, "the obsessional is inclined to aim at what we're calling the destruction of the Other" (1998a, p. 402).[3] For

Edon, the Other is both the source of his desire and the object he wants to destroy. Subsequently, as we will see below, there is a complementary split in the object of his affection. It seems important to add that this obsessional aggressivity tends to mostly play out in thought and fantasy. For males, it often has its origins in the combative dual relations between father and son as it plays out in the Oedipal Complex, a discussion that we will come to shortly. For the moment note that this rivalry plays out on what Lacan calls the imaginary and symbolic planes and especially in relation to prohibition, frustration, privation, and ultimately identification.

To further complicate things, it bothered Edon that he had hostile and "prejudiced" thoughts about Mindy, and he judged himself harshly for having them. Edon said of Mindy, "she *spoils* everything". I ask him to say more. He gives the example of Disney World, which, he said, *should* be a safe, fun, childhood place, but because Mindy told him she once took drugs there and was high on the rides, he said she "dirtied it, tarnished it", for him; she spoiled Disney World—one of his childhood dreams. But as he began to speak about his dilemma, he also doubted the fairness of this, and levied self-reproaches of unfairness. He wanted to be more tolerant, patient, charitable, and detached rather than judgmental and thinking others spoil things. In many ways, the person he was most hard on was himself.

He came up short, in particular, when he measured himself against his stringent ideals. Edon would continually relay to me how he is a "good person, who values life and works hard". He had internalised countless moral values and ethical ideals and wanted to "better handle the situation" in line with these ideals. He wanted to be less reactive and wished he could stand on the side-lines, "observe and not be influenced". He said if he did not act, perhaps he would not feel in such a power struggle. He wanted to remove himself from these struggles and "get out of the game". He often refers to Jesus and Christian values and wishes he could attain these more. When Christianity fails him, he turns to Indian philosophy and tries to use up a number of sessions to speak about the concept of the driver on a horse driven cart. As Edon explains it, the cart is the body, the driver is intelligence, the horses are the senses and emotions, and the reigns are the mind. Edon argues that in his case, the horses have too much control; he wants more command over his mind and emotions, particularly when tempted by sex. He wants the driver to command the horses and cart. He would also like his speech to stay at a philosophical level. I repeatedly encouraged him to speak more personally and specifically in an attempt to move him away from the obsessional strategy of engaging in a kind of pre-emptive strike that closes out any unwelcome input from his therapist as Other. Such a strategy is the obsessional's attempt and desire to "control" and regulate everything and be the master of his words, thoughts, and feelings—master, in the end, of his unconscious (and his horses). Equally, he wants an Other who does not desire, which equates to an Other that is dead.

When steered away from a philosophical rant, Edon's speech returns to his libidinal situation. In thinking of Mindy, he wonders aloud: "Do I deserve this?" I repeat back to him "Do you deserve this? Can you say more?" to which he replies that he meant, "Do I deserve better?" I hear the phrase on multiple levels: "Do I deserve this?" can point in many directions, does one deserve better, or does one *not* deserve this, or actually deserve worse? At first Edon could speak only to the former option—that he deserved better, but then came to also address and consider, via speech, the latter. The latter related to his strong superego and the prominent role of self-punishment. Edon felt he deserved to be punished. For what he was not sure, but he had in mind that it related, as will be discussed, to sex and how he was introduced to it. In this sense, Edon's unconscious was very present in his speech. He explicitly said, in no uncertain terms, that his need for punishment was related to his early introduction to sex. There was not a lot of affect attached to this felt need to be punished and he did not know the details, in fact, he doubted the details, but it was there, present in the moment via language, nevertheless.

While Edon doubted his love, sex was also a problem. Sex was "spoiled". Edon complained that he had to pressure Mindy for sex, which he felt badly about, and consequently could not enjoy it. As Freud observed, the failure to derive much pleasure from sex, or being "psychanaesthetic", is all too common, although not often publicly discussed.

However, the problem in Edon's case is not that he does *not* get pleasure from sex but that he gets too much pleasure from sex, or, for him at least, the wrong kind of pleasure, since it is illicit pleasure; it is pleasure as "contraband", to use Lacan's word for it. It is no surprise that sex with Mindy was a repeat performance of Edon's sexual relationship with his first girlfriend, whom he said he pressured into sex because he "got it into [his] head that [he] needed sex". But since sex was painful for her, Edon felt guilty, and thus did not enjoy it as he had hoped he would. The guilt also spoiled things—there were layers of spoilage—and it prevented him from enjoying his own pleasure.

He said *"something bad in me"* pushes for sex and he was concerned that this something bad was perverse and evil. He requested to understand it and, above all, to control what he felt controlled by. Furthermore, he said he wanted to understand how this something bad got there, inside him. Note the fundamental and thoroughgoing ambiguity here, so typical of the obsessional. While in his obsession to understand what was bad in *him*, he ultimately blames himself, and with his bewilderment at what it might be that is bad in himself he disarms the Other/therapist by adopting his place and worrying at *their* joint problem of how this bad thing ever got inside. It is a strategy that allows the obsessional to objectify the "problem" by looking at it with the curiosity of the spectator and thus avoid assuming it as his own.

Edon also focuses on his own desires, versus the Other's desire. It was on rare occasions that Edon spoke of his partner's desire or satisfaction. This was structurally significant and in contradistinction to the hysteric (think of the case of Mona), who blames the other for everything bad in life, and is mired in the Other's desire, with little mention of her own desire as separated from the Other's. Here, on the other hand, Edon blames his responses on himself but, in a second moment, is mystified by what is not part of his true self.

Love/desire split

Edon articulated how Mindy was "not [his] fantasy"; she was not pure and innocent, not like his "ideal love" would be, and because of her past of men and drugs, he said she never would or could be. As such Edon had set up an impossible situation: the woman he was supposed to love, he said he never could; he could, however, desire her. Because of her past, she was the debased woman, not the idealised woman he would love but the woman he could desire. Why engage in such a split between love and desire? Freud, in his essay "On the universal tendency to debasement in the sphere of love", speaks of a type of person who, unawares, seeks a romantic partner "they do not need to love, in order to keep their sensuality away from the objects they love" (1912d, p. 183). In order to protect the love object from being debased through sexual desire, the two currents of the "affectionate and sensual" are strenuously kept apart. As Freud states, "where they love they do not desire and where they desire they cannot love" (1912d, p. 183). This is not ideal, not, to be sure, because of any moral strictures, but because it often results in frustration, a lack of pleasure and satisfaction, and symptoms. Freud continues:

> People in whom there has not been a proper confluence of the affectionate and the sensual currents do not usually show much refinement in their modes of behaviour in love; they have retained perverse sexual aims whose non-fulfilment is felt as a serious loss of pleasure, and whose fulfilment on the other hand seems possible only with a debased and despised sexual object. (1912d, p. 183)

Edon seems caught up in this cycle in which the only woman he can desire is, like Mindy, one that is debased and degraded. This is the dilemma of the circuit of his desire.

Edon began to articulate how a part of him enjoyed the relationship with the debased object that Mindy represented for him because such discomfort and pain trained him to "sacrifice", to put the other's happiness before his own. As such it was good training (and good punishment). For Edon, sacrifice pointed to love, but sex and desire were relegated to a separate realm.[4] *Because* he sacrificed and suffered, he thought there was a better chance that "love [was] in the picture, not just sex". In this way it was "better" for him if sex was not altogether enjoyable and involved a sacrifice on his part. We might also say that he enjoyed that he was not getting enjoyment, thereby achieving a secondary satisfaction, a pleasure in sacrificing his means of pleasure and enjoyment. This paradoxical phenomenon of obtaining pleasure or satisfaction from the sacrificing of one's desires was initially analysed by Freud (in *Civilization and its Discontents*, 1930a) and relates to the relentless "gluttony" of the superego by Lacan, who gave this particular human peculiarity the name of jouissance. Jouissance is understood as this particular way of deriving satisfaction from sacrifice, which is why it is often understood as deriving pleasure from pain. Edon "sacrificed" his lust and desire in this scenario; as such, the paradoxical jouissance of his denial is caught up in this sacrifice. He says, "One reason I like the relationship is that I am *not* deriving happiness from it. It gives me a *weird* satisfaction." Thus, what he had begun by bitterly complaining about, he also, at another level, derived enjoyment from, and began to articulate as much.

Fantasy: sacrifice minus satisfaction and the "king of stupid"

Edon returned to the question of what he deserved, this time questioning whether he actually deserved the "whole picture"—the "ideal love"—for he himself was "far from good and pure". While he described his childhood fantasy in which he loved an innocent, moral, nice girl who loved only him, he worried *he did not deserve this fantasy* because he had made himself unworthy; he was spoiled as a result of "everything bad [he] did". I asked him to say more about the "everything bad he did." He said he had slept with too many girls—"it was sexual urges rather than love". And as long as he allowed his sexual urges to trump love, he was not worthy. It was a question of worth. Besides, he said it was better to enjoy without touching, that way you avoid "ruining something pretty".

Edon struggled to *impose this ideal* of loving without touching, of sacrificing without satisfaction, upon his fantasies because it conflicted with the opposing impulse to satisfy his lust on a debased object. Edon began the therapy speaking of his fears and doubts, and their insistence and intrusiveness, and then turned to his fantasies, which were equally captivating, fascinating, and yet invasive and devouring of his mental life and psychic activity. He continually attempted to impose restrictions on his active fantasy life. In a recurrent daydream, which Edon used to relax and to help him fall asleep, he helped a beautiful but troubled girl out of a bad and dangerous situation but did not have sex with her. In his fantasy he is the hero, the soldier, the knight, the rescuer, who sacrifices himself for the girl. He dies for the happiness of others. He remarks that of course he would like to "enjoy the fruit", post-sacrifice, but never does. But in his fantasy, he feels loved by the girl, who usually holds his wounded body as he dies, and it is worth the sacrifice to feel loved. Sex, even touching, he said, would lead to the destruction of the dream and its happiness; sex would spoil it. I ask him to say more. If you enjoy and help without touching, he said, you are less attached, which was better. He insisted the fantasy was about wanting to help, altruism, *not* about sex (or a fear of attachment), even though in the fantasy it is almost always a beautiful girl, sometimes a prostitute, he is helping. When he stressed the help factor as the important bit, I brought up that sometimes it is useful to look at things, in an all things considered manner, including the reverse or the opposite of what appears.[5] Edon was taken aback by this comment and found it odd. He would stick with the altruism plea.

However, Edon began our next session by saying he had been lying to himself for a long time. He said, "It is actually ninety per cent sexual, but with the sexual comes negative feelings." He felt even more depressed and confused. He said the helping "was a lie", a defence against lust and desire; "my mind is lying to itself. It's the king of stupid. The helping overlays a desire so it is never ever pure". The helping and sacrifice, which represented good, was always fighting with desire and sexuality, which was evil. That is what produces the fantasy daydream, Edon said. My client had become a Freudian overnight! Indeed, Freud particularly discusses how the "rescue-motif" is a rationalisation and secondary revision (1912d, p. 172), one that relates to a "parental complex", one's relations to mother and father, and attachments and fixations of libido, as will be discussed.

As therapy progressed, Edon said he was "tired of the same old story" and "need[ed] something new". His go-to rescue fantasy was no longer helping him fall asleep; it no longer relaxed him anymore. As a result of the therapy, it just was not working for him like it used to. He made an implicit request for a new symptom, one that worked better and provided more pleasure. As frustrating as it may be for clients when an old symptom stops working, it nevertheless shows that things are changing. Guilt over sexual feelings, leading to the repression of sexuality and its replacement by altruism, had reigned supreme as a reaction formation in Edon's psychic life for a long time. Now it was more transparent and thus not as ready-to-hand as a defence.

Let us explore this defence, this reaction formation that was so powerful, just a bit more. Regarding this defensive structure, there was likely another important moment, given what we know, what Freud and Lacan teach us about obsessional structure; it is likely that Edon had been over-whelmed by sexual feelings at a very young age, and that his secondary response was guilt and revulsion, a stance towards sexuality that he carried with him, unharnessed and misunderstood, and which contributed to his frustrating division between love and desire.

Our discourse then turned to why Edon thought his desire was "bad and evil" in the first place—why sexual desire was the enemy, shrouded in shame and guilt. He articulated that this sense had been there for as far back as he could remember. I asked him what he remembered.

A brief sexual history: the penis and the pumpkin seed

Edon recalled that after he masturbated, which he said began at age thirteen, he would feel such guilt that he would write a note to himself saying he would "*not* do this again for five years" (which of course never worked). He felt great anxiety over his masturbatory habits. He discussed a fear for his health. What if this activity was bad for him, what if you got sick, or if you ran out? He said it took him a couple of years to research masturbation and discover that it in fact does not make one sick and one does not run out of sperm.

This relates to how the obsessional measures his enjoyment and doles it out in portions. He never commits himself entirely, always preferring to keep something in reserve; he acts on the principle of "one for you and one for me", or, better, the principle of "one for you and the rest for me". We see this realised, in fantasmatic form, in Edon, who thinks that if he gives too much away through sex or even through masturbation, there may be none left for himself.

And here, with his masturbatory fears, we infer a threat of loss, a loss of potency. Edon did not know enough not to fear it. He also questioned why there seemed to be a religious prohibition involved. Of course there is a long history of religion deeming sexuality sinful, but Edon insisted that while growing up neither his family nor his country was religious, or allowed to be, yet he himself felt it was a sin— did he get this from his family? He vaguely recalled reading in the Bible (although he could not recall where, when, or why that would have happened, until later in his life when he adopted Christianity) about a man who "threw" (rather than spilt) sperm on the ground and was punished. He was "forever worried" after that. Such ideas stuck and produced conflicts. He tried actively not to masturbate but to no avail. He thought he was wasting his life. It was, he said, a "never-ending desire, a bondage. The more you do the more you want". He said, "This carries with me. I am still reading stuff [porn and then masturbating], but I feel really bad afterwards, and it really pisses me off. I wish I didn't always feel bad *or* that I didn't do it." He lives in fear that he will be punished for thoughts and acts of erotic desire, and thus finds himself in a tough, classically obsessional spot. Again we see the obsessional's struggle between his desires and the reaction against them. First this, then that; first the desire for sexual pleasure (masturbation), then the prohibition on sexual pleasure (punishment), in a veritable see-saw between satisfaction and prohibition, and the successive or dyphasic way in which it finds expression.

Edon spoke of not knowing about sex because it was censored and not discussed openly in his environment. He did not know how babies were made and, when asked, his mother told him he would eventually learn in biology class. He relayed a memory of being thirteen and a girl at school brought in a book illustrating naked men and women. He claimed, before seeing this book, he did not know there was a difference in sexual organs. He thought they were exactly alike and that everyone had a penis. He imagined when you had sex with someone two penises met and exchanged a seed, like a pumpkin seed, from one to another through the penises.[6] He looked at the picture of the woman in the girl's book and thought his classmates were playing a joke on him. He was stunned and confused. *Had they erased or hid the penis*? And here we glimpse a moment in his history where Edon discovers and precisely articulates a lack, something missing, an otherness. Was it a joke, he wondered? He doubted his knowledge and recalled it as a significant moment. It brought a sense of lack to the fore, and he had to know more.[7]

This moment when Edon fully acknowledges the reality of the sexual difference between men and women for the first time, was momentous for Edon. We can surmise that the fear of castration, which here clearly lies in the imaginary, induced by this recognition, was the trigger for the process of repression that turned Edon away from his sexual attacks on women (which will be described momentarily), leading to the repression of the aggressive desires, and their subsequent expression in symptomatic form (a return of the repressed) in his self-reproaches. Thus, the aggression towards women, as castrated objects, later fuelled the aggression of his own self-reproaches.

Edon recalled being introduced to pornographic materials at age thirteen; it was the first time for him and his country, which until then had censored pornography. His experience began with magazines, then movies, then phone sex, and finally he attempted to have intercourse with a prostitute but found himself impotent.[8] He hypothesised that pornography damaged him. He thought he was too perverted for his young age. He remembered liking a young girl in grade school and then saying to her in class, "should I be *on top* or should you?" He felt terribly ashamed when his comment was met by the girl's confusion and disgust; in retrospect he wondered, *still* embarrassed, what impelled him to say this. "I ruined it," he said. He tried to set rules, limits, and to regulate his intake of sexual material. For example, in graduate school, Edon tried to limit reading internet sex stories to every third day; but he would inevitably break the rule and feel guilty. He said his sexual urges ruined his relationships.

Present-day Edon equated touching and sex with sullying, and something in his earlier history had led to this equation. Freud offers insight when he says,

> He regards the sexual act basically as something degrading, which defiles and pollutes not only the body. The origin of this low opinion, which he will certainly not willingly acknowledge, must be looked for in the period of his youth in which the sensual current in him was already strongly developed but its satisfaction with an object outside the family was almost as completely prohibited as it was with an incestuous one. (1912d, p. 186)

Freud's words remind us to turn to Edon's youth to explore why everything to do with Edon's sexual desire was befouled, and why he *thought* that everything he touched became spoiled in its turn, as it were. It was as if Edon could not make use of his penis without feeling that it dirtied and defiled both the Other and himself. Where does this strange but also only too common obsessional feature of his sexuality originate? As we shall see, it arises from his relationship to his father. Edon needed to talk about this and he did not want to "waste" his sessions, his time; he wanted to "let things out".

Regarding "waste" and "letting things out", Edon also spoke through his bowels. In the session when he pronounced "this is my chance to let things out. I don't want to waste it. This is my one time. Other times I need to concentrate on school and work", and for many sessions thereafter, as he spoke, Edon polluted our therapy room air with his flatulence. He was "letting something out". As he put things into words, he expelled a rather aggressive assault from his sphincter into the room. Freud connected the obsessional structure with the anal phase, a phase in which a subject is caught up in a response to the Other's demand, which has to do with control and giving a part of oneself to the other.[9] I did not interpret nor even mention the smell, nor did Edon, but I did wonder about its connotations. Was this a regression to the anal stage? Was this his bodily response—his gift—to my desire and request for him to let go of his control over his words—to say whatever came to mind? Was he putting a part of himself into the room, that "bad and sullied" part that bothered him so much, and which he tried to keep in check via his ultra-neat and clean appearance? Did he need me to take in or accept this part of him? I encouraged Edon to say more.

Edon recalled being twelve years old and approaching women, asking them things like "do you want to have sex with me?" He waited on a deserted street, ran up to women, touched their breasts, and ran away. Some of the women ignored him, others cried. He would get what he called a "perverted satisfaction". At the time, he found this act both bad and exciting; he experienced an adrenaline rush. He did not know why this turned him on and was confused by it. He recalled this practice lasted around six months but was unsure of the precise time frame. I asked why he stopped. He said because he was afraid of being caught; he imagined the woman's brother would be waiting for him and would beat him up. He would feel afraid but also turned on.

Edon said since then—referring to sexually accosting women—"everything is spoiled".[10] I encourage him to say more. The street actions, he replied, were lust without love. The two were divided. He further bemoaned that as a young boy he found enjoyment from innocent pleasures like reading the *Iliad* (his take on this book was that it is about people falling in love and sacrificing for each other—a theme he gave much thought); why did he have to perform such sexually aggressive acts, he asked? The boy who ran up to unknown women and groped them, subsequently fantasised, as a man, via a reaction formation, that he was with women he helped and actively refused to touch. As his fantasies bespoke, Edon had put a taboo on touching. He also carried with him into adulthood the idea that if he were to be sexual, he would be punished.

I asked Edon to say more about being caught and beaten. He said, "Maybe this is *not* important" (which almost always means it is), and spoke of how an older man used to beat him up. One day he met this man in the apartment complex where Edon and his grandparents lived and the man made "sexual approaches". He unzipped his pants and asked Edon "where do you want it?" (recall Edon's question to the young schoolgirl). Edon said he "played the fool, kept [his] cool", and got away. He said he never told anyone and avoided thinking about it. He added that he "handled it well". I repeated this phrase. He said he "handled it", meant he pretended to go along with it, to know what he was doing, but then he got away. "Handled it?" He may or may not have put his hand on it, but said he knew it was *not* his fault.

Edon recalled being about twelve to thirteen when these various events occurred, but was confused as to the exact chronology regarding them (the forces of repression were at work). Edon thought the incident with the man was before approaching the women on the street, but he could not be sure. Either way, Edon had encountered sex and aggression together and was both frightened and turned on. He said between thirteen and sixteen years old he felt very sexually charged, and this charge was in turn strongly tinged with guilt and shame. He thought if people knew his thoughts and what he did, they would think ill of him, enough to want to punish him.

These were guilty pleasures indeed. There seems to be an evolution in Edon's behaviour. At first he engages in overt sexual actions of an aggressive kind and then, in what looks like a second moment, there is a repression and an associated guilt response with the fear of punishment. We see this in his narrative of being twelve, we see it in his twenties, and we can infer that it is likely a repeat of a dynamic from a much earlier childhood stage, a moment that has been repressed. In fact, Edon is the very embodiment of the classic obsessional dynamic that Freud described so long ago. We detect, with Edon, an initial, very early period in which there appears to have been a disturbingly overwhelming encounter with sexuality, the precise nature of which never became clear, followed by aggressive sexual behaviour towards women which subsequently undergoes repression, and, finally, the expression of the dual attitude towards women, with its erotic and destructive dimensions, in the form of his symptoms combined with his highly elaborate rescue fantasies.

A sexual history emerged, but it was still filled with gaps.[11] Edon questioned if and how all of this related to his current troubles; he felt it did but did not know how. He wondered if his past somehow related to why he could not enjoy being sexual and why sex and love seemed so separated (the answer was yes). He wondered if it related to his plaguing doubt about his girlfriend (the answer was again, yes). He wanted to sacrifice his own sexual enjoyment and then he would *know* it was love—then he could be certain. He wanted to purify his desire, to erase his doubt.[12] The unconscious answer to his problem was that he would love Mindy without enjoyment; he would find enjoyment elsewhere—"in a sacrifice". In so doing, he would also sacrifice his desire. One tenet of therapy is that we want to open more possibilities for someone to experience more desire and satisfaction from life. So I asked Edon to say more about "sacrifice", a signifier that seemed to index a restriction and castration of his satisfaction.

He associated that he "sacrificed for [his] parents' happiness". A recent example was that lately, rather than go out and have fun, he would stay home on Saturday nights and do schoolwork in order to make his parents proud. However, he added, that more often than not, he would end up looking at internet pornography, which would not make them proud. He imagined this would upset them. Note that this act is reminiscent of the Rat Man's midnight ritual. While dutifully studying, the Rat Man would leave the door open for his (dead) father to observe and then the Rat Man would take his penis out in front of the mirror, undoing the good with the bad. Returning to Edon, why, he asked, if he was trying to make his parents proud, did he also do things that would disappoint them?

And here we must address the importance of the subject's history. Edon began by talking about what worried him in the immediate present—his pervasive and invasive doubts—and then went into his fantasies, and then into his family background. As is the case with analytic work, we looked to his past to understand his present predicament. Not surprisingly, his early experiences, particularly those that concerned relations with his family, emerged as important.

The poisoned phallus

In myriad ways, Edon is a typical obsessional neurotic and his case shows the extent to which Freud's century-old account still has currency today. On top of this, though, there is the very specific predicament Edon struggles with concerning his libidinal relations. Anything to do with his sexual desire is tainted and everything he touches with what I will call his "poisoned phallus", becomes tainted in its turn, as it were. Why do I say "phallus"? Well, if as Freud said sometimes a cigar is just a cigar, a penis is never just a penis. *It always bears the mark of language and signifiers,* which is one major reason that we speak of the penis as a "phallus". The most important feature of the phallus is its status in the symbolic as carrying the mark of castration. It characterises the difference between the sexes, not by men "having" the phallus and women "lacking" it, but by the fact that *access to human sexuality*, for both a man *and* a woman, is via lack, loss, and castration, and for both, the particular way in which he or she engages in the field of sexual engagement and play is profoundly influenced by the way in which he or she relates to castration and the phallus. For the boy more specifically, the father, as Lacan says, is "bearer of the phallus" and "it's through identification with the father that virility is assumed" (1998a, p. 173). This is so very true of Edon. His access to his own sexuality as a male is contingent on the way in which his symbolic inheritance as a man and son of his particular father has been transmitted to him. As Lacan articulates, "Daddy is there, and he bestowed it on me" (1998a, p. 171). For a man, if things go well, he finds himself equipped to relate sexually to another person in a way that is more or less satisfactory. But things often do not go well for men, and *their sexual being in the world bears the marks of their history*. This is the case with Edon, for whom his "phallic inheritance", we might say, is marked by a sense of deficiency and illegitimacy, and hence everything he touches turns not to gold but to something rotten. His attempts to accommodate himself to this situation, and there have been many, have all been to no avail, and he found himself at the sexual impasse he was in at the time he came to see me for consultations. Where does this strange but only too common feature of his sexuality originate? As we shall see, it arises from his relationship to his father.

It is now time to explore the historical legacy, as it were, of the turmoil in Edon's life over sex. As will become clear, the transmission of the symbolic place that he comes to occupy as a man and owner of a penis has everything to do with his family matrix, but particularly to his relationship to his father and the place the father occupied for him. To better comprehend Edon's dilemma, the role of the father, and the import of this signifier "sacrifice" and how it originated in and came from the Other, we must turn to his family history more generally, and then focus on the particularities of the father's role.

The family matrix and the mother's desire

Edon lived with his mother, father, and paternal grandmother in a one-bedroom apartment in Eastern Europe. His parents slept in the bedroom and Edon slept in the living room with his grandmother. When Edon was three, his younger brother was born, and, shortly after his birth, Edon was sent to live with his maternal grandparents, whom he stayed with for nine years until his parents moved into a larger apartment when, at age twelve, Edon moved back in with his parents (we saw from the sexual history that age twelve proved to be a significant date). Edon's baby brother stayed with the parents. When Edon recounted the specifics, or not so-specifics, he said he lived with his grandparents from age three until he was about twelve, "about five to six years". Edon is very talented in his field of maths and sciences. Given that he likely knows that twelve minus three does not equal five, we can view this mathematical slip as a parapraxis. His unconscious had lessened the time of the arrangement. The slip exemplified how Edon's unconscious tried to minimise this part of his history.

Asked to say more about the move to his grandparents at age three, Edon began by emphasising that it was "normal" and "nothing big", and proceeded to provide many "logical" reasons why his parents, particularly his mother, wanted him to live with his grandparents at such a young age, rather than at home with them: Although the parents were professionals they made very little money and were not financially comfortable, their apartment was too small for all five of them (his paternal grandmother included), his grandparents' apartment had more room and was closer to his school so Edon did not have to walk so far, and the walk itself was less dangerous—there was less crime on that street.[13] Edon further hypothesised that his grandfather was a teacher and child psychologist and perhaps his mother thought by staying with a teacher, Edon would be better educated. Education was very important to his family, who were intellectuals, as Edon put it, and Edon couched this move as his parents' "sacrifice" for Edon's greater well-being, safety, and education. He said, "Mother didn't want me to stay there [their home]; she sent me to a teacher." He took pains to tell me that leaving his parental home was "fine", it did "not bother" him. I did not immediately attempt to remove the negation,[14] but I heard that he did protest too much. He had myriad rationalisations ready to hand to justify the actions of others that, in actual fact, he resented and felt as slights.

What did Edon's mother desire such that she had Edon move in with her own parents? Edon attempted to answer with certain answers: comfort, improved economics, more space, education, and safety for her son, for example. But such logical answers were ultimately unsatisfying for Edon. We do not see in Edon's case, so much a question of desire *for* the mother, as we see in some of the other cases in this book, but a question of what the mother desires, the desire *of* the mother. Edon, it seemed, on a certain level, was not her desire. A "sacrifice" was made, Edon insisted; was it a sacrifice of love (of him)? Edon, however, did seem to find a placeholder in his grandparents' desire.[15]

Edon enjoyed his grandparents and felt comfortable with them, especially when compared to being with his own father, a man Edon perpetually described as incompetent. About his maternal grandmother, Edon interpreted that she had already raised her own children and he was thus *"like a gift"* to her. This grandmother died during our therapy process. Edon said it was very hard on him to lose the "one who raised [him]" and added, "I lived for her". "Lived for her?" I asked. He said he *meant* to say, "I lived *with* her". In the exploration of this slip he said, "It can't be possible that I live for her. I'm *not* living to make anyone proud, *not* to make my grandmother proud. I do what I do for myself." And then he said, "Actually, she lived *for* me. She cared for me. I am doing what she wants me to do. I live for giving something back." And here we see Edon's life in respect to a symbolic debt to his grandmother.[16] Edon described their relationship as very close. He desired to make her proud, to make all three of his grandparents proud.

Edon loved his maternal grandfather and described him as both wiser and kinder than his father—better than his father. Edon disliked visiting his parents on weekends, in part because his father would "test him". Asked to say more about how his "father would test him", Edon could only reply, on schoolwork, which Edon found stressful. He wanted to play, but his father wanted Edon to work. Edon ended up doing neither. Within the family drama, his father was viewed as ineffectual. I enquired about other thoughts that came to mind about not wanting to go to his parents on weekends. He described how his mother perpetually fought with his paternal grandmother. Edon hated the conflict between "the bride and the mother-in-law". He would think, "Why do you [his parents] treat my grandmother that way?" She did not deserve it, he said, and he felt most "pissed off" towards his father for allowing the situation. His father had made the wrong choice such that neither of the women he lived with was happy—he failed to satisfy "his" women. Edon wondered if this was part of why his mother did not want Edon to live at home, and he "wished the situation were different". I punctuated this phrase with a questioning intonation. He wished his mother and father were kinder to his grandmother. He said, "I took my grandmother's side. I saw my parents through her lens"; which was to find his father lacking. And here we can detect a particular family matrix in which Edon became a mouthpiece of his (interpretation of his) grandmother's desire, and was angry with his ineffective father.

I asked Edon to say more about his paternal grandmother. He described her as his "shield" from his parents. Edon had a hard time communicating with his parents directly, and she helped him do so. His parents were like strangers to him. When Edon turned thirteen, his paternal grandmother died, and his first thought was of how he would deal with his parents without his "shield" and "barrier". He said he never learned to interact with them and that bothers him to this day. I asked if there were other ways he wished the situation were different. He found himself at a loss for words. The session ended there. It occurred to me that "barrier" was an interesting choice of words that displayed ambivalence.

Then Edon's discourse turned towards and focused on death. When Edon's maternal grandmother died during the course of our therapy, he expressed remorse over her death and said his parents were next in line; he paused and added that when they died, he would not feel grief for them. He could not say more about this statement other than the fact that they had a full life and thus he would not need to grieve. But was not his grandmother's life long and full? And he expressed remorse over her death. Edon indeed found that puzzling. He left our session pondering this question, and returned to our next session questioning why, when he wrote or emailed his parents, he was *unable* to bring himself to write "dear mother" or "dear father" at the beginning or "love Edon" at the end. He said something stopped him from including the words "dear" or "love". He wished he could, but he could not—he would not. He knew his parents wanted him to communicate and be more affectionate and effusive with them. They would have appreciated a "dear" or a "love" inclusion, but he did not want to give them that. He did not know why he did not want to give them what they wanted.

Edon was stuck. I asked him if he remembered his dreams, because often when you get to an impasse, a place where a client is stuck, dream work can help access more unconscious material in a way that is less threatening to the ego. Speaking about dreams frees the client to speak more candidly and allows access to the unconscious more readily as we feel less responsible (less direct ownership) for our dreams than our waking thoughts. Indeed, dreams have the striking feature of giving one's most intimate desires and thoughts a form of expression that appears alien, foreign and even mysterious to one. Freud spoke of dreams as occurring on "another scene" (the term is Fechner's) while Lacan, in turn, coined the term "extimate" (on this see J. -A. Miller, 2008). So Edon began to speak about his dreams. The dreams were micro-symptoms, filled with signifiers that proved fruitful; we used them to establish links, especially regarding the role of the father and the relation to the phallus.

Dreams of the father

Edon relayed a dream where he was at a table, having a family dinner, when he disobeyed his father. Edon associated to many aspects of the dream. Particularly productive was how Edon associated to the saga of shopping for family dinners, and then about a specific time when he was sixteen, and his father brought home a salami that was not on the list. Every week Edon's mother sent his father out with a grocery list that he was supposed to strictly adhere to (money was very tight), but rarely did. Edon's father justified that he bought the meat because it was cheap, not because they needed it. Another glitch was that the salami had expired; it was past its due date. If Edon ate it, his father would be responsible for putting the rotten thing, something bad, in Edon. The father would pass on the spoiled thing to the son.

Usually Edon's speech focused on "ruining" himself—that he ruined his dreams, his fantasies, himself, etc. Thus, this dream in which he disobeys his father leads via Edon's associations back to the much earlier childhood scene in which Edon disobeyed his father by refusing to eat the spoiled salami. They got into a fight; his father tried to insist, but Edon refused. Edon defied his father and refused to eat the salami. Edon remembered this instance as one of the very few times he was ever *verbally* angry with his father. He remembers often being very angry and disappointed in his father, feeling his father had failed to provide what was needed, but not verbalising it. He complains his father acted like a "little kid", the precise reproach Edon often levied at himself when he "did the wrong thing", a signifier of an identification with his father. When I asked, "a salami?", Edon laughed at the phallic imagery of the poison object—distancing it. Nevertheless the childhood scene of the spoiled salami incident brought up much anger and anxiety. It was not really a laughing matter. It pointed to the gift, the inheritance from the father to the son, in this case, not a poisoned chalice, but a poisoned phallus. The spoiled salami, which brilliantly represents the meaning of the tainted object that Edon has inherited, which is an inversion of the Midas touch that turns everything to gold, taints and sullies whatever it touches. It is a phallic symbol, to be sure, but poisoned by the father's imperfect role as the symbolic vehicle of the phallic signifier necessary for the young man's inscription in love and sexual relations between a man and a woman.

These nightly interruptions by Edon's unconscious aggravated and distressed Edon. He questioned why he would have such aggressive dreams about his father. He said, "something in me hates my father and I don't know why". Further associating, Edon noted that his father did not heed his mother's words, about the shopping list, for example, but also about most things; his father irritated Edon's mother, and again, Edon took his mother's side.

Further associating, Edon recalled in the dream it was as if he was supposed to be "thankful for something [he] didn't want in the first place. It puts [him] in an awkward position. [His father] is blind and ignorant". Edon remembered when his father bought a "cheap and crappy watch", and gave it to Edon as if Edon should be thankful for something that turned out to be "crappy". Edon said he *needed* a watch, *but not that one*. The father's gift was not valuable enough; it was subpar and less than desired.[17]

We see here more of the complicated family dynamic, particularly in terms of what Lacan highlights as the circulation of the phallus. The father is not adequate to the task of conveying the phallus to his son; he is doing things wrong, according to the mother's, paternal grandmother's, and then Edon's adopted narrative. As such, Edon is not able, it seems, to use the father as a successful access to the phallus.[18]

The dreams keep coming; in another, Edon's father wanted to take the bed linens from underneath Edon's bed to use for a houseguest. Edon was angry in the dream and felt his own sleep and well-being were being disturbed for a guest. His father put Edon out for another, putting another before him. Edon said "My father wants to take my blankets and sheets for a guest. I don't want him to do it. I want to have a conflict with him." In his dream, Edon rebelled from being put out.

Edon expresses that in these dreams he feels a desire to have a "weird contact" with his father. I ask him about this "weird contact"; he says he is unsure, but in the dreams he wants to be both aggressive with and close to his father.

Edon relays another in the series of dreams: "My father travels a lot in the dream. As soon as he comes home I just want to confront him. I just want physical contact. I went up to him. Then the scenery changed and he was with my mother on top. It was like a stage and I was down and he was throwing pieces of the wall at me after I confronted him. My mother took his side so I was alone. I wanted physical contact." The signifier "contact" keeps emerging and "taking sides" rears its head, Edon was down and alone, with his parents "on top".[19]

In yet another dream, Edon's family is sitting at the table and Edon wants to go somewhere, when his father says, "Stay a little longer". Edon disobeys in the dream, and upon waking, he says what stayed with him most strongly was the anger and animosity he felt towards his father. When hearing dreams, amongst other things, Freud taught us to listen for a desire or wish that may be fulfilled in the dream. In addition to a wish to argue with and confront his father, which Edon consciously recognised, I also heard a possible wish for the father to say, "stay". The dreams seem to indicate Edon wanted his father to act. In associating to this dream, Edon brought up the time his father offered to help Edon pack his luggage. Edon said, "My father was trying to be helpful. I said, OK, and handed him my books. Dad asked 'do you really need them?' It was one of my favourites! I said what are you doing? As if he was choosing for me, choosing what I should take or not take." Edon said his father does not know what Edon really needs—does not recognise his prized possessions—that his father's ideas and choices are erroneous.

The dream in the father series that produced the most useful material was the following: Edon was eating salad. "I ate all the salad [*not meat*] and my parents got pissed off. Father started chasing me around. I opened the door, jumped and started flying into weird places. Father was trying to catch me with a fork in his hands [as if Edon was a piece of meat himself]. I was trying to fly high but had trouble keeping altitude with *him beneath me* trying to chase me." I punctuated *Edon had trouble keeping [it] up because his father was beneath him.* Edon tenses up; "*He isn't good enough*", Edon associates, and we hear a paternal failure that angers and frustrates Edon and keeps him down. One might link this fault of the father in the transmission of the law to the rotten salami and the failure at the heart of the phallic order that confers the poisoned phallus upon Edon. We see a relationship to a defective father, one Edon cannot look up to, one who in fact, he looks down on, who is a rather pathetic figure. This failure at the level of the father may have resulted in the transmission of this poisoned phallus, epitomised by the dream, but not just in the dream. It permeates all the way through his relations with others and ramifies through other aspects of his way of being in the world. Edon cannot engage his phallus without feeling he has sullied something, himself included, as a result.

Where is the love: the blanket of aim-inhibited drive and doubt

Edon's libidinal relations affected his romantic, sexual, and family relations. There is a significant issue in all his libidinal relations (although it is especially pronounced with women) around the split between love and desire. It is interesting with the family members because *here we have an "aim-inhibited" drive,* as Freud calls it. Freud thinks of the tender feelings towards others as often inhibited in their aim, in the sense that their original aim of sexual satisfaction has been replaced by a loving attitude towards the other. In sensual love, the two forms (loving and erotic) are combined, but they can come apart to the point where they are mutually exclusive and the person can only desire where he does not love and vice versa. As Freud states, "Were they love they do not desire and where they desire they cannot love" (1912d, p. 183). At this point, and this seems relevant to Edon, a condition for someone to become an object of sexual desire is that she be degraded, with the inevitable consequence that the subject himself becomes tainted and dirty. The self-recriminations that Edon is susceptible to as a response to sex are better understood in this light.

In associating further to a desire for physical contact, Edon turns to how his parents try to show him affection but he will not let them. He both wants it and does not want it. He thwarts their affection and is reluctant to show them warmth, saying there is "weirdness". His speech turns toward his aversion to sharing personally with his parents. They would like him to be more open with them, to have more personal contact, but something in him shuts down; he comes to a halt and finds himself inhibited. I bring up the dream of the bed linens. He said, "I don't want to give them what they want. Because they want it, I'm reluctant." I say, "Retaliation?" He said no, not retaliation, I had gotten that wrong.

But in the next session he said perhaps he was retaliating and he had not recognised it. To be sure, my interpretation may not have been true, but it was productive. "So I'm angry and retaliatory, but why did I get so angry in the first place?" The effects of this anger rise to the surface of his speech, but wherein lay the cause? He demands to get rid of this "psychological thing", to get rid of the bad feelings within him and to find a "normal state". He wants to *not* feel like fighting, pointing again to the fact that he has a strong desire not only to fight others, but also to fight his desire in particular.

And here we note that *the obsessional often displaces or transforms affect (such as anger) into doubt*. As Edon spoke more in therapy, he moved toward the affect and emotional weight, that which had been displaced onto his doubting symptom when he entered therapy. He said, "I think I have a problem, I can't give affection to my father. There is nothing wrong with him; he has always given me affection. I cannot pinpoint a moment in my life when my parents didn't care for me. But something has had an effect. There is a barrier between us. I used my grandparents and dreaded to go home." I highlighted that he said he could *not* pinpoint a moment in his life when he felt they did not care for him. What if he took out the not? He replied, "Maybe the move to my grandparents damaged the relationship? Maybe that whole thing was damaging?"

In relating this case, it may seem strange to the reader that someone would not recognise what seems, from afar, obvious. However, for Edon his cemented, long-adopted, logical narrative that a "sacrifice" had been out of love, had been in place for a long time, and discussing that the move to his grandparents might have had negative as well as positive effects had a revelatory quality, in which *he assumed a part of his history* that had, prior to his talking, been closed to doubt. While he would explore the connections between his libidinal relations and familial past, it is also likely that the overall structure of what happened in his life as a child—his being given to his grandparents at age three for example, like a "gift" as he put it—took its toll, although he had rationalised it as at once both trivial and commonplace and also as the great "sacrifice" for the better good. *It seems this was his defence, not to doubt that it was the right thing to do, not to doubt his parents' love and his love for his parents, but rather to doubt everything else around him.*[20]

Something was thrown into question and began to be rewritten and taken up anew. At the beginning of the therapy, Edon took pains to tell me that he did *not* doubt that his parents loved him, *nor* that he loved his parents. *"How could you doubt you love your parents?"* he pronounced. Instead he spoke of doubting his love for his girlfriend and most other things, particularly his sexual and erotic desires and troubles, which he felt great guilt over. It became clearer, through speaking, that his guilt around sexuality, his rather tortured libidinal relations, and his doubt for his girlfriend were, in part, displacements and related to his parental complex. He began questioning whether his parents loved him, and if in his past, he felt loved and cared for. And in a number of dialectical reversals, Edon came to question whether he indeed felt a genuine love for his parents. This is where his doubt culminated. He began to ask the question, *"Do I love these people or not?"* The dynamic of "I love, I love not" rose to the fore. He continued, "I know I love my parents. *If I don't love my parents, what do I love?"* This was a profound question to be reckoned with for him. In asking, as he did, "Is it really possible (not) to love your parents?", he allowed himself a space in which he no longer had to excessively live out that question that he had been asking, not verbally, but with his very being for a long time.

Missing pieces: transference and the cause

To be sure, many threads were necessarily left unwoven into the fabric of this case study, but a question that remains and should be addressed is how Edon situated me in the transference.

At one point when Edon noted that he actively fought with his father in his dream (although not in waking life), Edon told me that *I* was "the cause". It was, he said, because we had spoken earlier that day during his session about the "weird contact" that he wanted with his father that Edon had that particular dream that night. Edon had previously said that he "could not see [himself] ever punching or kicking [his father]", but then had a *"not* uninteresting dream". I asked how it was interesting. He said he was "getting the hate away" and fought with his father in the dream, *because of* our conversations. In this sense, he had temporarily placed me as the cause of his desire and in so doing allowed a space for his desire to be less inhibited and rise to signification, at first in his dreams, and then in his speech.

Other ways in which the transference was implicated reared its head when, after speaking about a session prior in which Edon was waxing on about "living to give back to others", he expressed that it had occurred to him that he "should pay more" [money] than he did to see me. He was worried about me not receiving enough from him. He said he derived benefits from our work and was thankful, but at the same time he also worried that our work in some way harmed me. Indeed, in one session Edon brought in a daydream featuring "a girl who is really pretty, but looks tired"; he helped her tell her story and because of this act she changed as a person. Edon remarked, "She is different because someone helps her. I love her and after one year she would leave" (note we had one year to work together), but he did not touch her. He said in the daydream he was also trying to work through how in his life, "sex makes things unhappy", and the daydream "mixed helping through conversation and sexual feelings. She was beautiful, but I was afraid of ruining something pretty". With these utterances, I heard how Edon placed me in the transference on multiple staves of the score: at once as the woman who needed to be rescued (implicating me in his "rescue-motif"), second as the pure woman who is harmed or sullied by his desires, and third as the one who helps the other, but in so doing is wounded. These projections onto the transference mirrored the themes that continually repeated in Edon's dreams and fantasies. I did not interpret the transference, but rather allowed it its place, as I did not feel it was interfering with the work. In fact, it was good symbolic grist for the therapeutic mill.

These are snippets of a case focusing on the libidinal relations, the paternal function, and obsessional doubt. I present the above, not as a complete case, but as a modern day example of rather classic obsessional symptoms and structure. Edon clearly needed more time to narrate and elaborate upon his anamnesis than he was allotted—my time at the clinic had ended. He had run out, our work was cut off—in a way that defined-term therapy can be castrating and limiting. But the case also exemplifies how defined-term therapy can open up a space of desire. Edon wanted to further explore his anger toward his parents (particularly his father) and how it related to his conflicts regarding his sexual desires and his pervasive and troubling doubt—a doubt that poisoned his relationships, his sexual relations in particular, and to some extent his entire life. Edon began to wonder if there was one thing he could not remember, one traumatic incident in his childhood that had been repressed. He derived a fantasy that if he could remember this one thing, then the pieces would fall into place and release his doubt and his desire and then he could choose—without any doubt—his one true love and be happy.

A question that remained for Edon and for me is how much access we/he ultimately had to such material. As Lacan discusses in the "Function and field of speech and language in psychoanalysis" (in Lacan, 2006), there is a wall of language that acts as a barrier to translating our clients' experiences fully. Meanings hit against a wall, a limit. To stop hitting one's head against this wall would indicate an end to the process. However, there is difficulty in translating the real into the symbolic, and we as clinicians do not have privileged access to the real. I was on the same side of the wall as Edon. Given this, to what extent is a draining of the real into the symbolic fully possible? To what extent can the symptom be explained in terms of structural determination (this is taken up more completely in the conclusion of this book)? For we know in theory that there is a rewriting that takes place with the advent of language; for example, the Oedipal stage overwrites the pre-Oedipal. Freud likens this in *The Interpretation of Dreams* to a palimpsest where one thing is written over another and only traces remain (1900a, p. 169).[21] For Lacan these are traces of the real which can appear as holes in the story. What we do in our work, short and long term, is listen for the hole. I think even in short term work we can hear the incompleteness of the system and look for the "hole in the whole", as Fink has nicely put it. And our interpretations can try to hit this something that has been lost.

However, to further unravel the symptomatic knot and drain the real, Edon would need to speak more about the events that took place when he was younger, more about his sexual history, perhaps even the events that led up to his birth. It would have been much more favourable for our work to continue, but alas, circumstances were such that not only did his allotted sessions and my work at the clinic come to an end, I was also leaving the state. But our limited work together sparked Edon's desire to continue and he planned to see a psychoanalyst in town.

For all that was left unsaid, and there was plenty, in the end, I did not doubt that Edon took a certain enjoyment in our work. He enjoyed shaping his message for me and sharing his symptom. As J. -A. Miller discusses, Edon was "happy because [his] displeasure ha[d] been formalised" (1991, p. 15), and symbolised, to a certain extent. And thus for all that is left on the other side, it seems that even defined-term work can open up the can of worms that is desire and help move clients towards more integration of that which was experienced as most foreign, so that what begins as a major complaint becomes more meaningful and integrated into one's life story.

Notes

1. We also need to consider that Edon simultaneously derived pleasure from such thoughts of his girlfriend having sex with other men. We thus can also see these as everyday fantasies of a sort that cause both pleasure and pain.
2. This follows the trajectory Freud described in 1896, stating that we find "In a first period—the period of childhood immorality—the events occur which contain the germ of the later neurosis. First of all, in earliest childhood, we have the experiences of sexual seduction that will later on make repression possible; and then come the acts of sexual aggression against the other sex, which will later appear in the form of acts involving self-reproach" (1896b, p. 169).
3. The following citations for *Le Séminaire de Jacques Lacan, Livre V: Les Formations de l'Inconscient* correspond to the French pages. The translation is courtesy of the translation by Russell Grigg (forthcoming).
4. We will see how he made an unconscious connection between love and sacrifice based on his early family history.
5. I was using, albeit more liberally, Freud's idea that "dreams feel themselves at liberty to represent any element by its wishful contrary" (1900a, p. 353), and that whereas a wish sets the dream in motion, a fear can disguise a wish.
6. Edon also spoke of desiring a female cousin and wanting to have sex with her. He said when he thought about having sex with her, he imagined it was "with the same organ", that they would both have penises.
7. Note the women did have something; they had breasts. And Edon later ran up to random female strangers, and grabbed them to prove it, as will be discussed.
8. Edon said by sixteen he could no longer avoid temptation. He decided to see a prostitute with the hope that such an act would make his desire go away. But it remained. He thought if he fulfilled his curiosity, his want for knowledge, it would abate. He also wanted to be able to tell his friends he had sex (or rather not be lying anymore when he said he already had).

9. For more on the connection between the anal drive and obsessional neurosis see the second case in this book.

10. Hearing this, I remembered the way he used the word "spoiled" some sessions back. He said the people he "hung out with" in America were "spoiled", as in were given a lot but did not appreciate it, and because they had been given so much, they could no longer enjoy what they had, even though they had it good. His friends back in Eastern Europe were trying to survive, he said, but people here were spoiled. It is also in this sense that we can hear the signifier "spoiled". Once Edon got off on touching strangers, it was hard for him to get the same jouissance (this too becomes impossible for him at a certain moment). In other words, Edon was having a hard time mustering as much satisfaction and jouissance as he did as an adolescent.

11. For example, I asked him again to clarify his age at seeing the book the girl brought in, and he said it was after he viewed the pornographic magazines. I was wondering then, how, if he had viewed pornographic magazines, he had not seen a naked female. Edon denies that females do not have a penis, and yet according to his time line he was thirteen and had already been introduced to pornography. Was the castration threat forced out of his mind? It also could be the case that he had the order of events wrong, that he viewed the book before the pornography. There was something amiss in the history. There were gaps, I notice them and ask him to say more.

12. Edon also projected his doubt and desire to control his desire into the future. He worried about the future; what if when he is married he cannot control his lust? What if he still looks at pornography and has affairs? Will he hurt his future wife? His symptom spanned time.

13. Note that the sexual crime committed against him, that he narrated, happened at the grandparents' "safer" apartment complex. This was elided from his discourse.

14. See Freud's "Negation" (1925h), and Lacan's *Seminar I's* appendix on Hyppolite (1988a).

15. It seems the first son, Edon, is not the phallus for the mother. He did not see himself in this place—as that which is desired. Perhaps the younger brother was. Edon, however, did somewhat see himself as the maternal grandmother's desire, her "gift" she would call him, and used to say Edon "kept her young". But did Edon feel that this was his rightful place?

16. In yet another sacrifice of sorts, Edon had left his home and come to the United States for graduate school, in part to make his parents and grandparents proud. He does exceedingly well at school and work (Edon is quite talented at sublimation); his work future looks

promising, particularly monetarily—he already had offers in his field that would make his parents proud. He reports that he works terribly hard, seven days a week from morning until late at night. During the course of therapy he came to question why he worked so hard and for whom. He moves in his speech from a place where he says he wants to work more and be less distracted (recall his presenting problem—ruminations were intolerably affecting his work negatively), to questioning whether he truly likes his work. He arrives at a place where he can articulate that at times he does not like his work, is not passionate about it, and is "doing it as a matter of duty rather than personal fulfillment". It takes him numerous months of being able to put things up for question before he allows himself to utter such things.

17. Then Edon juxtaposed his father with the man Edon lived with, his maternal grandfather. He said unlike his father, his grandfather was wise, and handled things well. He and his wife were in harmony, unlike Edon's parents who, according to Edon, fought too much, were too pessimistic, and "sacrificed too much".

18. It seems Edon's maternal uncle potentially held the phallus, as Edon described him as particularly powerful. For example, when Edon would lock himself in the bathroom, the only way anyone could get him out was to say "your uncle is here", at which point, Edon would exit immediately. He said he was afraid of his uncle and the others used the uncle to get Edon in line.

19. Note that the "mother on top", could be heard as a potential primal scene image. It is also reminiscent of what Edon said to the young schoolgirl that shamed Edon.

20. From this point of view, Edon being "given" to his grandparents, as his "grandmother's gift", might also thus be seen as a poisoned chalice.

21. As Lacan states, "Hieroglyphics of hysteria, blazons of phobia, and labyrinths of *Zwangsneurose* [obsessional neurosis]; charms of impotence, enigmas of inhibition, and oracles of anxiety; talking arms of character, seals of self-punishment, and disguises of perversion: these are the hermetic elements that our exegesis resolves, the equivocations that our invocation dissolves, and the artifices that our dialectic absolves, by delivering the imprisoned meaning in ways that run the gamut from revealing the palimpsest to providing the solution of the mystery and to pardoning speech (2006, p. 281/232).

CHAPTER FIVE

Family ties that bind: the *wait*ress, lack, and loss

L ily's life was in a rut. She was in her thirties, not seeing anyone romantically, out of work, and living with her parents. Occasionally she worked as a waitress for her family's restaurant to both help out and earn money, which she found distasteful, especially because she had done so for much of her life, ever since she was a child. In fact, Lily disdained being a "*wait*ress", which was an apropos title in untold ways, for Lily was playing a waiting game, living her life as if always *waiting* for an alternative life to magically appear. And all the while, Lily complained bitterly that her "lust for life" had already been prematurely drained into her "father's business", the restaurant, and it was time for her to move on with her life.

Lily's case illustrates how we find the same existential dilemmas and powerful familial forces and ties that bind in the twenty-first century, as those that confronted Freud's patients in the nineteenth century, just in a different temporal and cultural context. Lily was strongly committed to her family, she was the glue that held things together, but, as we shall see, there was a risk she would never escape the whirlpool (or sinkhole) of the family structure that dragged her back and down.

Lily's presenting problem was that she wanted "out", to separate herself from her "overly enmeshed" family and move out of her parents' home, which she described as "chaotic" and (ironically for a family that dealt in the food industry) "without nutrients". But she found herself unable to move. Her opening question to me was *"when can I enjoy?"* She felt as though she had waited her whole life to enjoy, and said, "It never comes." She would cry out in sessions, "I am never going to get what I need!"[1] From the beginning and throughout our work, Lily would say that she wanted to "put things in place". This was her own stated goal for the therapy: to put things—what was out of place or missing—in place.

Lily described one all too brief period in her life—it lasted roughly three months—many years ago, when she had an apartment of her own, a job, money, clothes, and a boyfriend. This was a period, of very brief duration, when "everything was in place", when Lily was rendered more complete by what we think of as phallic attributes; she had those things that she saw as valued by our culture as stereotypical signs of the phallus, as what the Other desires. This is the phallus as a signifier, as the signifier of desire, and in this case what society, as the very big Other, encourages us to desire. But any feeling that she had the phallus quickly slipped out of Lily's hands; she said she "lost it all". She lost the job, then the apartment, then, the man. This loss of phallic attributes was a trauma that stood as a further obstacle to her moving out on her own and striving for love and work *again*. She repeatedly rehashed how she had tried and lost. All of these can be "lost", she emphasised, and the idea and experience of losing the object was very threatening for her.

Lily told me, "Now *nothing is in place.*" This utterance, pronounced in her second session with me, contained the wording of her conflict, a kernel of truth, for in this phrase, "now nothing is in place", one hears that if nothing is in place, then nothing can be lost. *Lily had unconsciously orchestrated her situation so that she had nothing left to lose. Also, inherent to this sentence, is the idea that in the very place where there should be something, there is nothing.* Lily's frustration, indeed her very being, was inordinately wrapped up in this sense of loss and losing.

"Broken and dirty"

In addition to highlighting her deep emotional frustrations, Lily also complained of extremely discomforting physical pain in her back and legs. After thirty years of life, she said, all she had to show for her work and existence was a "broken back and bad knees". She repeatedly described her life and body as "broken". Lily's bodily pain was in part related to her being quite overweight, a symptom she also wished to remedy. This symptom was also a factor that she said kept men, at least men other than her father, at bay. She related her "broken body" to the fact that her father "kept [her] back".[2] When asked how her father "kept her back", she said he made her work too hard, and moreover, had nothing for her but "*broken* promises".

Lily's father also spoke "*broken* English" (as an immigrant, English was his second language), which made him difficult to understand and had served as a source of embarrassment for Lily throughout her life. Her father's "broken" speech made it even more difficult for Lily to fit in at school and with peers. Thus, we find several verbal bridges from her father and his speech to Lily's body and feelings, and that bridge is "broken". In light of the case as a whole, as will become clearer, one might make the small stretch to "broken off".

Lily felt "like an old lady", she said, which was the way she described her mother: once youthful, but then shackled by work. The portrait Lily verbally painted of her mother was of a woman brought to her knees by work and, ultimately, by Lily's father. Lily saw and referred to her own self as a "worn out servant", another image and phrase Lily used to describe her mother. Thus, via her symptoms and her speech, Lily identified with and put herself in her mother's place, and did so in a manner customary with hysterics; the identification found expression in her signifiers and somatic symptoms.

Lily said being in her thirties, unmarried, with bad knees, a bad back, and no job or home of her own, was akin to being a "dirty dish rag", a worn out, de-valued object used to clean up other people's messes. Asked to say more, Lily described often feeling "dirty", particularly as a young girl, and associated that this was, in part, because her mother failed to wash Lily's clothes, hair, and body enough. Often Lily arrived for therapy sessions in sloppy clothes and once declared that she was dressing "like this" (in "dirty rags") because she "hate[d] herself". It was a message to society and to me, the Other, and signified the image she held of herself, a signifier she took from the Other. She articulated how although she desired to be clean, well groomed, and nicely dressed, as she would be *if* she had a career or a romantic date that required it, this "dirty" form of dress represented that she did not have these—they served as a sartorial index to her lack. She dressed in sullied rags as a symbol, or what Lacan calls a "semblant", of her existential status; it is a pretence that she herself is taken in by, and in fact she gets enjoyment from, even as, at some level, she knows it is pretence. As a rule, we can take a semblant to be some characteristic or feature that indicates a lack in the subject. And we see that Lily willingly, even pleasurably, takes on and gets an unconscious enjoyment from her rags as semblants of a lack that is more difficult for her to acknowledge.

Despite pointing to her mother's failings regarding cleanliness, proper housekeeping such as laundry and child grooming, Lily would nevertheless reiterate time and again that really, *"beneath it all"*, her father was to blame. Let us, then, examine her father's role more closely.

The role of the father as "only man"

Lily vented ample anger towards her father. He "caused [her] to be this, this dirty dish rag". She complained he had worked her "like a whore", and in the same stream of thought and speech added that she never had enough romance or sexual intimacy in her life. She repeatedly complained that her father made her work for years and years and then forbade her to go out and have fun—it was the tale of a servant, the frustrated young woman, wedded to the family, looking enviously from the family fortress to the outside world.

Lily was committed to her family, had worked hard, and felt entitled to more than she had received. She remarked in our very first session, "He did not fulfil my needs", pointing to both her disappointment and desire for her father to do so. Love for her father was clearly there, but so was the acrimony and rancour. Lily struggled with a strong love/hate split for her father, which manifested in animosity towards him.[3] Frequently, Lily's repressed love for her father reared its head in outright anger towards him, and above all resentment. It is as if she carries a grudge over having been wronged, as if she has a longstanding grievance arising from some past, vaguely perceived injustice. The French have a nice term, *"revendication"*, to describe the sense of unjust deprivation that the hysteric feels she has been subject to. The hysteric consequently demands the restoration of what, to her eyes, is rightfully hers.

From a "no-thing" to Oprah and back

Lily emphasises the sense of lack within her when she says her father made her feel "like a nothing". As a woman, especially, she felt she was nothing, which was particularly pronounced due to her family's traditional Indian heritage. Men held the power; women did not. However, Lily's internal status fluctuated between feeling like "a nothing", to expressing grandiose thoughts and everyday fantasies that she should be a celebrity, a star, like Oprah Winfrey (who is, of course, only one of the biggest personalities in the entire world). The problem, Lily said, was that her family "held her back". *And here, in the imaginary realm, we can see an almost static image of a fame-bound girl held back in the confines of the home by the family, in grimy rags—a Cinderella.* Lily complained that her family did not support her ambition to be an actress. They recognised her star potential, but failed to offer the encouragement she needed to "go out and do it".

At times Lily literally described herself as a "wanna-be"—her term as well as popular culture's, uncannily echoing Lacan's notion of the "want-to-be", the *manque-à-être*, as well as his metaphor of the something out of place, *qui manque à sa place*. There was clearly something lacking in Lily's symbolic order, something missing, which means, because only something that has a place can be missing, something was out of place. Lacan describes the subject, $ \$ $, as divided and lacking; at the heart of this division we find a lack of being and hence a "want-to-be", or even a "want-of-being".[4] Lily was desperate to be something, and in her very wanting, Lily's desire underlines her lack of being, her failure *to be* something. We can see, then, how the want-to-be points to the co-extensiveness of lack and want/desire, just as it equally points to her parents' lack.

Recognising her own stance and status as a "wanna be" infuriated Lily. To add insult to injury, she said her father was the "first to know that [she had] *nothing underneath*". She said he saw what she knew, that she had "no rod"—her words exactly: "I have no rod." I punctuated these phrases and asked her about the "nothing underneath" and the "no rod". She replied she lacked an inner strength, that she "meant" she had "no backbone". This was why, for example, she did not leave home. She said *if she had a rod, a backbone, she would not be in this position* (and here we see the unconscious, apparent right there, for all to hear, in her speech).

In one session, Lily announced, "There is a hole in me". When I punctuated this phrase, she brought up a man whom she adored, the only man with whom she had ever had sex, and said that he "filled up that hole". He was a married man, and hence, she said, unavailable to her. The married man whom she thought could have filled her up, left her empty, left her with a hole. It was her fantasy, as will be discussed below, that helped lead her to such an object choice that she chose a married man as the one partner who could fulfil her sexually.

Lily continued. Even more than wanting to be *with* him, to *have* him, she really wanted *to be* this man; he represented the phallus for her and her utterance pointed to a desire not only to *have* the phallus, but *to be* the phallus. Let me explain.

If we follow Lacan we can conceptualise the neuroses as both presupposing and entailing different questions of being. And, as discussed in chapter one, we must answer these questions of our being by reference to the Other, who holds the secret to all our desires. The child turns her attention to the Other's desire because she strives to find the answer to her own question and situate her own being, as Colette Soler remarks, via the Other's desire, that is, in the Other's lack. In other words, it is "with the Other's desire that the child tries to answer [her] own question and situate [her] own being" (Soler, 1996, p. 266). And what might the child take the Other to desire? In Lacan's schema, the symbol *par excellence* of the Other's desire, in the sense of what the Other desires, is the phallus. Lacan refers to the phallus as "the signifier of the Other's desire". The child may embody a desire to be the phallus, or a "want-to-be-the-phallus".[5] But in order for the child *to be* this phallus, the Other must lack. This logic remains particularly prominent in hysteria. Lily took up the position of the object that would fill the Other's lack; but in order to maintain herself in this position, she had to do whatever it took to maintain the Other as lacking.[6] Finally, while propping up and maintaining these positions, Lily made certain that her parents heard her complaints; and, actually, her symptoms were this complaint, albeit in the form of a silent or unarticulated protest.

Lily complained of being lost without "a man", however, she also suffered from lack more broadly, where it formed part of her general strategy towards the other. In this she identified with her mother. Both mother and daughter were missing what should be there—had a "hole". In their family dynamic, Lily's father held the phallic position of master and king. However, Lily constantly pointed to the slippage of this positioning, pointing, whenever she could, to the faults and failures in the father's position. She referred to her father as the "wizard of Oz", a being who supposedly holds all the power until you actually look behind the curtain or lift the veil. In some ways, Lily was obliged to uphold and maintain this wizard in the position of the phallus and take it all quite seriously; but in other ways, she articulated a disjunction between the person of the king and the phallus. Although she complained incessantly to her father and about him, she never actually told him where to shove it. She kept her father in a phallic position, even as she became his harshest critic. And all the while, Lily pointed to her mother's complicity in the pact, but not her own. Consequently, the more power Lily gave to her father, the less she had for herself, until there was very little phallic about her. She showed up dressed in dirty rags. We can see quite clearly here the hysteric strategy of revealing the other's, in this case the father's, castration, while maintaining him in the position of master all the same, "a master over whom she can reign", as Lacan describes in *Seminar XVII* (1991).

The brother, the phallus, and the family sinkhole

Part of the family dynamic concerned Lily's older brother, whom Lily described as somewhat pathetic and not nearly as talented as she was. Lily stated that, unlike herself, her brother was not impeded by the lack that Lily experienced so deeply, adding that her brother was more valued by her parents, particularly her father. The brother was encouraged in many ways that Lily was not. He went off to college. Lily's dream was to go away to school, specifically, to fly off to aviation school, but this, she said, would have been unacceptable to her father; so she did not go. I asked her, "Your father forbade you?" and she replied, "I didn't even bother to ask". In these ways and more, Lily maintained his position as well as her own.

And here we have a scenario that maps particularly well onto Freud's cases in the *Studies on Hysteria*: the girl who stays behind, "wedded" to the family, its constant support, a role she dutifully fulfils—*even as her neurosis is a protest against her fate*. Lily then watches as her brother leaves the nest and lives a freer life. In speaking about familial roles, Lily frequently pointed to sexual difference and to castration, without naming it as such. She circled around it, making herself dizzy in the process. Lily proclaimed: "I experience loss after loss and nothing will make up for it", "I've never known anything but loss", and "My life is a complete loss". She was extremely frustrated with her progress, in and out of therapy. About life and therapy, she pronounced, "I'm just going round in circles."

For Lily to find her way out of the rut that her spinning wheels maintained, it became ever more pressing and important for me to intervene, *to name the lack and introduce the missing link—the signifier that she could not speak* and that would, hopefully, allow for some transformation, some movement forward. For the process of symbolisation to go on, we needed to name the term that was excluded from the chain, the term that was not there for Lily when she needed it. Once we arrived at an appropriate stage in our work, and after I missed a number of ample opportunities, I began punctuating this "nothing underneath", which, it turns out presented itself every session. Yet this was not enough! So one session, when Lily repeated angrily "I would have gone to aviation school", I replied, "If you had a penis." She looked at me, paused (I worried that I had alienated her with what she might take to be some kind of Freudian hooey), but then said with an utmost seriousness, "Without a question. *Let's get this clear: I wouldn't be on this damn couch if I had a penis.*" And a lack was named.[7]

At our next session, Lily said, "I think we're getting somewhere. We hit upon something." Ironically, what we hit upon was a great loss.

Your money or your love

When and how did this intense loss of gratification come about? In filling out the ellipses of her anamnesis, Lily described her childhood. She related that until age four, she was a happy child. This was before her parents opened their own family business, and before, as Lily described, the children were put on the "back burner" for the restaurant. Before the family business, Lily felt she had a family, a mother and a father. They had family dinners and "everything was normal." And then her parents opened the business and it became the most important thing; it took over the family's life. What became most valued, to Lily's young eyes, was the money the business brought the family. Lily said the business "robbed and stole" from her, which nicely expresses, in monetary terms, the sense of unjust deprivation, or *"revendication"*, mentioned earlier. She "lost [her] mother and father to it", and lost her childhood and positive view of herself as a child. Ultimately she experienced a loss of herself as valuable, a loss of love. Nevertheless, the key place and central role in the family assumed by Lily also displayed her inability to separate herself from the family; even as she complained about her neglect, she supported the very arrangement that made it possible.

Ever since the "family became a business instead of a family," and she felt more like a servant than a beloved child, Lily tried desperately to recapture that lost sense of being more valued than money. She "scrambled to make up for that loss". Lily complained that her father put any money the family earned back into the business such that his wife and children were not able to use it for themselves. She said they "worked to the bone", but did not have a claim to the money and were in no way adequately compensated. Instead of buying new clothes, they went around in "dirty rags". Their dishevelled attire represented the not-having the phallus. We see the signifying chain (still) in motion here.

As she got older, Lily began identifying with her father around the desire for money. At times, Lily professed, "Money is my god", and that the most important thing was money. And although she did not seem to act upon this desire, she articulated that her desire was for the same object as she perceived her father's to be: money. In this way she identified with him. Lily also said, "Money is my husband." She described how her cousins moved from the security of their father's protection to the security of their husband's care. Lily, on the other hand, lacking a husband, felt unable to do this. She was stuck with and perpetuated an unsatisfied desire.

She was angry that she did not have money and said her father "owed" her. He "put [her] to work" her whole life. Indeed, maybe if she had been paid she would have at least been worth *something*—in her own eyes. She began working in the restaurant as soon as she was able to do the smallest of tasks. By the time we began our work, Lily tabulated she had been "serving others" for almost thirty years. Thus, at a young age, she became a servant to a boss, and this boss was her father.

Servile fantasies and the "indented servant"

Lily's dreams and daydreams were peppered with an image of a "boss", an image that was at first *not* consciously associated with her father. Lily reported daydreams about kissing "a boss". The boss scenario was a titillating one. In recounting one daydream, she described a boss "riding her". I asked her to say more about this phrase. Lily said she meant, "getting on [her] back". "*Getting on your back*?" I pursued the ambiguity. "You know, criticising", she responded. As I punctuated these phrases again—repeated the words, she associated to the potentially sexual nature of the terms, and then to the verbal bridges to her father, whom Lily said was always "getting on her back at work" and chastising her. It became clearer that taking up the position of serving her father, the boss, lay at the heart of the matter, and that it was quite a complicated mix of love and hate.

Before going further, permit me to detour to the preconditions of Lily's birth, for they play a role in the structure of the fantasy. We know that the most important signifiers for a person can be there in circulation even prior to her birth. Lily told the story of her parents' union as follows: Her parents had an arranged marriage. Her mother was to provide her father with entrance into the United States, via a green card. In marrying, Lily's mother provided both families, hers and his, a service. The plan was that the mother could soon divorce her husband and then she could marry for love, and her husband could likewise marry a more appropriate or desired woman, who, in this case, speculation was, would be a "good Indian wife". However, the plan fell through; they remained together, and the children were born. Promises were broken (rather ironically, the broken promise was of divorce in order to find true love) and neither parent was ever truly happy with the other. This was how Lily told it. This was Lily's story.

Thus, Lily perceived or interpreted her father's desire as being for that which he lacked, a "good Indian wife", a wife who would be an indentured servant to him (although Lily slipped, tellingly, and said an "*indented* servant"). Such a wife would, for example, be adept at serving tea for her husband, other Indian friends, and relatives, in the traditional way. This "servile wife" provided an answer to Lily's question about what her father wanted, needed, desired, and lacked. Lacan discusses how the subject is always caught up in the question "*Chè vuoi?*" or "What do you want?" (2006, p. 815/690), and how many of our ways of being in the world and with others (including the fundamental fantasy, which shall be discussed below, that also informs our more everyday fantasies) are intricate, unconscious responses to this question.

Lily felt that her mother was ultimately not what the father desired. Lily was not either, but she tried, from a young age, to fill her interpretation of her father's desire by being the good and servile wife she felt he lacked, and thereby also displace her mother. In this way she took the stance and positioned herself as the one who could potentially fill the lack in the Other.

But all the while, Lily also highlighted her father's lack by describing him as impotent in many ways, as a man who waited "for when the time comes", when the time never did. Hence, he did not fulfil his promises (especially to her). She called her father's non-responsiveness, these moments made up of broken promises, "little deaths".[8] He did not come through for her. Note, this image of someone who waits for a time that never comes also described Lily and her situation, and served as a further identification with her father.

Lily played a multileveled, intricate game in relation to her father. On the one hand, she saw herself as the only one who could fulfil his desire for a good wife. On the other hand, she did *not* do everything in her power to fulfil that desire. Rather, she complained about the lack in her father and said *she did not want to work*, at all, *not* in the restaurant, *not* in the home, *not* outside the home (unless she could be Oprah). The father had forced her to work too much, and now she was broken and tired.

The father's lack at once situated and greatly bothered Lily. This is part and parcel of the hysteric's strategy—the hysteric manoeuvres in such a way as to be situated at the centre of the Other's desire and then slips away from providing the satisfaction that would fill the gap, because filling it would make the Other's desire disappear—and then where would she be? Lacan posits that the neurotic's fantasy itself is caught up in the Other's desire; he states, "In the case of the hysteric […] desire is sustained in fantasy only by the lack of satisfaction the hysteric brings desire by slipping away as its object" (2006, p. 824/698). This is how Lily related to her father and others, eventually including me, as we will see. And how did Lily's mother fit into the picture, fantasy wise?

I'll take your place: the mother

During our work, Lily slowly weaved a narrative in which she needed to stay at home to take care of her father, in order to be the wife he did not have. What was going on with her mother? Lily recounted that at age eight, which we can speculate may have been at the height of her Oedipal attachment to her father, her mother was working both in the restaurant and at home and was not well. Lily saw her mother as worn out, tired, and ill. She remembered, around age eight, sending her mother to her bedroom one day. Lily said to her mother, "Go to your room. I'll take your place", and then thought to herself, "and will do a better job than you". On the one hand we can see a kindness in sending an exhausted mother to her bed and taking over her duties, and on the other, we can recognise Lily's (unconscious) wish to get rid of her mother. As we shall see, Lily paid a heavy toll for taking her mother's place.

A question arises concerning Lily's perception of her mother's desire. Did Lily interpret a desire on her mother's part for Lily to take her place, to ease her wifely duties? Did Lily smell a lack? I think the answer was yes. In Lily's estimation, her mother was not physically up to the task. Also, Lily spoke of how the broader Indian community viewed her mother (and by association herself), as a second-class citizen for not being bred and fluent in Indian traditions. Her mother also lacked the proper husband. Recall Lily's narrative of the arranged marriage. Her mother was meant to divorce her husband and then marry another man "out of love", as opposed to "out of an arrangement". So Lily's mother lacked as well. Lily thus positioned herself to potentially also fill a perceived lack in her mother.

In thinking this through, we can hypothesise that Lily perceived, in her mother, the castration of a woman, and that this unconsciously encouraged Lily to turn away from her mother and towards the father. It may be understood as such: Lily's initial attempt to be the phallus for her mother, and take her mother as her love object, collapsed when Lily realised that she herself did not have the phallus and thus must go and seek it elsewhere. So Lily turned away from the mother and towards the father from whom she strived to receive the phallus.

In this way, Lily's fantasy can be seen as a defence that veiled the lack in the Other, in other words, veiled castration.[9] There is something inordinately threatening about the lack in the Other. The child sees this lack as an inadequacy, one that affects the child's being, and hence runs from and defends against it in a valiant attempt to fight off this anxiety that arises in the face of the Other's lack. Lacan theorises that the subject directs the question of her being, and her reason for being, to the Other and the fact that the Other can never answer adequately, that is, lacks a definitive answer, is frustrating if not downright horrifying. Thus, Lacan tells us that the "refusal of castration [...] is first and foremost a refusal of the Other's castration" (2006, p. 632/528).

By taking up her position in the fantasy, *Lily filled two lacks with one stone, so to speak.* Lily both sought out her parents' lacks and refused them by constantly complaining about their lacks. Ultimately, she refused to let the lacks go unfilled; she refused to let lack well enough alone.

But it was not all bad. From this situation, Lily experienced a symptomatic jouissance, the jouissance of the martyr, a painful pleasure in renouncing her desire and giving it over to her father. Related to the jouissance of the martyr was Lily's discourse about how her family acted "under the guise of sacrifice", and how Lily's parents advocated that being a good person meant being a good Christian. Her parents' line was that if you sacrificed now, you would be rewarded later. This thoroughly annoyed Lily who said that she was always waiting to be rewarded but it never came. She argued that unlike her parents' life, her own life was *not* about sacrifice. However, we can remove the "not" from the sentence. We see how Lily desires desire, while her jouissance is tangled up in a renunciation of her desire, in favour of her being what she has interpreted as being her father's desire.

In this way Lily was again like her mother. Both seemed to display a passionate attachment to sacrifice and misery. Indeed, Lily expressed that while she had in the past gained significant satisfaction from her own complaining, by the time Lily began therapy with me, even she had become bored with her own groaning. This, she said, was unacceptable. If nothing else, she would have liked our work to return her to a state where she could re-gain some secondary satisfaction.

Lily played up the martyrdom aspect. She said she had to stay; if she left, it would kill her mother. I asked her to say more. Lily narrated that ever since she was a young girl, she fantasised that if she were to "escape" her familial home, her mother would die—actually keel over. Lily recalled this as a strong fear she lived with that paralysed her. The thought "If I leave, my mother will die" ran through Lily's head. The exact reason, according to Lily, would be from a *heart* attack.

I related that in this fear, we might also hear a wish. If Lily's mother died, then it would be easier for Lily to take her place. In many ways, Lily's mother was a stifling and needy figure. For example, when Lily was young, her mother would drive the children to school and instead of dropping them off on time, she would delay separation and take them out for breakfast. At first glance, this might sound playful and fun, but Lily said this was actually no help to her at all, rather it was a hindrance; Lily missed school because her mother wanted the company, company Lily's father failed to provide. One could detect a high level of separation anxiety from Lily's mother.

Lily related her reluctance to leave her familial home to her fear/wish that her mother might die. Another possible way to understand this was that Lily unconsciously punished herself for wanting her mother dead; in other words, because *of her wish, Lily unconsciously punished herself by never leaving*. She would stay and be the servile wife as an unconscious punishment.[10]

But why this death wish to begin with? Perhaps because Lily's mother held the place of the special object for the father and as long as she did, Lily could not fully occupy that place. In this way, the mother impeded Lily from being, being in the sense that is provided by the fantasy. For Lily it was something of a life or death struggle. One had to die for the other to live. This Oedipal wish to take her mother's place fuelled many of Lily's symptoms, including the rotting of her own body ("like an old lady's")[11] and a rotting and waning of her desire. Lily said she was "rotting inside and out". This rotting occurred on multiple staves of the score. As the years passed and she remained at home, she described her "lust for life" vanishing before her eyes.

The role of fantasy

Here it is helpful to more specifically and theoretically link the structure of Lily's desire to her symptom formation and the fundamental fantasy. First, we should discuss Lacan's concept of the fundamental fantasy more explicitly than we have so far. What is so fundamental about the fundamental fantasy and how does it differ from regular dreams and daydreams—those everyday phenomena we often call fantasies—thoughts, images, and vignettes that run through our heads for better and worse? Lacan proposes that in addition to everyday fantasies there is a fundamental fantasy that can be constructed in and through analysis. By *Seminar V* (1998a), Lacan provides a formula for the fundamental fantasy as it is encountered in neurosis. Lacan's matheme for neurotic fantasy is ($ \lozenge$ *a*), barred S lozenge *a*. This matheme can be read as $, the split subject, the subject split by language and the unconscious in particular, $\lozenge$, lozenge = in relation to, *a*, the object that causes desire.[12] Thus, fantasy concerns the divided subject's fundamental relationship to desire, particularly that which causes desire. Later, Lacan provides distinct formulas for the hysteric and obsessional fantasy, as well as specific fantasy formulas for perversion and psychosis.[13] Does every person harbour a fantasy that can be spelled out? Perhaps not, but the possibility of articulating an underlying unconscious working explanatory principle, that is making the neurotic's implicit fantasy, explicit, can be an integral part of Lacanian analytic practice.

One potentially helpful way to understand the fundamental fantasy is as the structure that supports or defines the subject's basic relationship to the Other and to desire. Lacan situates the fundamental fantasy on his graph of desire as a way of answering the question *Che Vuoi?*, what does the Other want? Specifically, what does the Other want from the subject? As Fink puts it, the neurotic seeks an answer to the question, "What is she wanted for?" (2007, p. 255). In attempting to answer this question, the subject's desire becomes "conditioned". Lacan says we can "abbreviate" the "neurotic's position with respect to desire" with the word "fantasy" (2006, p. 638/533), an indication that the fundamental fantasy structures the subject's desire and her relationship to the Other's desire. The permutations of the fantasy, which arise as daydreams, intrusive thoughts, masturbation fantasies, and the like, relate to and can even be reduced, so to speak, to the fundamental fantasy. They also point the way to the fundamental fantasy, which resembles a mould that we pour our experience into, or a paradigm that shapes a person's view of reality.[14] We see the world and desire objects within it through our fundamental fantasy, just as we view phenomena through our existing, often implicit, paradigms. While moulds help us make shape of formless substances, and paradigms help us make sense of the possibly overwhelming chaos, they also limit our experience. One often cannot experience or see that which stands outside of a given paradigm (Kuhn, 1962). In the spirit of a Kuhnian paradigm shift, *the traversal or crossing of the fantasy takes the aim of analysis beyond symptom and inhibition relief; it leads to a different perspective; it offers the potential for a different viewpoint, and it ultimately opens up many possibilities that may have otherwise been closed.*

Lacan speaks about the fundamental fantasy as over-determined and over-determining, both in terms of desire and symptom formation. The formula specific to the hysteric's fantasy can be written as: $(a \lozenge \bar{A})$, object a in relation to a barred or lacking Other (*Autre*). In situating Lily's position with respect to fantasy, I shall work with this matheme.[15] Based upon what we were able to piece together and construct during our work—and this work was not complete, so we must take this construction as preliminary—we can articulate that Lily's fantasy seems to have been that she wanted to be the object that served her lacking father. Her father was the barred Other (Ⱥ)—the divided and lacking Other. Lily aligned herself with the lack in her father. She positioned herself as the lost object—the servant who could potentially plug up his emptiness.[16]

Lily took up the position of the object that could potentially complete her father better than her mother could.[17] Fink puts it well: "In the hysteric's fantasy […] separation is overcome as the subject constitutes herself, not in relation to the erotic object she herself has 'lost' [as is the case with the obsessional], but as the object the Other is missing" (1997, pp. 119–120). Lily took up this position of the "object the Other is missing". She played mother; she served the tea (and more). This is not an uncommon role for hysterics, in part because the role of mother connotes, in general, satisfying the Other's desire. In *Seminar VIII*, Lacan states, "The satisfaction of playing the doting parent, which involves the wiping of tushies, is first and foremost the other's satisfaction" (2001, p. 246). In French, the verb *pouponner* means to play mother. The British have a saying, "I'll be mother", which means I'll pour the tea from the teapot and thereby take care of the other. This role fits in well with the hysteric position on multiple levels, for the hysteric's desire is so very caught up in the Other's desire.

The structure of Lily's desire was such that she wanted to be the being necessary to fill the lack, but also leave it unfulfilled. The problem was that she could not stop doing it, and a part of her longed to "move on" and out. But Lily's desire was fixated. We see an ossification of desire, which leads to a desire crisis; she was experiencing an enjoyment crisis. Lily repeatedly implored, "When do I get to enjoy?!" In order to do so, she would need to separate from the Other's desire and shift her (unconscious) subjective position that was based upon her interpretation of her father's desire. However, relinquishing this position, as painful a position as it was, seemed intolerable for Lily. After all, it provided her with *a sense of being*.

We can further view this situation as Lily having exchanged her desire for the sign of the lack in the Other (the sign of the phallus).[18] But all was not lost, by any means. For at the same time as desire is "exchanged", it is also propped up. We can see how Lily's desire was caught up in and weighed down by this fantasy, and at the same time, how this fantasy "props up desire" (Lacan, 2001, p. 293).[19] Lily's position at once stifled but also fuelled her desire. How so?

Although Lily considered her life to be missing a romantic component, there was an erotic aspect to her fantasised position that served her at an unconscious level. Aware that her father desired a servile Indian wife, Lily's status as servant to her parents gave expression to an erotic component that partly fulfilled Lily's desire. Recall her "boss" daydreams and the sexuality inherent to them. It also supplied a sense of being where there was nothing, "no rod". These were powerful lures, which indeed, did "keep [her] back". Again, while she got off on this position, experienced the pain and pleasure, she also knew, at some level, that she could do better.

In our work together, I tried to highlight how Lily was trying to be a better wife for her father, while at the same time keeping his lack in tack, by punctuating the aspects of her speech that revealed this dynamic. I did so in the hopes that through an articulation and recognition of this pattern, Lily might see and ultimately experience alternative positions and ways of being, ways of relating to others that might offer her more satisfaction and movement out of the rut. I tried to punctuate what I heard, that Lily had boxed herself in and that her father was taking up an awful lot of room in her life. For example, Lily cried out that she wanted a man in her life, *a love outside of her father*, but said there was "no room for one". She said the "only man in [her] life" was her father. I echoed her words back to her, "The only man is your father?" She was speaking the repressed. *She said she was terrified of becoming an "old maid", and worried that what she feared most had, indeed, already happened (we might say her unconscious wish came true).* She was an old maid to an old man, and it was no longer about her own desire. Her desire was too caught up in his, or theoretically speaking, to her unconscious strategy in relation to the Other.

We can think of fantasy as involving the way the subject positions herself in relation to the other/Other in terms of symbolic positions, which we can access via speech and, thus, theoretically via analysis or analytic therapy. We glimpse the client's fantasy by listening to her words, her stories, her signifiers, and mapping out the symbolic coordinates of her discourse. That the fantasy can often take the form of a sentence, such as Freud's classic example of "A child is being beaten" (1919e), points to the symbolic at work. In his seminar of June 14th, 1967, Lacan states, "The fantasy is [...] structured like a language. Since, when all is said and done, the fantasy is a sentence with a grammatical structure" (1966–1967b, p. 165). In this way, the fantasy helps to provide a subjective position for the subject from which she is able to desire.

A main goal or aim for therapy was to untangle Lily's desire as separated from her fantasised relation to the Other's desire, to move or change the obstacles in her way, to separate or at least shift her own stance as an object with respect to her (interpretation of her) father's desire. Why was this important? Because Lily suffered from her positionality; the sense of being that was provided for her by this fantasy was ultimately inadequate and unsatisfying. She could do better.[20] But getting to that something more, that something other, that something better, was no easy task.

We had gotten to the point of raising the question of formulating the fantasy. The fantasy is not something that is openly presented—it is something that has to be formulated or constructed in the course of therapy. The fantasy, like the anamnesis, is filled out and thus constructed through the analytic work.[21] Indeed, it is likely that by the time the fantasy has been thoroughly fleshed out, it has already morphed in one way or another. That is, in working with the fantasy, the fantasy is altered, which, of course, is the point. It is the same with symptoms. Once fully spoken, symptoms likely no longer affect the client in the same way and are changed symptoms. Such is the fate of the analyst's role and of the work: the client is always a step ahead of the clinician.

But with fantasy, Lacan reminds us there is also the element of the real that lies beyond interpretation and construction. On the one hand, it might seem quite obvious that Lily's fantasy was to be a servile wife to her father—she said as much, but an interesting question remains: what, if anything, was covered over by this fantasy? Freud shows us in "A child is being beaten" (1919e) that there are levels and phases of the fantasy, and like a dream, manifest content can cover latent material, displacements and condensations may occur. We did not get this far in our work together. Rather, we glimpsed the fantasy as well as the possibility that glimmered on the other side of it. And Lily and I both saw how Lily played a role in this scenario, *how she was also complicit*. More importantly, viewing herself as an active party, she *ideally* might have then chosen to position herself differently, as difficult and threatening a task as that entailed. And that is something; that is engaging the fantasy.

Lacan provides a formula for an aim and end of analysis that he calls "traversing the fundamental fantasy". This involves working through and moving beyond the fundamental fantasy. To cross the fantasy, Lily would have needed to be confronted by something. Lacan tells us that what she would need to be confronted by is the analyst's enigmatic desire. If successful, Lily would be on her way to accepting or owning her desire. In so doing, Lily would need to subjectify the cause of her desire. But this involves assuming responsibility. Fink states,

> Subjectification means that the subject assumes responsibility—not in words alone, that is, consciously, but at some "deeper" level—for his or her fate, his or her past actions, decisions, and accidents. The subject comes into being where his or her life was determined by outside or impersonal forces: the Other's desire, his or her parents' desire that brought him into the world. (1997, pp. 242–243, fn43)

And this leads us to another reason Lily might have positioned herself in this way. What else did she stand to gain? It became clear that *for Lily it was important to fail*. If she failed, which by her own definition she was doing, over and over again, she could continue to blame her parents. *In blaming them she could say it was not her fault and relinquish responsibility.*

Lily was living her life as determined by the forces, particularly the family drama, into which she was born. And while she could speak of this predicament quite eloquently, she was only slowly coming to see *her part* in the drama. Lily needed to verbalise and acknowledge the role she played in orchestrating the paths and even obstacles of desire. She was in her thirties after all (as she pronounced many times); how long would she play by these, the Other's, rules? She was asking this question with her being.

Lacan states that in analysis, "it is toward [the subject's owning of his desire] that he is directed and even channelled" (2006, p. 641/535). Thus another formulation for the end of analysis is an owning of one's own desire. Did we arrive at an owning of Lily's own desire? I wish. We were on the right path, but unfortunately, in the process of working through this fantasy to allow for something else to emerge, and even when confronted with my desire for her to continue, Lily ended our work together. What happened?

The termination: breaking it off

Bringing the outer world into the therapy room, Lily came to feel strongly that she was spinning her wheels, not only in life, but also in therapy. She asked if we could try a different approach. She had heard that some therapists give their clients homework (she had seen this on Oprah). Would I give her homework? "Like what?", I asked, and what would that do? She replied, homework to find a job, at least look for jobs, a certain amount per week and she would report back to me, as a pragmatic step towards independence from her family. She said it would help her free herself, one step at a time. I agreed to assist her in her search for work; she would look in the newspaper and online for job advertisements and report in our next session how it went. While on the surface of things, Lily seemed pleased that I would put her to work in such a way, and while this seems like an innocent enough move, retrospectively, I think this turn away from analytic work and towards a more behavioural model may have actually precipitated the premature end of our work.

Unfortunately, by engaging in this way of being with Lily, *I responded at the level of her demand rather than at the level of her desire. Lacan warns us against this.* Demand should be "bracketed", in an effort to keep desire in play. I forfeited what Lacan calls *the analyst's desire*, the "motor force" of analysis, which must be a pure, enigmatic desire for the analysand to speak, rather than a specific one—to get a job and move out of the parental home, for example, even if one can see that finding work, particularly meaningful work, would obviously be helpful in this case. I am not opposed to a more eclectic approach. Every now and then adding a behavioural technique into the mix works well. Clients have reaped the benefits in other cases. But in this case, I think it failed. I think I failed Lily.

Lily came to our next session with newspaper in hand. She had read the paper, circled potential jobs with a red pen, but had not made any moves. She said I needed to tell her to do more, to push her more (and I heard echoes of how she thought she could have been Oprah if only her parents had encouraged her more). Lily was situating me in the transference as the parent who had the opportunity to push her out of the nest (but also as the barred Other in her fantasy as will be discussed). Two sessions later, Lily called our work to a halt. She said she did not want to continue. I realised I had disappointed her at some level. I invited her to talk about it, talk about her wish to leave. But she had made up her mind. She said the perfunctory things: that I had helped, that she learned about herself and her predicament, etc., but that she was ready to move on and "take it from here". Somehow I did not quite buy that. Something had gone awry. I could see how I had misdirected the treatment.

Let us here recall the role and stronghold of fantasy. If the hysteric manoeuvres in such a way as to be situated at the centre of the Other's desire, and then slips away from providing the satisfaction that would fill the gap, because filling it would make the Other's desire disappear, and if Lily read my desire as being specifically for her to get a job, pure and simple (as opposed to the analyst's desire being enigmatic and hence fuelling the desire to speak more in therapy), then Lily could keep my desire intact by refusing to get the job. That was coming into play. And it was a repetition of what was happening at home. But it was also a more complicated dance than that. Why else, besides my own therapeutic blunders, which to be sure were plenty, did Lily "break it off"?

I would also suggest that, *in part*, Lily also "broke off" therapy when she did because she was confronting her subjective position and was moving towards a possible reconfiguration of the fantasy. She was speaking of *creating a life for herself*, separate from her family, and I think, at a certain level, such a notion *really turned her off*. As much as she said she "wanted" it, she could also not bear to give up blaming her parents for ruining her life. If she moved out, got a job and a partner (other than her father), she could no longer blame her parents, and she derived a significant amount of satisfaction from the set up as it was. As much as she suffered this positionality, as described above, it provided a reason for her being and was what she knew, on a very deep level.

Although she said things were shifting, there were big stakes involved regarding the position she held for her father. While Lily continually said that she "need[ed] things to change", when push came to shove, she chose to keep things relatively the same. The build-up of anxiety around relinquishing her position as the object that supposedly completed her father, the better wife, was too much. Lily had situated herself as a phallic object for her father. My interventions may have been taken as castrating. Lily would have needed to give up her semblance of a phallic position in order to take up a new position or come to have a new fantasy. Lacan discusses how the neurotic "figures that the Other demands [her castration]" (2006, p. 826/700). My suggesting things could be otherwise, could have been taken as castrating. Staring castration and possibility in the face, Lily chose to end our work, which could also be a message saying: "Nothing needs to change" and "Don't make me work", for she felt she had worked for the Other all her life and was "broken" because of it. Despite or perhaps because of my encouragement to continue and my attempts to keep up the pressure, telling her we were getting somewhere and that our work could help, she told me she did not want to continue further. I do believe in encouraging clients to continue and tried to use my desire to sustain our work, but my attempts failed.

Why was it so difficult? Because Lily got something out of her fantasised position. For one, Lily's positioning within the fantasy provided her with an answer to the all-important question of where she fit in, within the family structure and within *the world in general* and that is a powerful thing. Lacan discusses how the subject "butt[s] up against the question of his essence" (2006, p. 815/690), and how the fantasy, in turn, provides a form of an answer to this question. Her unconscious answer was that she was a servant to her father. This was the "image set to work in the signifying structure", as Lacan (2006, p. 637/532) defines the fundamental fantasy. And Lily played this to the hilt, while she yelled and hollered about what a disappointing and lacking father she had. *Indeed, Lily lived her life in such a way as to emphasise this lack in her father so that she could maintain and secure a place for herself.*

To be sure, whether clients (and therapists!) are conscious of it or not, there is always both a pull towards *and* a fear of doing the analytic or therapeutic work. I do believe Lily's departure may have been avoided if I had stayed at the level of desire and fantasy, at the level of speech in particular, rather than go along with her demand for a more behavioural therapeutic approach that focused on a very concrete, specific goal. Regardless of why Lily broke off our work, we must view Lily's therapy as incomplete. This is not at all uncommon. Often times, clients end therapy when the analyst or therapist believes there is still work to be done. However, sometimes it is a much more grey area. Sometimes it feels like continuing therapy may be, for pragmatic reasons, a case of diminishing returns. This leads us to the interesting question: is there even such a thing as a complete analysis or a complete therapeutic process? Of course different approaches to therapy and even different psychoanalytic approaches have different answers. Freud and Lacan have somewhat different answers from each other. Indeed, Lacan provides different formulations for what constitutes a proper or complete "end" of analysis at various stages of his work. In the following concluding chapter, I discuss these pertinent issues.

Notes

1. During an early session, in response to this cry, I replied, "And yet what you need now might change." This remark, of course, pointed to a desired therapeutic outcome, and was perhaps too swift a move. The thought of an alternative possibility and framework, the idea that Lily indeed might not be able to attain what she desires now, but that what she desires may shift and even that she might desire differently, was an implicit aim. I return to this issue and the more general one of what we can hope to achieve from an analysis or therapy in this book's conclusion.

2. One can also hear a polyvalent meaning to "kept [her] back", as in "got your back". For while Lily bitterly complained about her father, she was a "kept woman"; he did provide her a roof over her head, food to eat, etc., when she did not have a job or means to provide these things for herself. In this way he also "kept [her] back".

3. Note that in obsessional desire, as in the previous case of Edon, there is a strong love/desire split that the obsessional attempts to suture by one means or another, whereas the hysteric, as here, often engenders a love/hate split that she then employs to undermine the other.

4. See Schneiderman (1980, p. vii).

5. Lacan states, "What the neurotic most commonly wants to be is the phallus" (2001, p. 250). In "The direction of treatment and the principles of its power" (in Lacan, 2006), Lacan states, "[T]he receiving and giving of [the phallus] are equally impossible for the neurotic, whether he knows that the Other does not have it, or that the Other does have it, because in both cases the neurotic's desire is elsewhere—to be it. And whether male or female, man must accept to have and not have it, on the basis of the discovery that he isn't it" (2006, p. 642/537).

6. And although Lily gave over a certain jouissance to her parents, at the same time, she refused to let them enjoy what she had given up. As Lacan observes, "What the neurotic does not want, and what he strenuously refuses to do right up until the end of his analysis, is to sacrifice his castration to the Other's jouissance, by allowing it to serve the Other" (2006, p. 826/700).

7. Theoretically speaking, I embraced what Lacan calls "an opportunity to get the patient to grasp the function the phallus as a signifier serves in [her] desire" (2006, p. 632/528).

8. In French, *la petite mort* means the moment after orgasm. Of course, for Lily, the moment after orgasm rarely, if ever, came; we will get to the connections between waiting, lack, promises, and sexuality.

9. The fundamental fantasy, which will be theoretically articulated more explicitly later in the chapter as well as in the conclusion of this book, is conceptualised in myriad ways. One way is as a defensive strategy related to the ego. Lacan, in his first seminar, states that to comprehend human relations, we must take into account the "human ego, namely that set of defenses, of denials, of dams, of inhibitions, of fundamental fantasies which orient and direct the subject" (1988a, p. 17). Fantasy, as an ego defence, serves to defend against the threat of castration, in particular. However, Lacan warns us not to take up fantasy solely in terms of its egoic or imaginary functions, not to get too mired on the imaginary realm, but to simultaneously acknowledge the symbolic dimension of fantasy. Thus, my hope is that this case offers one example of what both can look like in the life of a subject.

10. We might view this thought, "If I leave, then my mother will die", as an obsessional thought, and view it as an obsessional trait in an otherwise hysteric structure. The "decision" to stay, can be read as a reaction formation to the contempt that finds expression in Lily's desire for the mother's death. Punishing the other by punishing oneself can also be viewed as an obsessional mechanism in which the hatred is expressed towards the object of her identification. But again, this potential obsessional strategy is adopted by an otherwise rather clearly hysteric structure.

11. Here we can detect the "mortifying effect" of the signifier penetrating the body (J. -A. Miller, 1996b, p. 425). Miller states: "The signifier penetrates the body. When we speak of the mortifying effect of the signifier, we note that Freud himself highlighted the fact that the human body is progressively mortified, to such an extent that jouissance is required to take refuge in the well-known erogenous zones. This mortification is so complete that Lacan makes the body the locus of the primordial Other, that is, the locus in which the signifier with its mortifying effect is first inscribed" (1996b, p. 425).

12. On this formula see also Lacan's seminar of November 16, 1966 from his course entitled *La Logique du Fantasme* (1966–1967a).

13. The formula for the perverse fantasy is $a \lozenge \$$ (Lacan, 2006, p. 774/653). There is a question as to whether the notion of a fundamental fantasy is applicable in terms of a psychotic diagnosis. Can we put the fantasy to use in analytic work with psychotic patients? In this book, I am limiting myself to speaking about clinical work with neurotics, but the question is an interesting one that deserves more attention. Some argue that in psychosis, the delusional system or what Lacan calls the

delusional metaphor, stands in for the place of the fundamental fantasy (see Freud's "Constructions in analysis", 1937d; and Fink, 2007; and Vanheule, 2011).

14. See Dunand (1995, p. 253).

15. In *Seminar VIII, Le Transfert* (2001), Lacan discusses a more complex formula, one that he does not seem to make much use of after *Seminar VIII*. The more complex formula is:

$$\frac{a}{(-\varphi)} \Diamond A$$

Which we can read as little *a* over minus lower case phi in relation to (or desire for) the Other (capital A). In this chapter, I will explicate the simpler version ($a \Diamond Ⱥ$).

16. And here we can understand fantasy as J. -A. Miller defines it when he says that fantasy is a mode of the "subject's relation to the lost object" (1996b, p. 425).

17. And in clinging to herself in the position of object *a*, she could ignore herself as split subject, she could ignore castration. In *not* making her way in the world, she could try to avoid castration anxiety.

18. Lacan discusses that the hysteric aims "to be the procurer of this sign in an imaginary form", and she "always exchanges her desire for this sign" (2001, pp. 293–294).

19. In *Seminar XI*, Lacan states, "The subject situates himself as determined by the fantasy. The fantasy is the support of desire; it is not the object that is the support of desire. The subject sustains himself as desiring in relation to an ever more complex signifying ensemble" (1978, p. 185).

20. For as Fink reminds us, the "sense of being that is provided by fantasy is 'false being', as Lacan refers to it in the mid-1960s, suggesting thereby that there is something more" (1995, p. xii).

21. Lacan claimed, "When all is said and done, it is less a matter of remembering than of rewriting history" (1988a, p. 14). In the therapeutic field there is much debate as to whether reliving affect is more or less important than symbolic reconstruction. Lacanians have been criticised at times for not "getting to the feeling", or the affective level of the work, and remaining too intellectual. In *Seminar I*, Lacan states, "The stress is always placed more on the side of reconstruction than on that of reliving, in the sense we have grown used to calling *affective*. The precise reliving—that the subject remembers something as truly belonging to him, as having truly been lived through, with which he communicates, and which he adopts—we have the most explicit indication in Freud's writing that that is not what is essential. What is essential is reconstruction, the term he employs right up until the end" (1988a, p. 14).

CHAPTER SIX

More or less rough around the endings: the diverse ways therapies end

It is my hope that the previous case studies, for all their specificity, reveal that while our cultural climate differs substantially from nineteenth century Europe, whence Freud set us on this course of psychoanalysis, when we listen closely, *just as he did*, to the words of those who undertake talk therapy because they are suffering, we find the same existential dilemmas that confronted his patients. We hear deep-rooted questions about how to love, work, and grapple with the inevitability of loss, lack, and ultimately death.

Furthermore, we witness how the two classic existential and diagnostic structures of hysteria and obsessional neurosis are still very much alive (if not always well) and relevant to our current clinical work. The five cases in this book provide contemporary versions, forms, and expressions of the psychic structures that were observed and theorised by Freud and then Lacan, and illuminate how a working knowledge of these structures can guide us in both our understanding and treatment of clients. While we must always be careful not to pigeonhole people into diagnostic categories nor have psychological theories *stop* us from actually hearing fully, at the same time, *ethically*, we must employ a theoretical framework to help us navigate the chaos that is another's suffering, and these diagnostic formulations provide fruitful treatment directions that allow and encourage us to hear and interpret from something other than our own personalities, egos, beliefs, and values.

Given the presence of these existential phenomena and structures, clinicians do well to turn to the tools that Freud and Lacan provide us. We can still confidently employ the radical power of free association and other analytic techniques to alleviate affliction and open new possibilities for those who, when confronted with these dilemmas, find themselves stuck and unable to move forward to live more satisfying lives. Lacan noticed that paying attention to formations of the unconscious, to phenomena such as parapraxes, dreams, memory disturbances, jokes, verbal bridges, etc., had rather gone out of fashion. In presenting these cases, my aim was to remind readers that bringing our attention back to such material, lies at the heart of the transformative aspects of talk therapy.

Indeed, the main aim of this book has been to show how engaging the unconscious through speech helps transform people's lives, their relations to themselves and others, their impact on the world around them and how that world impacts them, and to show specific examples of what that can look like in practice.

To be sure, each person, each case, is always unique. However, granted the singularity of each individual's therapeutic journey, there must be some similarities in the aims and ends of analysis or therapy. What is it that these tools, which Freud and Lacan provide, aim to accomplish? Are these goals and conceptions of ends of analysis the same for Freud and Lacan? Is there even such a thing as an "end" of analysis? Fully answering these pertinent questions would comprise a book in itself (one which I plan for a future project), but here I will *briefly* take up these questions and sketch the different formulations that Freud and Lacan offer on the aims and ends of analysis, how the cases presented in this book relate to these questions, and finally, examine where "happiness" may or may not fit into such equations.

Ends of analyses: Freud and Lacan

Analyses and therapies end for a variety of reasons, as we see in the cases presented in this book; some reasons are quite pragmatic,[1] others less so. This leads us to ask an important question, though one that is difficult to answer: what constitutes a bona fide "end" of analysis or therapeutic ending? Is there even such a thing as a "complete" analysis or therapy? And what are suitable aims? There is little consensus on these questions; different psychoanalytic schools provide varying replies. Even when limiting our discussion to a Lacanian perspective, we do not arrive at one easy answer.

One reason for this aporia is that, in contrast to the caricatures made of their work, Freud and Lacan take seriously the idea that analysis, or for our discussion, therapy, must be a unique venture for each individual. An analyst or therapist, for all her or his training and expertise, should not enter into a particular therapeutic process with a prior notion of how it should proceed and turn out. Rather, Freud and Lacan offer *guidelines* for the direction of treatment and formulas for worthy goals. Let us begin with Freud's and then see how Lacan both follows and diverges, and where the previous case studies fall along the spectrum of possible therapeutic endings.

Freud's pessimism

In "Analysis terminable and interminable", Freud asks, "Is there such a thing as a natural end to an analysis—is there any possibility of bringing an analysis to such an end?" (1937c, p. 219). His response is less than an absolute, enthusiastic "yes". Rather, he says it would behove us to "decide what is meant by the ambiguous phrase 'the end of analysis'", and acknowledges that practically (and humorously) speaking, an end is achieved when the "analyst and the patient cease to meet each other for the analytic session" (1937c, p. 219). In other words, an end is when a final session takes place. Lacan echoes Freud's humour when he provides a definition of psychoanalysis as "the treatment one expects from a psychoanalyst" (2006, p. 329/274).

Humour aside, Freud comments that an analysis may be considered complete when,

> First, the patient shall no longer be suffering from his symptoms and shall have overcome his anxieties and his inhibitions; and, secondly, that the analyst shall judge that so much repressed material has been made conscious, so much that was unintelligible has been explained, and so much internal resistance conquered, that there is no need to fear a repetition of pathological processes concerned. If one is prevented by external difficulties from reaching

this goal, it is better to speak of an *incomplete* analysis rather than
of an *unfinished* one.

The other meaning of the "end" of analysis is much more ambitious. In this sense of it, what we are asking is whether the analyst
has had such a far-reaching influence on the patient that no further
change could be expected to take place in him if his analysis were
continued. (1937c, p. 219)

Here Freud presents a juxtaposition of two kinds of endings. The first
entails a resolution of psychopathology, an alleviation of symptoms
and inhibitions. The second specifically asks what analysis can accomplish when pushed to its limit. This has to do, not solely with removing pathology, but with making a substantial modification to a person's
way of living in the world with others—a veritable shift in subjective
positions for the person, into the future. Freud describes these long-
term effects and this ambitious ending where no further change can be
expected even if continued, where a limit has been reached, as "a real
achievement", and reminds us that this is no easy task.

Truth to tell, Freud's words do not tell us what these changes are
(for that we will turn to Lacan). Rather, Freud provides a negative-like
description (relief from symptoms, etc.) but then, when it comes to giving a positive definition, Freud is unusually silent. A complete analysis,
defined as one where no more material can be analysed, does not tell us
much. In any case, Freud declared the first ending much more common
than the second. Every analyst will have a "few" of these, he says (1937c,
p. 220) and we are likely to find a "variability in the effect of analysis"
(1937c, p. 228); that is, oftentimes a "transformation is achieved, but
often only partially: portions of the old mechanisms remain untouched
by the work of analysis" (1937c, p. 229).[2] Results are often imperfect,
mirroring life itself, but myriad beneficial changes, on a spectrum, have
occurred during the process.

So, as Freud describes, some analyses end by mutual agreement when
it is thought that the analysis has gone far enough and a law of diminishing returns has come into play; this is a pragmatic decision. Then
there are those analyses that end as a result of "external difficulties"—
one or other party has to leave, for work, relationships, or for other
life callings. Most often it is the client who has to terminate for these
practical reasons (as we see in the case of Mona), but sometimes the
therapist must end the process because of life's circumstances (as with

Lisa and Edon). And in the third, there is this "ambitious" or "ideal" ending where no further change is possible.

Then there are also internal obstacles to contend with; remembering and working through all the repressed material would be quite a challenge, because a) there is just so much of it, and b) "what has once come to life clings tenaciously to its existence" (Freud, 1937c, p. 229). Regarding the limits of the "efficacy of analytic therapy" (1937c, p. 231), Freud also draws attention to the challenge of working through the castration complex, which, according to Freud, occurs more or less thoroughly depending upon the circumstances and the patient's sex. He states,

> We often have the impression that with the wish for a penis and the masculine protest we have penetrated through all the psychological strata and have reached bedrock, and that thus our activities are at an end. This is probably true, since, for the psychical field, the biological field does in fact play the part of the underlying bedrock. [...] We can only console ourselves with the certainty that we have given the person analysed every possible encouragement to re-examine and alter his attitude to it. (1937c, p. 252)

Thus even when a client is given every opportunity to speak about things "all things considered" and thus alter her or his perspective, there remains, for Freud, an obstruction to complete transformation: the "bedrock of castration", which we can think of as essentially a refusal, by both men and women, to accept lack in both the sexual and more existential dimensions of their lives.

Because full acceptance of lack is the most significant and universal obstacle to a complete end, resistance may rear its head in various ways. In speaking of a certain male patient, Freud says, "His riddle is *almost* completely solved [...] at the moment a residue of his symptoms remains. [...] I hope that this residue will not prejudice the practical success" (1937c, p. 215). This "residue" has manifold meanings. One is the very obstinate nature of the repression process itself. If repression worked we would not have the pathology we witness, but there is constantly a battle between what Freud called "the return of the repressed" and the myriad obstacles to putting the material into words.

In addition to repressed material that remains unspoken, Freud states, "In every phase of the patient's recovery we have to fight against his inertia, which is ready to be content with an incomplete solution"

(1937c, p. 230). A person's ego is also part of the problem (though for some, including Freud at times, and certainly the ego psychologists led by Anna Freud, but excluding Lacan, the ego is also part of the solution). Theoretically, the ego is a compromise between the id and superego and is often content with and even keeper of the status quo, no matter how unpleasant that status might be. Not only are we, after all, at least comfortable, if not happy, with what we know, we cling to it for the satisfaction that we unconsciously derive from it. Our symptoms are a secret source of jouissance, despite our complaints, and thus, as Freud says, we find "*resistances* against recovery [...]. The ego treats recovery itself as a new danger" (1937c, p. 238), and we continually butt against the powerful forces of ego-defences at work keeping the repressed at bay.

Impediments to "complete" analyses are by no means located solely on the side of the patient. The analyst's or therapist's own counter-transference issues also get in the way. As Freud states, "Among the factors which influence the prospects of analytic treatment and add to its difficulties [is] [...] the individuality of the analyst" (1937c, p. 247). Freud of course recommends analysis for the analyst to help overcome the analyst's resistance. Although the following advice is rarely heeded, Freud states, "every analyst should periodically—at intervals of five years or so—submit himself to analysis once more, without feeling ashamed of taking this step" (1937c, p. 249). For the analyst, analysis really is interminable.[3] So for Freud, in addition to the external factors that can cause an analysis to come to a premature end, there are considerable internal barriers as well: the bedrock of castration, ever more layers of repressed material to unearth, ego-defences, and the counter-transference.[4]

Lacan's unique take on ethical and unethical endings

Lacan agrees with many but not all of Freud's assertions regarding the end of analysis, but diverges from Freud's position that psychoanalyses end mainly for practical reasons, when one gets to a point of diminishing returns, for example. Lacan is rather exceptional in conceiving of analysis as indeed terminable, and throughout his oeuvre, he proposes a number of definite formulations about possible endings.

To be sure, there are many analytic goals Lacan does *not* advocate and that are to be avoided. Lacan emphasises that a client's ego-defences and ego itself get in the way of analysis; he refers to the ego as a compromise solution on par with symptoms. The ego is our public face, and for Lacan, a cause of suffering, *not* an ally. His "Mirror stage" essay (in Lacan, 2006) conveys how our immediate bodily experiences are superseded by imaginary identifications with others. We start to see ourselves, and then experience ourselves, through another's eyes, as if looking at ourselves in a mirror. Indeed, this is the creation of the ego. Lacan's early theory of aims in analysis involves a working through of these identifications that can be so very alienating. The mirror phase is the initiation of our alienation, and Lacan warns that analysis needs to scrutinise and reverse, not continue, this estrangement from our own experience. We saw in the cases how useful it was to recognise and articulate the role clients' imaginary identifications unconsciously played in their lives.

Identification with the analyst, specifically the idea of an analysand's ego identifying with the ego of an analyst, which Lacan dubs "ego-ego" analysis is viewed as a pernicious conclusion. Lacan makes this argument via his critique of ego psychology.[5] While some analysts and therapists encourage clients to model their behaviours and cognitions on the "proper" behaviours and cognitions displayed by the analyst, Lacan argues that this is a repetition of the disease of conforming to the Other's desires and demands and should be actively forestalled.[6]

Through identification and subjugation, we all too readily hand over our autonomy to the Other. Therapy needs to move in the opposite direction, which is why analysts or therapists need to keep their counter-transferences to themselves. For Lacan, like Freud, also locates resistance on the analyst's side of the couch, emphatically stating, "There is no other resistance to analysis than that of the analyst himself" (2006, p. 595/497). Lacan implores the analyst to maintain the "pure" desire of the analyst, the analyst's desire, and keep her or his counter-transference, defined by Lacan as "the sum total of the analyst's biases, passions, difficulties, and even inadequate information" (2006, p. 225/183), in check, out of the process, to be worked-through in the analyst's own analysis and supervision.

Some analytic schools encourage the use of counter-transference as a view into a client's psyche, as a mechanism to glean important information about a client, but Lacan is clear that information gathered from the counter-transference is about the analyst, and should remain on that side of the couch, *not* be projected onto the client. I believe Lacan states his assertion so emphatically in order to clearly make his point, but truth be told, resistance is, of course, located on both sides of the couch, because on both sides are human beings, and resistance is inherent to speaking beings.[7]

Also unsatisfactory, and for Lacan, unethical, meaning it runs counter to the ethics of psychoanalysis, is working towards pre-set goals based upon certain moral or superego demands, that is prescribed, culturally sanctioned ways of being.[8] Lacan is adamantly against any kind of "normalising." Any process whereby we lose the uniqueness of the individual, destroy separation, and encroach upon subjective freedom and responsibility, should be averted.[9] As Lacan states, "there's absolutely no reason why we should make ourselves the guarantors of the bourgeois dream. A little more rigor and firmness are required in our confrontation with the human condition" (1992, p. 303).

In addition to Lacan's critiques of certain aims, we can also locate numerous analytic endings that Lacan discerns, conveys, and champions. Why does he provide different formulations at varying times? One answer is that the broader theory in which Lacan is thinking, changes through the years. But there is also a sense in which these diverse expressions describe the same outcome in different terminology. It is as if each of Lacan's formulations for the end of analysis sheds light on what an analysis is, from a particular place within Lacanian theory. While it is beyond the scope of this conclusion for me to take up *all* of the formulations Lacan provides, I will discuss those that are the most important.

Early to middle years: fall of the imaginary, emergence of signifiers, and subjective destitution

In the early years, Lacan articulated that analysis must examine and call into question the imaginary identifications and relations that hold and bind a person. And it is via speech and the realm of the symbolic that an analysand loosens these imaginary ties. Through the symbolic we affect the imaginary of a subject; through talking, a slow process of dis-identification or de-identification takes place.[10] We, of course, can never be completely free of identifications (we have egos after all), but we can more consciously articulate how these identifications have moved us in ways we were unaware of previously. Russell Grigg refers to the vacillation or fall of semblants in analysis as a "controlled decline of the imaginary", or even more poetically put, "a slow burn" of identifications, which allows an analysand to re-orient herself towards the real.[11]

At the heart of Lacanian theory is the idea that speech changes the subject. As our discourse changes, so do we. Thus, Lacan proposed working at the level of the signifier, and attending to the gaps in the patient's history, that is filling out the anamnesis. Lacan states, "Analysis can have as its goal only the advent of true speech and the subject's realisation of his history in its relation to a future" (2006, p. 302/249). And here we see the importance of the fundamental rule of analysis—free association or saying whatever comes to mind, free from censorship alongside an aim of integration, that is, including what has been excluded—repressed, speaking about things "all things considered". The point is to speak fully and well, not just use what Lacan deems empty egoic speech, which is parroting what we have been saying to the public or told by others, but allowing for something new to emerge, saying something we have not said before, speaking our truth if you will. The ability to articulate one's history in full speech is, to be sure, a worthy goal. Lacan claims, "When all is said and done, it is less a matter of remembering than of rewriting history" (1988a, p. 14). *It is striking that this full speech is achieved, not through being honest or rigorous, but through free association. This is truly the faith or trust that psychoanalysis places in language.* Just speak freely and truth will emerge. This, of course, is much easier said than done.

As we speak, we progressively see how our destiny is tied to the signifiers of the Other. As we speak more, we encounter the emergence, repetition, and insistence of signifiers, and how we must move beyond the signifiers of the Other, further take hold of our destiny, and assume more responsibility for our discourse and lives; Lacan calls this "subjective destitution".

By verbalising we give voice to and own our unique desires and further our Eros. In 1961, Lacan told his seminar attendees, "What is at stake in analysis is nothing other than bringing to light manifestations of the subject's desire" (2001, p. 238). A most significant part of the process revolves around a separation and unknotting of one's unconscious desire that is so very tightly tied to the Other. In turn, there is a freeing of desire. Lacanian theory guides us to view the cast of characters involved in clients' lives in relation to the overall circuits of desire and the clients' positions within them. We saw in all the cases how helpful it was to encourage an articulation of the unconscious determinants of the structures of desire.

In the "middle" Lacan, we also encounter a spotlight on grappling with the existential givens of loss and lack (we of course only desire that which we do not have or have lost). One must, in analysis and therapy, deal with loss and lack, what Lacan formulates as an acceptance or "subjectication of castration" (see *Seminar XV*, 1967–1968). Here Lacan and Freud diverge.[12] While Freud does not rule out a working through of the castration complex, he does highlight the immense difficulties involved. Lacan does *not* share Freud's pessimism on this point. Instead, Lacan sets a subjectification of castration during the therapeutic process as a precondition to a complete analysis. *For Lacan, analysis at its heart involves a subjectification of loss and lack, and a taking responsibility for one's destiny.*[13] Subjectification (of desire, of signifiers, of jouissance) plays an essential role in Lacanian analysis in myriad ways. Once a subject has come to terms with castration and the integration of the possibility of loss, an end of analysis is in sight and possible. *A coming to terms with and ultimately a letting go of the irretrievable loss and lack experienced in being human and the inevitable anxiety that accompanies this state of affairs, is key.*

Of course, the ultimate acceptance of loss involves the coming to terms with the existential given of our and our loved ones' impending death. Lacan refers to this in Heideggerian terms as working towards an assumption and subjectification of our "being towards death" (see *Seminar VII*, 1992).

Fantasy as progression of the aims of analysis

But it does not all end with signification and symbolisation, for desire is caught up in and expressed by means of the fantasy. The interrelationship between desire and fantasy is specifically addressed by Lacan in the middle to later period of his work, when, investigating the question of the aims of analysis, he emphasises the importance of the construction of and then so-called traversal of the fundamental fantasy. Traversing the fantasy refers to altering a client's fundamental viewpoint or way of looking at the world, a paradigm shift, in terms of the subject's relation to desire and jouissance such that the client is no longer quite the obstacle to her or his own satisfaction. For we saw in these five cases, how the clients were their own worst enemies when it came to achieving satisfaction. In Lily's case, I discussed what makes the fundamental fantasy so fundamental, the fantasy as the means by which we cipher and make sense of phenomena, in other words, how it (always uniquely) at once helps us both make sense of the possibly overwhelming chaos of life and limits our experience of and satisfaction from it. Importantly, going back to Freud's potential endings, traversal of the fantasy takes the aim of analysis beyond symptom and inhibition relief and offers a potential for different viewpoints and opens up many possibilities that may have otherwise been closed off.

In 1964, Lacan's formulation of traversal of the fantasy as a worthy analytic aim moved the discussion from the symbolic realm (as it relates to signifiers and desire) further towards the real.[14] Here we find the aspect of the Freudian unconscious as it is implicated in the production and limitation of jouissance and is related to the real. A crossing of the fantasy allows an opening up of jouissance, a widening of the ways of enjoying available to the subject, since the analysand's mode of jouissance is caught up in and limited by the fantasy. On the one hand the fundamental fantasy is portrayed as an underlying sentence, explored via the symbolic, and on the other, there is the real aspect of the fantasy. As Lacan states, "to a certain degree, fantasies cannot bear to be revealed in speech" (1992, p. 80). It is this real aspect that leads Lacan to call fantasies "bothersome" (2006, p. 779/657).

Russell Grigg discusses how fantasy points to the position the analyst occupies in the *real*, and states the fundamental fantasy is "not interpretable" (2008, p. 66). There is a difference between a subject's relationship to a fantasy and to a formation of the unconscious. There is a purely symbolic dimension to a symptom, of course; it is what Lacan calls its "formal envelope", and this *can and should* be analysed via the work of analysis relying on free association.[15] But fantasies are different. They are sometimes conscious, sometimes unconscious, sometimes not entirely either, and can be both either conscious or unconscious at different times (this last point is found in Freud's work). People tend to be ashamed of their fantasies but often know quite a bit about them, which they will divulge in analysis but often with embarrassment; indeed, they have to overcome a reluctance to share them with the analyst, in part because fantasies are often typically politically incorrect—peppered with violent acts, cultural taboos, and so on. At the same time there is an enjoyment, a jouissance, in recounting them to another, despite the shame and embarrassment. Fantasies are necessary for a person's sexual life to find expression and are often most obvious around masturbatory practices. Moreover, even as people know quite a bit about their fantasies as the source of their enjoyment, the material is impoverished; fantasies do not produce the rich material by way of association that symptoms do, but rather exist as a sort of island in the middle of all that. Thus, analysing a fantasy is more like giving a construction than interpreting formations of the unconscious.[16] Indeed, we see a distinct shift in Lacan's later years from a focus on interpreting symbolic unconscious formations, towards engaging the realm of the real, and his work with fantasy is part of this turn.

The later years: jouissance, the drive, and identification with the symptom

In his later response to the question of the aims and ends of analysis, Lacan is still concerned with separating from the Other, but desire, as inextricably tied to the signifier in the early and middle work, is superseded by jouissance and the drive. The drive lies beyond desire, as desire is always harnessed to the Other, while the drive is not. Lacan's later articulated aim concerns an identification with, acceptance, integration, and ultimately subjectification of the drive and jouissance in order to attain more satisfaction, separated from the Other.[17] Paying attention to the myriad forms of jouissance—that pleasure and enjoyment which we do not want to own, and which may be distasteful to our ego and our own conscious desire—is highlighted in therapy and brought to the fore.

But why does Lacan move from a focus on dialectising desire to the drive and obtaining more jouissance? By focusing on jouissance and the drive, Lacan was, in part, attempting to avoid the trappings of identification and the discourse of the Other, which are inherent to the imaginary and symbolic registers. It is too easy for the analysand to identify with the analyst's desire, even if the *analyst's pure desire* is continually in play, for that, as speaking beings, is how we are made.

That said, how are we to understand that one of Lacan's last formulations actually *involves* identification? Lacan conceptualised that if the analysand is to identify with something, then it should not be with the analyst, but rather with that which is most one's self. By the conclusion of analytic work, the analyst's role should move from a subject-supposed-to-know position to something no longer needed or useful to the analysand (Lacan says a "waste product"). At this point, if an identification is in play, it is with what at the commencement of therapy seemed most alien—that is, one identifies with, makes the most of, and best lives out one's own symptom. Lacan formulates this as identification with the symptom as real: "To know how to handle, to take care of, to manipulate [...] to know what to do with the symptom, that is the end of the analysis" (1977b, p. 7). This is how Lacan situates the place of identification at the end of analysis.

Moving in on the real

While Lacan was always interested in gleaning more knowledge about unconscious formations and how they move one and about unconscious knowledge, there came a point in his later teachings where he questioned such knowledge. Aspiring to ever more influence on the real, Lacan believed that working at the level of knowledge and the symbolic left something to be desired. Lacan states, "the subject in himself, the recalling of his biography, all this goes only to a certain limit which is known as the real" (1978, p. 48). For there *remains* that which is not included in or is excluded from the signifying network, which we so carefully attempt to map out in analytic work. Charting the signifying network allows us to close in on the real, the traumatic nucleus, that which has not been put into words. But ultimately the real exists beyond the symbolic and outside of language. Lacan portrays the real as "the impossible" (1978, p. 167). It is impossible to speak the real and therefore to grasp it through knowledge. Lacan states, "the real, or what is perceived as such, is what resists symbolisation absolutely" (1988a, p. 66).[18] *While the real resists symbolisation, we still attempt to symbolise it. We approach the real in therapeutic work by putting experiences into words.* Words are precisely what we have to work with. Jacques-Alain Miller has formulated the notion of a progressive draining of the real into the symbolic.[19] The more a client fills in her or his anamnesis, the more she or he drains the real into the symbolic—up to a point. And what we can hope for, in so doing, is *a shift in a client's relationship to the real*, a worthy aim. However, there is always a limit—perhaps this is the "residue" of which Freud spoke.

In this book, I have focused on the symbolic over the realm of the real because I have found Lacan's early and middle work particularly useful to my clinical practice. Perhaps another reason why the earlier and middle Lacan was so prevalent in conceptualising these cases was that the cases themselves were rather "new" or "young" therapies versus "older" analyses that have been conducted for longer periods of time. An articulation of history, a filling in of gaps, and a dialectising of desire serve well as aims of younger therapies. Such aims allow for more freedom and desire, and promote less fixation, anxiety, and symptomology.

Also, the symbolic realm is inherently easier to speak about and capture in words and hence write about! Even in focusing on the symbolic, there was always more to say. For all of the case studies, I could have said more, struggled to say what I meant, and said more than I thought I was saying. Such is always the case with language; it outruns our intentions, and we give expression to our desire, without even realising it. In this way, writing case studies could be an interminable affair, but at a certain point one discovers that one has said something, perhaps enough, and something that was previously implicit has become explicit. We can view this too as draining the real into the symbolic. And to be sure, *a change in the symbolic, in turn, affects the real. This is the movement of talk therapy.*

Do differences make a difference? The procedure of the pass

Yet another question to be raised is whether these diverse formulations of technical aims and endings make any practical difference to the way analysis is actually conducted. Here we arrive at Lacan's invention of the "pass": when an analysand explicitly narrates or reports to a minimum of two other analysands who are more or less at the same stage of their analyses about his analysis—how it began, ended, and how it affected his relations to unconscious knowledge. While the pass refers to the professional "passage" of becoming an analyst with a particular standing in an analytic institution, it is first and foremost a method Lacan introduced in the late 1960s to investigate whether what he was describing and prescribing actually worked.[20] The pass was created to collect data that allows us to observe how different aims might work out for people—pragmatically speaking. At least in theory (and there is much controversy as to whether the pass is a worthy endeavour; even Lacan had his doubts), the pass would lead to and encourage the idea that there is some common understanding and outcome that is shared by Lacan's various formulations of the end of analysis.

It seems to me that there is indeed a unity amongst Lacan's different ways of thinking about analysis and they need to be thought of as different facets of essentially the same thing. Each conception throws light, albeit from a different theoretical standpoint and a place within the theory, on what analysis is or could be. While the cases presented in this book are not the first-person testimonies of the pass, they do offer narratives of therapeutic work based on a Lacanian approach; how do they thus fit into this discussion?

The cases: "variability in the effect"

I have presented a series of cases with quite specific endings, the sorts that are not particularly widely discussed in the literature, and yet are ways of terminating analysis and therapy that anyone who works clinically has some experience with. Someone leaves before you think they should because of what is happening in the therapy (Lily and Max for example); or departs for practical considerations, because it is not possible for the therapist and client to go on seeing each other (Edon and Lisa for example). These are cases where the therapy has not been brought to the point of diminishing returns, as Freud refers to it, or to the bedrock of castration, nor to the point of the pass, as Lacan theorises it, and all the different ways in which he thinks about the matter.

So, on the one hand, there is the ideal as it were, of the end of analysis as Lacan formulates it, and as briefly discussed above, and then there is the practical termination of particular treatments, on the other—what Freud refers to when he speaks of the "external difficulties" that prevent one from reaching the end of analysis. What are we to say about those cases that do *not* go through all the way to the aforementioned ideal ends? Are they valueless? Clearly not! Should we never undertake an analysis or therapy with someone who might not see it through to a complete end? Again, clearly not. Freud himself saw many patients who came for short periods of time, often just months, and yet goals were achieved and benefits obtained. In this book's cases, we find people who have come for therapy and have been engaged in that therapy for varying periods of time, so what benefits have they gleaned?

What therapeutic betterments did my clients specifically derive from their respective treatments? In many of the cases the therapy was able to lift depressive phenomena and either alleviate or resolve somatic complaints. Romantic prospects arose, and for some, work goals were furthered or achieved. Sometimes it was just an opening up of possibilities, a matter of putting more choices before them going into the future. Let us return to each case very briefly.

Mona began therapy complaining that she was unable to concentrate on her graduate school studies or much of anything. She was disconcertingly tired and not her usual spirited self. Rather than focus on these depressive states per se, we worked with Mona's unconscious desire, which consequently came to relieve many of these phenomena.

Looking back at the wording of Mona's presenting problem, at her phrase that she had "lost [her] *fight*", we see the signifying chain that constituted Mona's desire from the very beginning. Her desire was caught up in a fighting dynamic that fuelled both her jealousy and her need to identify with the Other's love object in an attempt to answer the question, "Am I desirable?" Mona had done a lot of unconscious identifying with others in her life, but by the end of our work, many identifications had loosened and Mona was prepared to fight more for what *she* wanted, as further separated from the Other's desire. She was generally less caught up in the unconscious circuits of desire, particularly her triangulating tendencies, which when she first came to see me had her running around in circles (or rather triangles) in fits of jealousy. Through speech, she made explicit her role in these shenanigans, what she garnered from them, and what she stood to gain by relinquishing them to make room for alternative subjective positions, to choose to engage in her libidinal relations in this way, or not. In a nutshell, Mona was able to work and love more freely—she planned to attend graduate school for a newly decided upon career, and was seeing a boyfriend with whom she felt things were going well enough—"it would do"—which is a classical Freudian formula for secondary benefits of analysis, as I will discuss in the last section of this conclusion.

When Max entered therapy he felt depressed (lethargic and lacking motivation in particular), and as if his life was going nowhere (or worse, down the toilet). Through speech he examined the unconscious role that his go-to defence of withholding played in his life and expressed how his family matrix, including a symbolic debt, that had remained veritably unspoken in his family, profoundly affected him. We saw the extent to which Max was subjugated by his father's signifiers—"a pain in the ass", for example—and how Max needed to reclaim his own thoughts, body, desire, will, and ultimately destiny, and release himself from the subjugation of the signifiers of the Other. He needed to articulate and realise that he was indeed alive. As incredibly tragic as it was that his brother before him had died, it was indeed his brother who died, *not* Max; there did not *need* to be two dead (one playing dead). This needed to be brought to the fore and worked through in Max's own words, versus Max unconsciously living out the words and silences of his parents. Max narrated important parts of his history that had previously been left out of the conversation, but were unconsciously moving him to *inaction*.

Max ended our therapy abruptly. In the chapter I addressed some potential reasons, but these can only be hypotheses. The point was that one needs to keep the obsessional hystericised, involved with the Other, and this did not happen. Max reverted to shutting the Other (myself) out, right when we were most engaging his unconscious in the process. Our last sessions exemplified how, at least in his dream life, and by associating to the "fertile dream", Max was becoming more aware of the far-reaching role that loss played in his life and how unconscious knowledge was coming to the fore. The dream also pointed most acutely to the work being done around lack versus empowerment, and the relationship between death and castration.

Recall that Max had begun therapy to receive psychotropic drugs, but ended up going off the drugs, stating that what he really needed was to talk. That stance was sustained for some time, although there was much more to talk through. But ultimately the transference was not worked through and Max left stuck in his obsessional position, perhaps in the heat of a transferential crisis as described in the case.

In writing Lisa's case, I focused on our work with a very specific isolated symptom—a phobic response to vomit and vomiting accompanied by elaborate avoidance strategies. We connected the signifier "throw up" to Lisa's familial history. Associating to this symptom encouraged Lisa to remember childhood scenes that had not been adequately integrated into her adult psyche. The work with this symptom did a great deal for us, for Lisa; it loosened her fixated and unarticulated stance with respect to desire, in particular how her desire was unconsciously wrapped up in revulsion. As an impactful secondary benefit of fleshing out the ellipses of her strange symptom (and the other work she did in therapy), Lisa felt stronger in love and work. Instead of giving up on her doctoral program, she was well on her way to finishing her dissertation and had successfully applied for academic positions. She planned on moving to her new location with her partner, and generally felt much more confident in both realms of work and love. Lisa moved from a subjective position in which she frequently felt "worthless" to one in which she felt much more "worth" it.

With Edon, we began to unravel the knot of his obsessional doubt and ruminations and followed the various threads of his story such that he concluded our sessions with a greater understanding of how his symptoms and troubled libidinal relations connected to his specific history. Edon's doubting symptom, which was a major complaint that seemed most alien and disturbing to him at the start of therapy, became much more meaningful and personal for him.

Additionally, Edon questioned his long-adopted, logical narrative that a "sacrifice" had been made out of love when he moved from his parental home to his grandparents', and he allowed himself to articulate the negative as well as positive effects. In so doing *he assumed a part of his history* that had, prior to his talking, been closed to doubt. We thus grappled with a doubt and aggressiveness that had come to permeate most of his relations, and we did so by symbolising and putting into words what had previously been unspoken. The more Edon spoke, the more he moved toward a wider range of affect, which had been limited and displaced onto his doubting symptom when he entered therapy.

And via dream associations we started to untangle the knots of Edon's phallic inheritance, as it related to his relationship with his father, and as it tainted his sexual life.

As outlined in the case, Edon's therapy ended for practical reasons, just when he had temporarily placed me as the cause of his desire and in so doing allowed a space for his desire to be less inhibited and rise to signification in his dreams and speech. It was unfortunate that our work ended when it did, for there was much more to say. Hopefully Edon continued the work with another therapist. At the very least our limited work together sparked his desire to continue to examine the role his unconscious played in his life.

A major part of the work with Lily involved the process of symbolising, in particular, naming the term that had been excluded from the chain, the term that was not there for Lily when she needed it. By speaking frankly of sexual difference, a lack was named, a lack that haunted, pervaded, and meddled in most aspects of her life and being. And her family romance was further symbolised through speech and thus acknowledged on a more conscious level. In formalising how Lily was unconsciously playing the "servile wife to her old man", we saw how Lily orchestrated her role in the scenario that she heartily complained about, *how she was also very much complicit*. And we saw how she gained intense satisfaction from blaming others, but that, ultimately, that satisfaction was limiting and she could do better. We formulated and worked with, but did not traverse, the fantasy.

While Lily could speak of her predicament quite eloquently, she was only slowly coming to actually accept responsibility for *her part* in the drama. Viewing herself as an active party, she *ideally* might have then chosen to position herself differently, as difficult and threatening a task as that entailed. Sadly this did not occur and, as I observe in the chapter, my missteps may have resulted in a premature termination of the work.

And there we have some variations of possible endings: not ideals and "complete", but very real nonetheless. One last question remains, were the clients' happier for their work in therapy? And should happiness even be part of the equation?

Forging on, dare we say, towards happiness?

At this point, some readers may inevitably and fairly ask, "What, if anything, does all of this have to do with happiness? Does this form of talk therapy make us happier?" As described above, Lacan presents these burgeoning number of technical formulations for the aims and ends of analysis, but what good are they if they do not have at least the by-product of allowing a person to have a better life (if not a good one!). These are philosophical questions, but are pragmatically important nonetheless.

Psychoanalysis has always had a rather strange relationship to its aims. On the one hand, it can be legitimately inscribed in the philosophical tradition, from Socrates, Plato, and Aristotle onwards, that ponders the examined life, the purpose of a human life. Aristotle spoke of how a meaningful philosophical inquiry involves questions around what kind of life activities lead to human flourishing. One cannot just say, "I will flourish!" and do so, one must cultivate habits, ways of thinking, and ways of being with others. For the Greek philosophers the question of what leads to the good life was a substantial one. In one sense, we can locate psychoanalysis in this tradition, in that analysts do speak of vitality along with resilience to life's misfortunes, and Freud spoke of winning back "some degree of capacity for work and enjoyment" (1912e, p. 119).

But Freud also stressed that we cannot aim directly at a cure, or we will miss the boat. Psychoanalysis—certainly Lacanian analysis—does not aim at happiness as a goal in and of itself.[21] We may think of this in relation to the old adage, one cannot directly aim to be happy, rather one can do the particular things in life that matter to one and, if all goes well, one may find that these endeavours bring happiness as a *secondary benefit*. Meaningful work and caring relationships, for example, bring happiness as secondary benefits. Of course, here, as in any other aspect of living a life, there are no guarantees. Likewise, one does not aim, specifically, to make someone happier via Lacanian therapy, but these secondary benefits can indeed be the result of the techniques presented here. Otherwise, what would really be the point? In contradistinction to some caricatures of Lacanian analysis, Lacan's is not an intellectual exercise, however intellectually it may be presented. The process is a therapeutic one, *via words and speech* with another person, that ultimately helps people live freer, more satisfying lives.

It is my hope that the presentation of Lacanian case studies such as these will encourage more clinicians to consider utilising or integrating a Lacanian approach into their practices, at least present the option and open the possibility. Case studies are invitations for other clinicians to consider our methods and to open a dialogue regarding what we do behind closed doors. In presenting such clinical material, practitioner-researchers engage in the greater conversation about how theoretical models deeply influence our practices and how therapeutic interactions differ when approached from diverse theoretical perspectives. Such dialogue eventuates in the demystification of the therapeutic process for clinicians and clients alike. In a time abounding with technological communications and physiological fixes, it is all the more important to speak of the work that speaking can accomplish. In this age of biological treatments, there is still much we can gain and achieve through talking; call me old fashioned, and I will take it as a compliment. In this vein, I do hope clinicians and students will consider a Lacanian approach to be a viable alternative, one that truly keeps the value of speech in treatment alive. The point is we may and perhaps must emphasise speech as a means of symptom relief, a working through of the existential dilemmas we inevitably face as human beings, a pathway to greater personal freedom and growth, a furthering of Eros, and dare I say it?—Yes I do, via the secondary benefits described above, a dose or more of happiness.

Notes

1. A few of these cases came to a premature end because of external difficulties such as changes in work and residence, on either my or the client's part (or both), which is far from ideal. These days, with better access to telecommunication systems, cell phones, computer-to-phone, or computer-to-computer technologies (such as Skype), this happens less often. Therapists and analysts may continue therapeutic work from various places, even time zones, which allows for more consistent work. At the time when these cases took place, such technology was both less available and less commonly used.
2. Perhaps surprisingly, Freud himself characterised "complete" psychoanalyses as taking "months, even years" (1926e, p. 187). Even today we consider months or years quite normal in terms of "longer term" work. Many of Freud's famous cases indeed took place over a matter of months, which we would now consider brief work.
3. I was surprised to find that in the United States, in psychology doctoral and masters programs, one's own counseling, therapy, or analysis is *not* a requirement for someone to become a therapist or counsellor.
4. While not relevant to this particular passage in Freud, one might view this residue, which Freud could not quite put his finger on, in a more positive light. This residue might be interpreted as the fact that analytic work continues even after an analysis has officially or technically ended, and, this "residue" hopefully continues to positively affect a person's life. There is also yet another possibility, which is that perhaps the problem is that one suffers when one's symptom works against one, and that rather than abandon one's symptom altogether, it is a question of finding a way to work with it in a more satisfactory, less painful way than before, which relates to Lacan's final position as will be discussed below.
5. Lacan's critique of ego psychology is peppered throughout his work, but can be primarily found in his first and second published *Seminars*.
6. Later in his theorisation, Lacan goes so far as to say that if the analysand is to end an analysis identifying with anything, it would be best to do so with her or his own symptom, as will be discussed below.
7. Lacan also states, when discussing the goal of analysis as owning one's unique desire, that "resistance to this owning [of the subject's

desire] can, in the final analysis, be related here to nothing but desire's incompatibility with speech" (2006, p. 641/535).

8. On the ethics of psychoanalysis in relation to Lacanian goals, see Baldwin, "Lacanian Psychoanalysis as a human science" in *Invitation to Psychology as a Human Science* (forthcoming).

9. For an interesting discussion on what psychoanalysis might be aiming towards, particularly in relation to freedom, as a "final cause" of psychoanalysis, and one that takes into account Lacan in juxtaposition with three other psychoanalytic approaches, see Lear (2009).

10. On this term see Rivka Warshawsky's "Dis-identification applied to the end of analysis" (2004). This term also refers to the idea of specifically not identifying with the analyst, but rather encouraging a lack of such an identification.

11. Grigg presented these ideas in his paper at the 2013 Affiliated Psychoanalytic Workgroups (APW) Conference on the Imaginary.

12. Unfortunately many contemporary psychologists and students are turned off by Freud's biologism around issues of castration. Lacan reads the fear of castration figuratively, not literally, having to do with our relationship to lack and loss, and takes the phallus to be a signifier, par excellence, of desire and power. Thus when one "wants to be or have the phallus", it is not the organ; it is about one's relation to desire, the Other's desire, and power. I hope this became clear in the specifics of the cases, as it can be an obstacle for clinicians, students, and readers.

13. In a talk given at PULSE in 2011, Eric Laurent read a letter from Lacan to his analyst Rudolf Lowenstein, six years after Lacan's analysis ended. In it Lacan told Lowenstein that when he was to see Lacan in London he would "find there [in London] a man [Lacan] more certain in his duties and his destiny". This is a quite a nice description of an aim of analysis.

14. In *Seminar XI*, Lacan describes a positive analytic outcome as when "the experience of the fundamental fantasy becomes the drive" (1978, p. 273). A problem, as is often the case when we enter "real" territory, is that here we enter unchartered waters, unchartered in the sense of not yet put into the symbolic register, and these phenomena become difficult if not impossible to talk about. Trying to discuss it, however, Lacan asks, "How can a subject who has traversed the radical fantasy experience the drive? This is the beyond of analysis, and has never been approached" (1978, p. 273). It involves moving through the screen of fantasy into the space of the real. This crossing, theoretically speaking, leads to a living out of the drive.

15. Verhaeghe and Declercq nicely phrase it, "Thus considered, the symptom is a Symbolic construction built around a Real kernel of jouissance.

In Freud's words, it is 'like the grain of sand around which an oyster forms its pearl'" (2002, p. 2).

16. For all its intricacies, as with all of Lacan's concepts, the concept of traversing the fantasy has its inherent usefulness in guiding the clinician, generally, among the always very unique features of each case. The clinician works with the particular fantasy of each client. Although when working in the Lacanian tradition, one would be aware of this notion of the fundamental fantasy, and be equipped and ready to hear, think about, and utilise it, one should not be on a quest for the fantasy with an eye to traverse it, so to speak. We too often only find what we are searching for, when what we should be listening for is ultimately neither about us, nor the theory, per se, but about the client. That said and kept in mind, when working within a Lacanian framework, it is useful to keep an ear out for the fantasy, how it works, how it shifts and undergoes permutations in therapy, and how it might be worked through or reworked by the client, which is considered one worthy end to the analytic process.

17. On the drive versus desire and working with the drive see Lacan's *Seminar V*, trans. R. Grigg (forthcoming).

18. Lacan knew very well the possibilities and limits of language. As early as his "Mirror stage" essay, Lacan pronounced "[P]sychoanalysis can accompany the patient to the ecstatic limit of '*Thou art that*', where the cipher of his mortal destiny is revealed to him, but it is not in our sole power as practitioners to bring him to the point where the true journey begins" (2006, p. 100/81).

19. J. -A. Miller discusses this notion in his "Orientation Lacanienne" lectures that are unpublished. Fink also utilises this formulation; see Fink (1997, pp. 47–49) and also Fink (1995, Chapter Three).

20. See Lacan (1968), Fink (1997), Nobus (2000), and Soler (2014).

21. In *Seminar VII* (1992), Lacan describes the demand for happiness that the analyst will be met with by the analysand and even society, and reminds his readers that here psychoanalysis differs from Aristotelian ethics, and does not look towards happiness as a goal in and of itself, does not take up this demand.

REFERENCES

American Psychiatric Association. (2013). *Diagnostic and Statistical Manual of Mental Disorders* (5th edn). Washington, DC: Author.

Baldwin, Y. (forthcoming). Lacanian psychoanalysis as a human science. In: R. Brooke, C. Fischer, & L. Laubscher (Eds.), *Invitation to Psychology as a Human Science*. Pittsburgh, PA: Duquesne Books.

Baldwin, Y. (forthcoming). Reading "On ex post facto syllabary". In: D. Hook, C. Neill, & S. Vanheule (Eds.), *Reading the Écrits: A Guide to Lacan's Work*. New York: Routledge.

Baldwin, Y., Malone, K. R., & Svolos, T. (Eds.) (2011). *Lacan and Addictions: An Anthology*. London: Karnac.

Bernheimer, C., & Kahane, C. (Eds.) (1990). *In Dora's Case: Freud—Hysteria—Feminism* (2nd edn). New York: Columbia University Press.

Breuer, J. (1895d). Fräulein Anna O. In: *Studies on Hysteria. S. E., 2*: 21–47. London: Karnac.

Dor, J. (1997). *The Clinical Lacan*. New York: Other Press.

Dor, J. (2001). *Structure and Perversions*. S. Fairfield (Trans.). New York: Other Press.

Dunand, A. (1995). The end of analysis (I & II). In: R. Feldstein, B. Fink, & M. Jaanus (Eds.), *Reading Seminar XI: Lacan's Four Fundamental Concepts of Psychoanalysis* (pp. 243–256). Albany, NY: SUNY Press.

Fink, B. (1995). *The Lacanian Subject: Between Language and Jouissance.* Princeton, NJ: Princeton University Press.

Fink, B. (1997). *A Clinical Introduction to Lacanian Psychoanalysis: Theory and Technique.* Cambridge, MA: Harvard University Press.

Fink, B. (2003). The use of Lacanian psychoanalysis in a case of fetishism. *Clinical Case Studies, 2*(1): 50–69.

Fink, B. (2004). *Lacan to the Letter: Reading Écrits Closely.* Minneapolis, MN: University of Minnesota Press.

Fink, B. (2005). Lacanian clinical practice. *The Psychoanalytic Review, 92*(4): 553–579.

Fink, B. (2007). *Fundamentals of Psychoanalytic Technique: A Lacanian Approach for Practitioners.* New York: W. W. Norton.

Freud, S. (1895d). Fräulein Elisabeth von R. In: *Studies on Hysteria. S. E., 2:* 135–181. London: Hogarth.

Freud, S. (1896b). Further remarks on the neuro-psychoses of defence. *S. E., 3:* 157–185. London: Hogarth.

Freud, S. (1900a). *The Interpretation of Dreams. S. E., 4–5.* London: Hogarth.

Freud, S. (1909d). Notes upon a case of obsessional neurosis. *S. E., 10:* 151–318. London: Hogarth.

Freud, S. (1910h). A special type of choice of object made by men (Contributions to the psychology of love, I). *S. E., 11:* 163–175. London: Hogarth.

Freud, S. (1912b). The dynamics of transference. *S. E., 12:* 97–108. London: Hogarth.

Freud, S. (1912d). On the universal tendency to debasement in the sphere of love (Contributions to the psychology of love, II). *S. E., 11:* 177–190. London: Hogarth.

Freud, S. (1912e). Recommendations to physicians practicing psycho-analysis. *S. E., 12:* 109–120. London: Hogarth.

Freud, S. (1912–1913). *Totem and Taboo. S. E., 13:* ix–162. London: Hogarth.

Freud, S. (1916–1917). *Introductory Lectures on Psycho-Analysis. S. E., 15–16.* London: Hogarth.

Freud, S. (1919e). A child is being beaten: A contribution to the study of the origin of sexual perversions. *S. E., 17:* 175–204. London: Hogarth.

Freud, S. (1923b). *The Ego and the Id. S. E., 19:* 1–66. London: Hogarth.

Freud, S. (1925h). Negation. *S. E., 19:* 235–239. London: Hogarth.

Freud, S. (1926e). *The Question of Lay Analysis. S. E., 20:* 177–258. London: Hogarth.

Freud, S. (1930a). *Civilization and its Discontents. S. E., 21:* 57–145. London: Hogarth.

Freud, S. (1937c). Analysis terminable and interminable. *S. E., 23:* 209–253. London: Hogarth.

Freud, S. (1937d). Constructions in analysis. *S. E.*, *23*: 255–269. London: Hogarth.

Freud, S. (1963). *Dora: An Analysis of a Case of Hysteria*. New York: Macmillan Publishing [Original work published 1905].

Freud, S., & Breuer, J. (1895d). *Studies on Hysteria*. *S. E.*, *2*. London: Hogarth.

Gherovici, P. (2003). *The Puerto Rican Syndrome*. New York: Other Press.

Grigg, R. (2002). Enjoy-meant of language and jouissance of the letter. *Psychoanalytical Notebooks*, *8*: 57–65.

Grigg, R. (2008). *Lacan, Language, and Philosophy*. Albany, NY: SUNY Press.

Grigg, R. (2013). Treating the wolf man as a case of ordinary psychosis. *Culture/Clinic*, *1*: 86–96.

Guéguen, P. -G. (2013). Who is mad and who is not? On differential diagnosis in psychoanalysis. *Culture/Clinic*, *1*: 66–85.

Kuhn, T. S. (1962). *The Structure of Scientific Revolutions*. Chicago, IL: University of Chicago Press.

Lacan, J. (1966). *Écrits*. Paris: Éditions du Seuil.

Lacan, J. (1966–1967a). *Le Séminaire de Jacques Lacan, Livre XIV: La Logique du Fantasme, 1966–1967*. Unpublished.

Lacan, J. (1966–1967b). *The Seminar of Jacques Lacan, Book XIV: The Logic of Phantasy, 1966–1967*. Translated by C. Gallagher from unedited French manuscripts.

Lacan, J. (1967–1968). *Le Séminaire de Jacques Lacan, Livre XV: L'Acte Psychanalytique, 1967–1968*. Unpublished.

Lacan, J. (1968). Proposition du 9 octobre 1967 sur le psychanalyste de l'École. *Scilicet*, *1*: 14–30.

Lacan, J. (1977a). Desire and the interpretation of desire in *Hamlet*. J. -A. Miller (Ed.) & J. Hulbert (Trans.). *Yale French Studies*, *55/56*: 11–52 [Original work published 1959].

Lacan, J. (1977b). *Le Séminaire de Jacques Lacan, Livre XXIV: L'Insu que Sait de l'Une Bévue, s'Aile à Mourre*. *Ornicar?*, *12/13*: 6–7.

Lacan, J. (1978). *The Seminar of Jacques Lacan, Book XI: The Four Fundamental Concepts of Psychoanalysis*. J. -A. Miller (Ed.) & A. Sheridan (Trans.). New York: W. W. Norton [Original work published 1973].

Lacan, J. (1983). *Le Séminaire de Jacques Lacan, Livre VI: Le Désir et son Interpretation, 1958–1959*. J. -A. Miller (Ed.). *Ornicar?*, *26/27*: 7–44.

Lacan, J. (1988a). *The Seminar of Jacques Lacan, Book I: Freud's Papers on Technique, 1953–1954*. J. -A. Miller (Ed.) & J. Forrester (Trans). New York: Cambridge University Press [Original work published 1975].

Lacan, J. (1988b). *The Seminar of Jacques Lacan, Book II: The Ego in Freud's Theory and in the Technique of Psychoanalysis, 1954–1955*. J. -A. Miller (Ed.) & S. Tomaselli (Trans.). New York: Cambridge University Press [Original work published 1978].

Lacan, J. (1991). *Le Séminaire de Jacques Lacan, Livre XVII: L'Envers de la Psychanalyse, 1969–1970*. J. -A. Miller (Ed.). Paris: Éditions du Seuil.

Lacan, J. (1992). *The Seminar of Jacques Lacan, Book VII: The Ethics of Psychoanalysis, 1959–1960*. J. -A. Miller (Ed.) & D. Porter (Trans.). New York: W. W. Norton [Original work published 1986].

Lacan, J. (1993). *The Seminar of Jacques Lacan, Book III: The Psychoses, 1955–1956*. J. -A. Miller (Ed.) & R. Grigg (Trans.). New York: W. W. Norton [Original work published 1981].

Lacan, J. (1994). *Le Séminaire de Jacques Lacan, Livre IV: La Relation d'Objet, 1956–1957*. J. -A. Miller (Ed.). Paris: Éditions du Seuil.

Lacan, J. (1996). On Freud's "*Trieb*" and the psychoanalyst's desire. B. Fink (Trans). In: R. Feldstein, B. Fink, & M. Jaanus (Eds.), *Reading Seminars I and II: Lacan's Return to Freud* (pp. 417–421). Albany, NY: SUNY Press [Original work published 1966].

Lacan, J. (1998a). *Le Séminaire de Jacques Lacan, Livre V: Les Formations de l'Inconscient, 1957–1958*. J. -A. Miller (Ed.). Paris: Éditions du Seuil.

Lacan, J. (1998b). *The Seminar of Jacques Lacan, Book XX: Encore: On Feminine Sexuality, The Limits of Love and Knowledge, 1972–1973*. J. -A. Miller (Ed.) & B. Fink (Trans.). New York: W. W. Norton [Original work published 1975].

Lacan, J. (2001). *Le Séminaire de Jacques Lacan, Livre VIII: Le Transfert, 1960–1961*. J. -A. Miller (Ed.). Paris: Éditions du Seuil. [Forthcoming in English as *The seminar of Jacques Lacan, Book VIII: Transference (1960–1961)* (B. Fink, Trans.) Cambridge, UK: Polity 2015; page references here are to the French pagination.]

Lacan, J. (2002). *Écrits: A Selection*. B. Fink (Trans.). New York: W. W. Norton [Original work published 1966].

Lacan, J. (2006). *Écrits: The First Complete Edition in English*. B. Fink (Trans.). New York: W. W. Norton [Original work published 1966].

Lacan, J. (2013). Columbia University: Lecture on the symptom. *Culture/Clinic, 1*: 8–16 [Original work published 1976].

Lacan, J. (translation forthcoming). *The Seminar of Jacques Lacan, Book V: The Formations of the Unconscious, 1957–1958*. R. Grigg (Trans.). London: Polity Press.

Lacan, J. (translation forthcoming). *The Seminar of Jacques Lacan, Book VIII: Transference, 1960–1961*. B. Fink (Trans.). London: Polity Press.

Laplanche, J., & Pontalis, J. -B. (1988). *The Language of Psycho-Analysis*. D. Nicholson-Smith (Trans.). London: Karnac [Original work published 1967].

Leader, D. (2011). *What is Madness?* London: Penguin.

Lear, J. (2009). Technique and final cause in psychoanalysis: Four ways of looking at one moment. *The International Journal of Psychoanalysis, 90*: 1299–1317.

Leclaire, S. (1980). Jerome, or death in the life of the obsessional. In: S. Schneiderman (Ed. & Trans.), *Returning to Freud: Clinical Psychoanalysis in the School of Lacan* (pp. 94–113). New Haven, CT: Yale University Press [Original work published 1956].

Malone, K. R. (2000). The place of Lacanian psychoanalysis in North American psychology. In: J. -M. Rabaté (Ed.), *Lacan in America* (pp. 3–24). New York: Other Press.

Miller, J. -A. (1991). Reflections on the formal envelope of the symptom. J. Jauregui (Trans.). *Lacanian Ink, 4*: 13–21 [Original work published 1985].

Miller, J. -A. (1994). Love's labyrinths. T. Radigan (Trans.). *Lacanian Ink, 8*: 7–13.

Miller, J. -A. (1996a). An introduction to Lacan's clinical perspectives. B. Fink (Trans.). In: R. Feldstein, B. Fink, & M. Jaanus (Eds.), *Reading Seminars I and II: Lacan's Return to Freud* (pp. 241–247). Albany, NY: SUNY Press.

Miller, J. -A. (1996b). Commentary on Lacan's text. B. Fink (Trans.). In: R. Feldstein, B. Fink, & M. Jaanus (Eds.), *Reading Seminars I and II: Lacan's Return to Freud* (pp. 422–427). Albany NY: SUNY Press.

Miller, J. -A. (2008). Extimity. *The Symptom, 9*.

Miller, M. J. (2011). *Lacanian Psychotherapy: Theory and Practical Applications.* New York: Routledge.

Nasio, J. -D. (1997). *Hysteria: The Splendid Child of Psychoanalysis.* S. Fairfield (Ed. & Trans.). Northvale, NJ: Jason Aronson [Original work published 1990].

Nobus, D. (2000). *Jacques Lacan and the Freudian Practice of Psychoanalysis.* London: Routledge.

Nobus, D., & Downing, L. (Eds.) (2006). *Perversion: Psychoanaltyic Perspectives.* London: Karnac.

Parker, I. (2003). The unconscious love of Elisabeth von R: Notes on Freud's first full-length analysis. *Psychodynamic Practice: Individuals, Groups and Organisations, 9*(2): 141–151.

President's Council on Bioethics (2003). *Beyond Therapy: Biotechnology and the Pursuit of Happiness.* New York: HarperCollins.

Roudinesco, E. (1990). *Jacques Lacan & Co.: A History of Psychoanalysis in France, 1925–1985.* J. Mehlman (Trans.). London: Free Association Press [Original work published 1986].

Schneiderman, S. (Ed.) (1980). *Returning to Freud: Clinical Psychoanalysis in the School of Lacan.* New Haven, CT: Yale University Press.

Schneiderman, S. (1983). *Jacques Lacan: The Death of an Intellectual Hero.* Cambridge, MA: Harvard University Press.

Schwartz, A. (2013). Drowned in a stream of prescriptions. *The New York Times,* 2 February.

Soler, C. (1996). Hysteria and obsession. In: R. Feldstein, B. Fink, & M. Jaanus (Eds.), *Reading Seminars I and II: Lacan's Return to Freud* (pp. 248–282). Albany, NY: SUNY Press.

Soler, C. (2003). The paradoxes of the symptom in psychoanalysis. In: J. -M. Rabaté (Ed.), *The Cambridge Companion to Lacan* (pp. 86–101). Cambridge: Cambridge University Press.

Soler, C. (2014). *Lacan—The Unconscious Reinvented.* E. Faye & S. Schwartz (Trans.). London: Karnac.

Spinelli, E. (1997). *Tales of Un-Knowing: Eight Stories of Existential Therapy.* New York: New York University Press.

Svolos, T. (2001). The great divide: Psychoanalytic contributions to the diagnosis and management of psychosis. *Lacanian Ink, 18:* 42–59.

Swales, S. (2012). *Perversion: A Lacanian Psychoanalytic Approach to the Subject.* New York: Routledge.

Turkle, S. (1978). *Psychoanalytic Politics: Jacques Lacan and Freud's French Revolution.* New York: Basic Books.

Turkle, S. (2011). *Alone Together: Why We Expect More from Technology and Less from Each Other.* New York: Basic Books.

Vanheule, S. (2011). *The Subject of Psychosis: A Lacanian Perspective.* New York: Palgrave Macmillan.

Vanheule, S. (2014). *Diagnosis and the DSM: A Critical Review.* New York: Palgrave Macmillan.

Verghese, A. (2008). Culture shock—Patient as icon, icon as patient. *New England Journal of Medicine, 359*(26): 2748–2751.

Verhaeghe, P., & Declercq, F. (2002). Lacan's analytical goal: "Le Sinthome" or the feminine way. In: L. Thurston (Ed.), *Re-Inventing the Symptom: Essays on the Final Lacan* (pp. 59–83). New York: Other Press.

Warshawsky, R. (2004). Dis-identification applied to the end of analysis. Originally presented at the Seminar of the Freudian Field on Lacan's *Direction of the Treatment.* Tel Aviv, January 2004.

Whitaker, R. (2010). *Anatomy of an Epidemic: Magic Bullets, Psychiatric Drugs, and the Astonishing Rise of Mental Illness in America.* New York: Random House.

INDEX